JEWISH WRITING IN THE CONTEMPORARY WORLD

Series Editor: Sander L. Gilman, University of Illinois

Contemporary Jewish Writing in Canada

An Anthology

Edited by Michael Greenstein

University of Nebraska Press : Lincoln and London

Acknowledgments for the use of copyrighted material appear on pages 231–32, which constitute an extension of the copyright page.

Manufactured in the United States of America

Library of Congress Cataloging-in-Publication Data
Contemporary Jewish writing in Canada : an anthology / edited by Michael Greenstein.
p. cm. – (Jewish writing in the contemporary world)
Includes bibliographical references.
ISBN 0-8032-2185-1 (cloth: alkaline paper)
1. Canadian literature – Jewish authors. 2. Jews – Canada – Literary collections. 3. Canadian literature – 20th century. 4. Canadian literature – 21st century. I. Greenstein, Michael. II. Series.
PR9194.5.J48C66 2004 810.8′08924071–dc22 2003023399

For Anita,

In the bow,

And by my side.

Contents

ACKNOWLEDGMENTS

I wish to thank the following:
Irving Abella,
William Abrams,
Phyllis Aronoff,
Henry Auster,
Rachel Brenner,
Michael Brown,
Iris Bruce,
Mervin Butovsky,
Usher Caplan,
Adam Fuerstenberg,
Sander Gilman,
Harold Heft,
Sara Horowitz,
Gershon Hundert,
Doug Jones,
Jon Kertzer,
Shel Krakofsky,
Monique Martin,
Seymour Mayne,
Richard Menkes,
Ira Nadel,
Ruby Newman,
Ruth Panofsky,
Zailig Pollock,
Norman Ravvin,
Ira Robinson,
Ken Sherman,
Ron Sutherland,
Harold Troper,
Gerald Tulchinsky,
Harold Waller,
and Seth Wolitz.
Special thanks
to all the editors
of *Parchment* and
Viewpoints.

Michael Greenstein

Introduction

Sambation to Saskatchewan

Writing at the end of 1968, Mordecai Richler describes Canada as the 'ghetto of the north' and repeatedly quotes W. H. Auden's phrase about the dominions being *tiefste Provinz*—places that have produced no art.[1] Richler concludes that the former colony of Canada with its governor general, a vestige of the British Empire, is still a fragmentary nation of regions, not yet bound by a unifying principle, distinctive voice, or mythology of its own. Well-known Canadian novelist Margaret Laurence has referred to Canadian writers in general as 'the Tribe'; how much more so do Jewish writers in Canada belong to their own tribe. Jewish writing in Canada is doubly ghettoized and regionalized between Montreal and the prairies, yet there are a number of distinctive voices during the course of the twentieth century who find mythologies outside of national boundaries.

In 'The Music of America' Sacvan Bercovitch, a native Montrealer who translates Yiddish-Canadian writing and specializes in American literature at Harvard University, distinguishes between prevalent mythologies in Canada and the United States. Among the differences is Canada's status as a colonial country without a mythology in contrast to 'America' with its indigenous, imperialist sense of identity. In addition to Canada's 'rhetoric of absence,'[2] Bercovitch draws upon Northrop Frye's image of the 'bush garden' with its Laurentian Shield and River that contrast with the Atlantic seaboard of the United States: 'The traveler from Europe edges into it [Canada] like a tiny Jonah entering an inconceivably large whale . . . the Gulf of St. Lawrence. . . . Then he goes up the St. Lawrence and the inhabited country comes into view, mainly a French-speaking country, with its own cultural traditions.'[3] At the confluence of Frye's biblical metaphor and the St. Lawrence River (which irrigates the bush garden and initiates the immigrant's rite of passage) lies the island of Montreal—birthplace of Canadian-Jewish literature. Tired, huddled masses arrived at Ellis Island to be greeted by the welcoming words of Emma Lazarus on the Statue of Liberty; later immigrants to Montreal would see a large electric cross on the top of Mount Royal, a reminder of the Christian past that they thought they had left behind.

Despite the relative absence of a dominant mythology comparable to the American model, Frye mythologizes his northern country in another key: 'As I write, the centennial of Confederation in 1967 looms up before the country with the moral urgency of a Day of Atonement. I use a Jewish metaphor because there is something Hebraic about the Canadian tendency to read its conquest of a promised land, its Maccabean victories of 1812, its struggle for the central fortress on the hill at Quebec as oracles of the future. It is doubtless only an accident that the theme of the most passionate and intense of all Canadian novels, A. M. Klein's *The Second Scroll*, is Zionism.'[14] Frye's 'music of Canada' points to the centrality of *The Second Scroll* (1951), Klein's earlier poetry, and his final silence (1955–1972) in any consideration of Canadian-Jewish literature that begins, for the most part, after the Holocaust. The year 1967 marks Canada's centennial but is also the year of Israel's Six-Day War, which changed the political consciousness of many Jewish writers in Canada. Frye's dominant Canadian metaphor is the garrison: 'Small and isolated communities surrounded with a physical or psychological "frontier" . . . develop what we may . . . call a garrison mentality. . . . Novelists of our day studying the impact of Montreal on Westmount [the city's privileged district] write of a psychological one' (225–26). Where the American frontier spirit is more aggressive, the Canadian garrison is more protective, and despite the differences between a militant garrison and a defensive ghetto, Canadian-Jewish writing internalizes the ghetto-garrison mentality as each writer seeks a means of escaping the ghetto while adhering to its traditions. Faced with a northern landscape, muted music, and a belated history, Jewish writers in Canada often look elsewhere for their founding myths—sometimes to Europe and Israel, sometimes to America, where Canada is part of and apart from the *goldeneh medinah*.

Montreal: Yiddish Sources

A. M. Klein, the father of Canadian-Jewish literature, produced a rich body of writing prior to his career-ending silence, which lasted from 1955 until his death in 1972. When Klein's family settled in Montreal in 1910, they arrived just a few years before the family of Saul Bellow, who describes his birthplace as a medieval ghetto around St. Dominique Street with its Orthodox synagogues, ritual baths, and gloomy yards surrounded on the west by kilted Highlanders and on the east by nuns from the parish school.[5] In this uniquely neo-Victorian city characters walked out of the nineteenth century—'in Westmount out of Dickens or Thackeray, in Montreal East out of Balzac. And in between, figures biblical, or characters created say by Israel Zangwill.'[6] Amid Galician, Rumanian, Lithuanian, or Russian immigrants, a circle of Yiddish writers who were familiar to Klein formed an insular enclave in the 1930s and 1940s. Foremost among them was the prolific poet Y. Y. Segal (1896–1954), who became editor of the Yiddish-language daily, *Der Kanader Adler* (*The Canadian Eagle*, 1907–1987).

In 1945 Segal referred to Montreal as 'a Vilna of Canada' because of its vibrant Yiddish culture, which started early in the century. Looking back to eastern European centers of learning, Montreal's Yiddishists carried forward a legacy ranging from secular radicalism to Chasidism, which manifested itself in nostalgia for the Old Country and a utopian vision of Zion. Other contributors to the *Eagle* included Reuben Brainin (1862–1939), Ida Maze (1893–1962), Moishe Shaffir, Israel Rabinovitch, and Yaacov Zipper, who formed a Montreal school of Yiddish letters. In 1942 Klein wrote an editorial commemorating thirty-five years of creative journalism at the *Eagle*: 'Mainly a first-generation community, Montreal Jewry had flesh-and-blood ties with many parts of Eastern and Central Europe. The *landsmanshaften*, the old-town brotherhoods which flourished everywhere, and which have persisted to this day, always knew the *Eagle* to be their house-organ.'[7] In the same breath Klein moves easily from this Yiddish socialist vision of helping refugees after pogroms to a critique of French journalism: 'The *Eagle* has never, as certain Parisian papers, adopted as its slogan the omniscient *Je suis tout*—but it can, without exaggeration arrogate to itself:

Je suis partout!'[8] In his distinction between metropolitan chauvinism and Yiddish egalitarianism, Klein's sense of justice invokes the entire Diaspora and gives wider flight to the *Eagle*.

Montreal's Jewish Public Library, founded in 1914, further promoted political, educational, and cultural needs of the new immigrants, as did the Jewish People's and Peretz Schools (founded in 1913) and the United Talmud Torahs. In contrast to the New York Public Library, where Jewish intellectuals read themselves into America, Montreal's Jewish Public Library offered a forum of continuity with the Old World's Yiddish roots. As late as 1956 Director Dora Wasserman organized a dynamic and innovative Yiddish drama group under the auspices of the *Folk Shule*. It is the only permanent Yiddish theater company in North America and has adapted the work of Isaac Bashevis Singer for the stage and performed contemporary French-Canadian plays in translation.

Segal arrived in Montreal in 1911 from Ukraine and began publishing in the *Adler*. He became its editor from 1938 to 1945 while Klein was coeditor at its English equivalent, the *Canadian Jewish Chronicle*. Their poetry and personalities overlapped as they both straddled Old and New Worlds, and Klein merged them in his poem 'Diary of Abraham Segal, Poet.' Klein also translated and praised the poetry of Melech Ravitch (1893–1976), who became director of the Jewish Public Library in 1941 and translated Kafka's *Trial* into Yiddish. Like Segal and Klein, Ravitch writes of divisiveness and the need to unify a lost world with the present. Similarly, Rochl Korn (1898–1982), who came to Montreal after the Holocaust, writes about her lost home and generational links.

Jacob Zipper (1900–1983) arrived in Montreal in 1925 and set down his impressions in his journal. When he lands in Quebec City he longs for his Polish hometown, and on the train to Montreal he confuses Canadian and Polish landscapes. Zipper complains about the quality of Yiddish in Montreal and the city's preoccupation with materialistic values. He notes the differences between secular and Orthodox members of the community and despairs of the low intellectual levels compared to those he had left behind in Europe, but after he lectures to a full hall at the Jewish Public Library, his hope is renewed, and he is excited by the warm response contrasting with Montreal's cold climate.

Another early community figure is Rabbi Yudel Rosenberg (1895–1935), who was born in Poland and came to Canada in 1913, living in Montreal from 1919 until his death. A prolific writer in Hebrew and Yiddish, he edited and translated the *Zohar* and composed the story of the Maharal of Prague and the Golem, the legend that Rosenberg's grandson, Mordecai Richler, would later use in his post-Holocaust novel St. *Urbain's Horseman*. At the opposite pole to Rosenberg's orthodoxy is the secular fiction of Solomon Ary (1911–1997), who conveys the sexual side of the Yiddish world in a manner reminiscent of Isaac Bashevis Singer's fiction. Carrying the Yiddish tradition in Montreal through to the end of the century are the novels of Yehuda Elberg (b. 1912), who came to Montreal in 1956 from Poland, and whose novels, *The Empire of Kalman the Cripple* (1997) and *Ship of the Hunted* (1997), have been translated and published in the United States. Likewise, Chava Rosenfarb's two novels, *Bociany* (2000) and *Of Lodz and Love* (2000), have been published in the United States and convey the flavor of Polish life before the Holocaust.

Bociany returns to the eponymous Polish *shtetl*, named after the storks that nest on the roofs of the village. The town takes on a kind of borderline quality between this world and a fantasy world. 'There, at the mysterious Sabbath River, the Sambation, lived the dragons that guarded the land of the eternally happy little red Jews, who knew nothing of exile.'[9] The Diaspora's legendary river cannot be crossed because it flows too violently six days of the week and rests only on the Sabbath when crossing is forbidden by law; on the other side of the river live the lost tribes of Israel. The novel's epigraph, 'The end of reality is the beginning of legend,' signals a Yiddish affinity for magic realism, from the quaint water carrier to the source and mouth of Sambation. By the end of *Bociany*, with the future of Poland in doubt, Rosenfarb envisions America and associates it with the utopian state of Jews in Diaspora. Jewish writing in Canada frequently aligns Sambation with local rivers from the St. Lawrence to the North Saskatchewan in the west; these river systems mediate between home and exile, branching out from ghettoes to cosmopolitanism and to other minorities within a multicultural society. It remained for A. M. Klein (1909–1972) to translate this Yiddish milieu literally and figuratively into the surrounding English and French cultures of Montreal.

Montreal: A. M. Klein

Educated at Baron Byng High School with its majority of Jewish students, and later at McGill University and the Université de Montréal, where he studied law, Klein absorbed French and English to add to his historic knowledge of Yiddish and Hebrew, the four languages making their way into most of his polyglot poetry and prose. What Robert Alter has written about Saul Bellow applies equally to Klein: '[F]rom his ghetto childhood in Montreal he retains enough Hebrew to make proper use of biblical and liturgical motifs in his fiction, enough genuinely literate Yiddish to have produced admirable translations.'[10] Some of his earliest poems were published in 1927 in the *Menorah Journal*, and his first collection of poetry, *Hath Not a Jew* (1940), was published by Behrman House with a foreword by Ludwig Lewisohn, who describes him as 'the first Jew to contribute authentic poetry to the literatures of the English speech.'[11] Lewisohn continues his praise: 'Abraham Klein, the most Jewish poet who has ever used the English tongue, is the only Jew who has ever contributed a new note of style, of expression, of creative enlargement to the poetry of that tongue.' Despite such accolades, Klein was ultimately disappointed at not reaching a larger Jewish audience in the United States (twenty times the size of Canada's), and in being misunderstood by non-Jews in Canada. Lewisohn's verdict notwithstanding, Klein's contribution is belated in comparison to Emma Lazarus's nineteenth-century sonnets and Abraham Cahan's editorials and novel *The Rise of David Levinsky* (1917), which preceded the rise of Canadian-Jewish literature by at least one generation, in line with immigration patterns of both countries.

Instead of turning to contemporary American models, Klein returns to earlier British writers from Chaucer to Shakespeare and Milton, and to neoclassical, Romantic, and Victorian poets. On the one hand, his writing is often formal and archaic; on the other hand, as he moves toward modernism by the middle of the twentieth century and becomes increasingly influenced by Joyce's experimental style, his writing takes on a different character. Circumscribed by streets bearing the names of Catholic saints—St. Lawrence, St. Dominique, St. Denis, and St. Urbain—Klein and the

Jewish writers who follow him transcend the ghetto's confines and reach out linguistically and culturally to a broader cosmopolitanism and secular messianism.

While Klein's poetry and editorials in the weekly *Canadian Jewish Chronicle* from 1938 to 1955 are concerned with the rise of Hitler in the 1930s and with the Holocaust in the 1940s, he turns to French-Canadian subjects in his last collection of poetry, *The Rocking Chair* (1948), where he finds common ground between Jews and French Canadians in his bilingual poems about the province of Quebec. Shortly after completing these poems, Klein traveled to the newly founded State of Israel and subsequently wrote his novel *The Second Scroll* (1951), which covers Jewish history in the Diaspora and Zion from early in the twentieth century until mid-century. In the five chapters of this compact novel from 'Genesis' to 'Deuteronomy,' the nameless Montreal narrator searches for his uncle Melech Davidson. Each chapter is followed by a 'gloss' consisting of a variety of genres—poetry, a play, and an essay that interprets Michelangelo's paintings on the ceiling of the Sistine Chapel. The nephew's quest takes him to Europe, North Africa, and Israel, but he never meets his messianic uncle, whose face is never revealed, for all the photographs of him are double or multiple exposures. These blurred images suggest the multiplicity of interpretations within *The Second Scroll*—a novel that challenges the tenets of Christianity and Islam in their historic injustices toward Jews.

Klein writes between two rivers—the realistic St. Lawrence and the legendary Sambation. Fascinated by the impassable, mythological Hebrew river, Klein invokes this symbol at a critical historical juncture between Uncle Melech's escape from the Holocaust and his preparation for Israel: 'then was there fashioned Aught from Naught. . . . Sambation raged, but Sambation was crossed. . . .'[12] In his redemptive imagination Melech traverses this river, but his crossing may be an illusion or mirage for a lost tribe of Canadian Jews who adhere to the realistic presence of the St. Lawrence River. 'In Praise of the Diaspora' (1953) personifies the exile in 'Uncle Galuth,' who encounters Sambation and concludes that even the pre-Exodus experience in Egypt is not entirely negative, for the 'mind, too, is a Nile,'[13] benefiting from exposure to foreign cultures. Mindful of these intersections, Klein recreates Sambation ex nihilo to fill absence with 'Aught,' to retrieve lost uncles and tribes, and to compensate for the history of *galut* and the Holocaust.

The allure of Sambation resides in its paradoxical bipolarity: it rages and rests as if frozen, it isolates, yet protects, the tribes of red Jews in their exile on the other side; apocalyptic and demonic, it throws up stones that may be destructive or energetically constructive in edifices of the imagination. On the one hand, Sambation mythologizes the abject side of exile (*galut*); on the other, it characterizes a more comforting sense of Diaspora and has the added appeal of transforming the negative aspect into a positive one. A staunch defender of the Diaspora, Klein maintained his transcendent view of its mythical fluid boundary and messianic potential for the return of lost tribes. As a utopian river, subversive Sambation is everywhere and nowhere, a critical impasse or aporia, comic and tragic—hence it may be situated in Canada, where significance is always elsewhere. With its ubiquitous absences Canada partakes of a certain utopianism: during the Holocaust 'Kanada' was designated as a place of plenty in the concentration camps.

As Leslie Fiedler puts it, Canada is a 'no-man's-land,' invisible from both the United States (with its Jewish 'significance') and the United Kingdom (with its 'great tradition' from Shylock to Daniel Deronda).[14] Canadian-Jewish literature finds itself in between New York and London, simultaneously belonging and not belonging to Jewish culture south of the border and British culture on the other side of the Atlantic. Caught between the extremes of American mobility and English conservative rootedness, Canadian-Jewish literature charts a middle course between the ironic and the iconic, wandering and fixity, so that the margin becomes an all-encompassing center. In the guise of the St. Lawrence River, Sambation flows through no man's land. To the traditional mirror along the roadway, this body of writing adds a reflection in rivers where questing antiheroes or nobodies mime Everyman.[15]

Just as Klein turns to the redemptive powers of Sambation after World War II, so he turns to Canadian thematics in his final volume of poetry, *The Rocking Chair* (1948)—specifically, a French-Canadian heritage that overlaps in complex tension with his own Jewish past. Although Klein identifies with the rocking chair as a symbol of French-Canadian tradition, its oscillations also symbolize the Jewish poet's ambivalence toward Quebec's antisemitism, which he caricatures in a number of poems. In 'The Break-up,' 'St. Lawrence lies / rigid and white and wise'—simultaneously dead and awaiting rebirth.[16] With its repeated 'crack,' 'The Break-up' is a harbinger of the poet's impending psychological dilemma, for its thawing leads not to a rebirth but to the river's yielding 'last year's blue and bloated suicides.' The color red that shouts 'from all the Aprils hanging on the walls' is a reminder of crucifixion during the cruelest month. In this instance, Klein's St. Lawrence resembles a frozen Sambation with its collision of Christian and Jewish myths; real and imaginary rivers are metaphors of his mind.

Klein also conflates two streams in 'Grain Elevator,' a symbol imported into Montreal's harbor from prairies out west, whose 'oriental' origins are 'babylonian / like something out of a legend' (7). The static elevator opens up a number of biblical possibilities for the poet's imagination. In a series of rhetorical questions he wonders if it is a Leviathan swamped on the shore of the St. Lawrence or a 'blind ark lost and petrified.' At once local and legendary, Klein's river is Canadian as well as historic and diasporic, '[t]he cliffs of some other river.' Sometimes other races claim the 'twinship' of his thought, 'as the river stirs / restless in a white Caucasian sleep.' A whale within a whale, his two-hearted St. Lawrence always doubles in its cosmopolitan flow between ambiguous origins and wide-mouthed silence. The river sides (but never resides) with city or country; for the Jewish stream of unconsciousness, extraterritorial rivers of lost tribes come to mind. Combining east and west, 'Grain Elevators' concludes with the universal, colored faces of all mankind.

'Montreal' demonstrates the multiple streams that make up Klein's Jewish geography, for its opening line, 'O city metropole, isle riverain!' (29) recalls Joyce's Liffey. With Yiddish and Hebrew streams added to the English-French 'bilinguefact' and 'multiple lexicons,' his 'riverain' fixation recurs throughout Canadian-Jewish literature that follows in his wake. Just as Klein's river reaches out to the French, so he also identifies with the Indian tribe paddling along the St. Lawrence in 'Indian Reservation: Caughnawaga': 'This is a grassy ghetto, and no home.'

In an extensive study of 'the river' in early American life and literature, John Seelye comments, '[A] transfiguring threshold, the river is a defining agent in the metamorphosis of colonies to republic, serving as entrance or border but always a symbol of what might be obtained beyond, whether a more fertile land or a water source in India.'[17] Seelye turns his attention to Canada where the St. Lawrence participates in the transformation of provinces to dominion: 'Columbus in Canada is Jacques Cartier, his quest also a compound search for gold and the Northwest Passage' (13). Reminding us that Jacques is Jacob the supplanter, and Cartier the man of maps charting not the coast but the interior route, he highlights French and biblical origins that are also unique to Klein's Montreal. Canadian-Jewish quests originate in Eden's Tigris and Euphrates, continue in Babylonian exile, and flow through a number of European tributaries before crossing the Atlantic to the St. Lawrence and ultimately the Saskatchewan River, which traverses the prairies. If a Northwest Passage lies beyond the Saskatchewan, so too do lost tribes of a northern, peaceable kingdom. Seelye notes the primacy of rivers to the imperial process; for Jews historically conditioned to being conquered and exiled, the invention of a river beyond reality affords an escape route to compensate for conditions of conquest and exile. Diasporic and postcolonial rivers abound in Canadian-Jewish literature as sites of cultural exchange, translation, and transformation.

Whereas Seelye offers an American-Hebraic slant, Simon Schama presents the British side of a Canadian-diasporic preoccupation from his childhood on the Thames. 'Though lines of imperial power have always flowed along rivers, water-courses are not the only landscape to carry the freight of history. When not paddling in the currents of time, I was gumming small green leaves to a paper tree pinned to the wall of my *cheder*, the Hebrew school. . . . The trees were our proxy immigrants.'[18] His Zionist education on the Thames would have been familiar to Klein and his followers on the St. Lawrence. As a transfiguring threshold, the river acts as a frontier in North America, a space of contestation and accommodation for the multiple voices of Canadian-Jewish literature.[19] When the Fathers of Confederation mediated between empire and colony, they turned to the Seventy-second Psalm, importing Hebraic origins from England and the United States: 'Let his dominion also be from sea to sea, and from river unto the world's end.'[20] Rivers are reminders of exile as well as of a longing for home in the lesser Promised Land of Canada; to the three thousand miles of Canadian geography from the St. Lawrence to the Saskatchewan, Jewish writers add three millennia from the Euphrates, Nile, Jordan, and Sambation.

Montreal: Irving Layton and Leonard Cohen

Only a few years younger than Klein, but seemingly of a more modern generation, Irving Layton (né Lazarovitch) doubts that he would have become a poet had it not been for Klein's example and instruction. Layton cultivates an outspoken persona—a mix of prophet and clown (he claims to have been born messianically circumcised)—to compensate for his mentor's silence and Canada's rhetoric of absence. In 'Requiem for A. M. Klein,' the younger poet joins hands with Klein, whom he sees as a medieval troubadour, and leads him out of a labyrinth of silence. Layton concludes by immortalizing poets of Montreal's island against those of the British Isles and, unlike Klein, he increasingly looks to contemporary American poets for his own stylistics. Layton's 'Epigram for A. M. Klein' is more upbeat: 'They say you keep the devils laughing by your wit / And all the furnaces stilled that they may hear it.'[21] Like Klein, Layton attended Baron Byng High School and describes his background in familiar terms: 'In Montreal the dominant ethnic groups stared at one another balefully across their self-erected ghetto walls. Three solitudes.'[22] Layton remembers his feelings of anxiety when crossing St. Denis Street, the border between Jewish and French-Canadian territories, 'hostile Indian country densely populated with church-going Mohawks' (145) waiting to ambush him. If he feels like a warrior on the eastern front, on the west he feels like a trespasser on tree-lined and privileged aloofness of Anglo-Saxon settlement. Layton's ghettoization requires a twofold escape: (1) he uses satire and the morality of prophetic tradition to denounce enemies on either side; (2) he seeks cosmopolitanism and romanticism around the Mediterranean, especially on Greek islands, which offer an escape from harsh Canadian winters and equally harsh Canadian puritanical values, so abhorrent to his Nietzschean sensibility. The Mediterranean haven with its sense of

Hellenic and Hebraic origins provides a displaced Semitism for several Canadian-Jewish writers.

In his other genealogy, 'Keine Lazarovitch 1870–1959,' Layton pays tribute to the memory of his fierce mother and concludes by saying that he continues to sing '[w]hile all the rivers of her red veins move into the sea.' Having inherited his mother's defiance, he passes it on to the next generation in 'For My Two Sons, Max and David,' where he lists stereotypes from the wandering Jew to 'the Jew to gas,' and concludes defiantly, admonishing his sons to be none of those humiliated Jews but instead be gunners in the Israeli Air Force. By 1967, when Canada's centennial culminated in Montreal's Expo '67 and in a subsequent rise in Quebec nationalism, which many Jews in the province found threatening, Layton begins focusing in his writing on militant support of Israel. From leftist politics of the 1930s and 1940s to post-Shoah cosmopolitanism and humanism to identification with Israel after the Six-Day War, Layton's ideological trajectory to the right reflects the directions of other Jewish writers in North America.

Like his close friend Layton, Leonard Cohen, an 'uptown,' or privileged, Westmount Jew, who is critical of that very privilege, pays homage to Klein and navigates the St. Lawrence. In a 1964 lecture about Klein at Montreal's Jewish Public Library, 'Loneliness and History,' Cohen distinguishes between the roles of prophet and priest and argues that Klein should have distanced himself more from his community.[23] As editor, public political figure, and speech writer for the Bronfmans at Seagram's business empire, Klein lost that distance. Cohen also sees his poet-prophet figure as a traitor to his community, and this complex interrelationship revolves around the common derivation of traitor and tradition. In this dialectic the traitor is at once part of the community and apart from it.

Cohen's rare lecture in 1964 marks a watershed in the history of Canadian-Jewish literature: Klein had been silent for a decade, Cohen had published his modernist first novel the year before and would go on to publish his postmodernist second novel two years later. Cohen, Layton, and other Canadian-Jewish writers adopt the stance of prophet or traitor to their community, and their involvement risks rejection. Cohen salutes Layton in 'Last Dance at the Four Penny,' where they dance a *freilach* and revive the rabbis of

Prague and Vilna. Cohen's dance with 'Reb Israel Lazarovitch' takes place 'in this French province, / cold and oceans west of the temple.' This polarity becomes more expansive in 'The Genius' as Cohen lists Jewish stereotypes from the ghetto Jew who dances to the apostate Jew, banker Jew, Broadway Jew, doctor Jew, and finally Dachau Jew, whose 'twisted limbs' in the final stanza return to the twisted limbs of the first stanza to emphasize history's distortion of all Jewish stereotypes. With Klein and Layton, Cohen condemns local and universal antisemitism that culminates in the Shoah. Since he identifies with Jewish suffering and its moral heritage, he feels alienated from the bourgeois comforts of Montreal's Jewish community. His anticolonial rejection of the Governor General's Award for poetry in 1968 coincides with Cohen's identification with the rise of Quebec's nationalism.

Cohen's first collection of poetry, *Let Us Compare Mythologies* (1956), establishes his interest in Hellenic and Hebraic polarities, which recur throughout his career. Embedded in the epigraph from Faulkner's 'Bear' is an allusion to Keats's 'Ode on a Grecian Urn': 'She cannot fade, though thou has not thy bliss. . . . Forever wilt thou love, and she be fair.' Cohen's lyricism owes much to the Greek aesthetic of beauty and truth, while his Jewish heritage provides him with ethics and irony, and this hybrid mythology makes him feel out of place in Canada's cold pastorals: 'I belong beside the Mediterranean. My ancestors made a terrible mistake. But I have to keep coming back to Montreal to renew my neurotic affiliations. Greece has the true philosophic climate—you cannot be dishonest in that light.'[24] Between Montreal and the Mediterranean, Cohen composes 'The Song of the Hellenist': 'O cities of the Decapolus across the Jordan, / you are too great; our young men love you.'[25] Greek statues are too tall for the people of Jerusalem, who are 'small and ugly, / blemishes on the pedestal.' Jonathan is opposed to Theodotus; brilliant scholars with dirty fingernails are opposed to carved marble gods with straight noses; and the Protocols, Bleistein's cigar, and Passover cake are juxtaposed with 'their tall clean women.' Cold Greek models are inhuman, Jewish blemishes are all too human, and Cohen charts an ironic course between ideals and reality. His intertextual strategies form part of a larger intercultural and interethnic pattern—the translation of traditions.

In his first novel, *The Favorite Game* (1963), Cohen identifies with the St. Lawrence River by naming his poet-protagonist Lawrence Breavman, whose apprenticeship reflects the coming of age of Montreal's Jewish community. Breavman plays some of his favorite games in his garage near the garbage can, which is a step removed 'from the mysterious stinking garbage heaps by the edge of the St. Lawrence' (16). Some of these children's games mimic torture techniques of the Nazis; other adolescent rituals alienate him from his family and French Canadians. When he leaves Montreal for Manhattan, Breavman studies the Hudson River ignited by the sun. Failing to discover an epiphany written on the fiery water, he finds instead a monotonous glare off the Hudson. Neither New York nor Montreal satisfies Cohen's artist-hero, who comes of age, as in many Jewish novels in Canada, transgressing borders. The favorite game is a ritual in snow: in spring the winter's game runs into the St. Lawrence, melting place of rituals and communities.

Cohen's second novel, *Beautiful Losers* (1966), also explores rivers, from its epigraph of Ray Charles's singing 'Ol' Man River' to its opening portrait of Catherine Tekakwitha (1656–1680), Iroquois Virgin, or Lily of the Shores of the Mohawk River. Book 1, 'The History of Them All,' refers to a postcolonial recuperation of seventeenth-century native Canada, complicated by and aligned with a 'postdiasporic' Jewish sensibility. That is, Cohen deliberately marginalizes those Jewish concerns that are central to his first novel in favor of early and contemporary Canadian history. Jewish tribes lie behind Indian tribes, and the first-person narrator, who 'comes after' Catherine Tekakwitha, tries to avenge colonial and diasporic history. The narrator is an old anthropologist, who studies plans for a birch-bark canoe to 'rescue' Catherine from the Jesuits, yet he does not want to carry on with his belligerent life on his 'journey up the Mohawk River.'[26] Cohen's obsession with birch recalls Birkenau, one of the many references to the Holocaust in the novel's displacement of Jewish history with Indian tribes. Naming of individuals, tribes, and systems lies at the center of this novel about identities and the absence of centers. One long paragraph mixes them all: rivers, constipation, Tekakwitha, Dachau farmyards, dietary Nazis, and death camps. This paragraph of loss culminates in 'One is ready to stake everything on a river' (40). Cohen stakes much, if not all, on Jewish-Canadian rivers, for the beautiful lost tribes of Indians are on the other side of their own Sambation, and Cohen tries to cross these rivers in his postcolonial prose and poetry.

In book 2, 'A Long Letter from F.,' he introduces the 'New Jew' with a question: 'Are you aware of the Ganges you insulted with a million mean portages?' (160). In that question the British Empire writes back, erasing distinctions between beautiful losers and ugly winners. F. (a radical politician and friend of the narrator) documents the last four years of Tekakwitha's life from her canoe trip along the Mohawk River to the Hudson, Richelieu, and finally the south bank of the St. Lawrence River, where she kneels at her favorite spot at the foot of a cross. In the winter of 1678, beside the frozen river, she burns herself with hot coals, and her mortification is compared to 'newsreel Belsen' (194).

Beautiful Losers ends with a bilingual Jesuit statement: 'Canada and the United States will achieve a new strength from contact with this purest lily from the shores of the Mohawk and the banks of the St. Lawrence River' (243). Old and new interact in complex patterns of translation throughout Cohen's novel, where Ol' Man River irrigates and interrogates the North American imagination. Like the old-new pattern, beginning and end intersect in preposterous postmodern configurations. Before the final trip to the end, F. imagines the following: 'Like a numbered immigrant in the harbor of North America, I hope to begin again. . . . Not the pioneer is the American dream. . . . The dream is to be an immigrant sailing into the misty aerials of New York' (215). Breaking down national and colonial boundaries in this migration up the river, F. demonstrates that the past is prophetic: St. Lawrence and Sambation, Indian and Jew, interact in Cohen's mystical allegory.

Montreal: Mordecai Richler

Montreal's other major Jewish writer, Mordecai Richler (1931–2001), uses satire and social realism to capture his city and critique his community. Like Cohen and Layton, he belongs within a prophetic tradition of writing that alienates him from the parochialism of his milieu. 'To be a Jew and a Canadian is to emerge from the ghetto twice.'[27] Double emergence means looking to the hum and buzz of implication in other cultural capitals: 'Like Jews again, Canadians are inclined to regard with a mixture of envy and suspicion those who have forsaken the homestead (or *shtetl*) for the assimilationist flesh-pots of New York or London.'[28] At home and not at home on St. Urbain Street, Richler also feels displaced from both the British and American mainstream: 'Looking down on the cultural life of New York from here, it appears to be a veritable yeshiva. I won't even go into the question of Broadway or television, but from *Commentary* by way of *Partisan Review* to the *Noble Savage*, from Knopf to Grove Press, the Jewish writers seem to call each to each, editing, praising, slamming one another's books, plays, and cultural conference appearances.'[29]

In his second novel, *Son of a Smaller Hero* (1955), Richler maps his territory: 'The ghetto of Montreal has no real walls and no true dimensions. The walls are the habit of atavism and the dimensions are an illusion. But the ghetto exists all the same.'[30] Richler constructs and deconstructs those walls in his social satire, which examines family and Jewish community, displaces the protagonist's father, and initiates a struggle with his Kleinian precursor. A local poet (namely, Klein) composes an ode for the funeral of the protagonist's father, the eponymous smaller hero: 'Now David Lerner, who was also there was a horse of a different colour. Formerly a communist and still a poet, Lerner was famous for his lyrics throughout Outremont. Possessor of a real rhetorical gift, he wrote speeches that were read by philanthropic millionaires at Zionist banquets.'[31] Richler's quarrel with Klein continues in *St. Urbain's Horseman* (1976), where he borrows the messianic quest motif, with Cousin Joey Hersh replacing Uncle Melech Davidson. From his cosmopolitan home in London and his colonial home in Montreal, Jake Hersh hunts Nazis and relies on his Jewish 'allsorts bag,' which contains Rabbi Akiba, the Thirty-six Just Men, Maimonides, the Golem, Trumpledor, and Leon Trotsky.

Richler's most extended treatment of Klein occurs in *Solomon Gursky Was Here* (1989), with biographer and fly-fisherman Moses Berger, son of L. B. Berger (who is loosely based on A. M. Klein), involved in a dual quest for trophy salmon and the wealthy Gursky family (loosely based on the Bronfmans). Richler engages in postcolonial appropriation in his history of nineteenth-century Canada as the novel opens in 1851 in Ephraim Gursky's igloo on the frozen waters of Lake Memphremagog. More than a century later Moses Berger traces this history on two maps: one of Canada with its Laurentian ice sheets of circa 10,000 B.C.E.; the other, a surveyor's map of the Northern Territories with Ephraim Gursky's journey traced in red ink.

Again, rivers course through the vast historic and geographic terrain of *Solomon Gursky Was Here*. Their Arctic trek takes Ephraim and his grandson Solomon along the Coppermine River, where they share stories from the Bible alongside native tales, comparing oral and written mythologies of loss. Just as Jewish and Eskimo traditions appear side by side, so Richler juxtaposes the historic Coppermine of the northwest with the contemporary Restigouche River in New Brunswick, where Moses fishes for salmon. Even the border between Canada and the United States takes the form of a biblical river for the Yiddish literati who end up in the north of North America: 'They were still this side of Jordan, in the land of Moab; the political quarterlies as well as the Yiddish newspapers they devoured coming out of New York.'[32] Similarly Moses and Richler long for that Promised Land of letters on the other side of the border. Their postcolonial quest takes them back to 1845, when Sir John Franklin departs from the Thames in search of the Northwest Passage. Franklin chooses a biblical passage from chapter 17 of 1 Kings for his passage, 'which tells how Elijah the Tishbite hid himself by the brook Cherith, that was before Jordan' (36).

After Franklin's expedition fails, Hebrew artifacts are discovered in the Arctic. Moses studies these as well as Solomon's journals, which are equally exotic in their descriptions of watersheds of the Yellow and Yangtze rivers. At the same time as Gursky keeps track of the world, Richler turns to British imperialism in the Canadian West early in the twentieth century and conflates Jewish and Canadian history in a postcolonial fiction. This connection with bifocal postcolonialism recurs when intoxicated Moses examines a copy of *Life with the Esquimaux: A Narrative of an Arctic Quest in Search of Survivors of Sir John Franklin's Expedition*. The double displacement of narrative and navigation leads to the identity of the portrait of Prince Henry the Navigator, who in 1415 left Land's End to seek the legendary kingdom of Prester John. This mythical realm of underground rivers that churns out precious stones is in the vicinity of Sambation (147).

Richler may scorn Klein, but he respects Saul Bellow, who has absorbed and translated the same milieu of Mount Royal, St. Lawrence, French, and Yiddish from his childhood. Lamenting that Bellow's fame does not extend as far as Montreal's old working-class Jewish quarter, Richler describes the Nobel laureate as 'a big cultural fisherman [who] casts his line both high and low, covering all the water'[33]—a standard to which Richler aspires. Richler may also envy the status of Bellow, Malamud, and Roth as the Hart-Schaffner-Marx of Jewish-American fiction, whose popularity is unmatched by any Jewish writer in Canada. Bellow's *Adventures of Augie March* preceded Richler's *Apprenticeship of Duddy Kravitz*: Augie conquers America, Duddy tries to possess land in Quebec. Similarly, *Herzog* with its universal letters preceded *St. Urbain's Horseman* with its more limited journal. The lag between Bellow's *To Jerusalem and Back* (1976) and Richler's *This Year in Jerusalem* (1994) is yet another instance of American overshadowing and Canadian belatedness.

With all of his American and international successes, Bellow still remembers his Montreal roots. Bellow's first novel, *Dangling Man* (1944), begins with a confession of origins: 'I have lived here eighteen years, but I am still Canadian, a British subject.'[34] His memories of Montreal also include a French influence unknown in the United States: 'I have never found another street that resembled St. Dominique . . . the French and immigrant women, the beggars . . . whose like I was not to meet again until I was old enough to read of Villon's Paris' (57). French, English, Hebrew, and Yiddish are his and Montreal's unique inheritance.

Born in Lachine, Quebec, Bellow describes Moses Herzog's neo-Victorian train ride across the St. Lawrence River. Moses sees the river frothing: 'The water shone and curved on great slabs of rock, spinning into foam at the Lachine Rapids, where it sucked and rumbled. On the other shore was Caughnawaga where the Indians lived in shacks raised on stilts.'[35] As in Klein's poem 'Indian Reservation: Caughnawaga,' *Herzog* juxtaposes the poverty of Indians and Jews with a biblical sensibility, for Moses' childhood is forty years behind him, 'his ancient times, remoter than Egypt' (140). His reminiscences are 'Jewish antiquities originating in the

Bible' (148). Montreal's Jewish 'cave dwellers' differ only slightly from Indian shack dwellers not so far away.

Montreal: French Connections

On the Francophone side of the city three distinct voices have emerged since World War II to interact with the majority of Anglophone Jews. Just as Yiddish has diminished in Montreal over the course of the century, so more recent immigrants from North Africa have added to the Sephardic and Francophone part of the Jewish community. Although Moroccan Jews may be linguistically comfortable in Quebec, they nevertheless remain wary of nationalist and separatist movements in Quebec politics, which Mordecai Richler strongly denounced. Where once the Anglophone Ashkenaz community of Montreal reacted to antisemitism around the middle of the century, now Francophone Sephardic Jews are equally mistrustful of the government's referenda to separate from the rest of Canada. Monique Bosco, Naïm Kattan, and Régine Robin confront these political insecurities by problematizing their own Jewish roots prior to their settling in Montreal. While they are able to cross previous ghetto boundaries into the French part of the city, they are more interested in a broader cosmopolitan picture that takes them to Paris and more eastern origins. This broader base also applies to a sense of Jewishness that draws on and integrates Sephardic and Ashkenazic sources. Thus, Naïm Kattan, a native of Iraq, sees A. M. Klein as both Sephardic and Ashkenaz, oriental and occidental—a Jew of the Diaspora.[36]

Bosco, Kattan, and Robin choose their rivers of (be)longing, with the Seine serving as an intermediate stage between more eastern roots and their western destination of Montreal. Their multiple backgrounds result in polyphonic sensibilities. Robin intermingles Jewish history and Montreal's signs of the times in a lesson on Sambation in her novel *La Québécoite* (1983) (*The Wanderer*). Exiled from origins in Ukraine and Paris, she settles in Montreal, only to find more shifting sands in names and translations of a fluid identity. 'The Dinour River is said to be the river of Becoming.'[37] Never fixed, the Bergsonian river is ancient and postmodern, a flowing frontier between past and future, an absence and a presence, a mirage of crossings. For the landlocked inhabitants of ghettoes the river offers hope and a means of escape; for North American Jews it may be a site of nostalgia, a connection to the Old Country, a transnational wanderer. Robin's migrant writing combines Yiddish and French in pre- and postmodern modes to explore her multiple identities as an 'allophone' from France. Fluent in French as well as Yiddish in her urban territory, she looks over her shoulder to Freud, Kafka, Canetti, and Perec and senses her ethnic camaraderie with Cohen and Richler.

Like Robin, Monique Bosco confronts the situation of exile from Vienna, Paris, and Montreal as woman, Jew, and writer with a non-Quebecois accent. Having lost her mother tongue, German, she writes in translation, in the fluid margins between various identities and cultures. Translation leads to transformation, a theme central to her writing, especially in the biblical example of Lot's wife, the nameless woman who looks back and is turned into a pillar of salt or petrified tears. To identify with that transformation is one source of Bosco's lamentations: the desire to return home, but the impossibility of doing so. In *Babel-Opéra*, Bosco composes polyphonically a series of metamorphoses; in her second metamorphosis she exchanges the Danube for the Seine in her western trajectory and transformation. In 'Métamorphose VI' she moves further west to Canada, where she encounters Eskimos and Indians and adapts to English: 'I do speak white, you know.'[38] She also meets her revolutionary lover, who speaks '*Paroles-fleuves*': 'An endless flow of words, like the immense Saint Lawrence River, the other shore of which we sometimes do not see' (59). A revolutionary, he insists that he will not render unto Caesar what is Caesar's, but instead will overthrow thrones and empires. In this postcolonial metamorphosis white speech becomes colorful as Bosco layers the present with past texts to accompany her displacements.

For Naïm Kattan, too, the Seine is an intermediate point between origins and the St. Lawrence. At the end of his first novel, *Farewell, Babylon* (1975), the protagonist leaves Baghdad for France, and through the windows of the bus heading for the desert he sees the faces of friends and family, but also the howling dogs pursuing him. At the end of its sequel, *Paris Interlude* (1977), he arrives in New York from Paris and looks both forward and backward with transatlantic bifocal vision. 'I already had a double skin. Soon it would be triple, an impassable carapace.'[39] In North America he carries Europe with him—'Jews reconstructing, in the framework of the new continent, an ever-receding Europe.'[40] When Kattan first arrives in Montreal, he discovers a migratory city that stretches between river and mountain, a space for translating dreams: 'But the Montrealers, shut into their villages, didn't even know the river was there, that they could walk to Verdun and sit on its banks. Some Sunday afternoons you found a few solitary people there . . . who found in the wild, untamed waters of that inland sea an image of the force and power they were looking for.'[41] The St. Lawrence acts as a correlative for the immigrant's imagination; mountain and river provide the city with a frontier. Kattan, Bosco, and Robin reinvent Old and New Worlds and are in turn invented by them.

Whereas a number of Jewish writers have left Montreal in response to political and linguistic pressures, others such as Robert Majzels have remained and adjusted to the Francophone shift, or 'bilinguefact.' Majzels is both a novelist and translator, reflecting the need to be part of his French milieu. His experimental postmodern novels challenge traditional categories and classifications; their intertextual and intergeneric mélange reflects and refracts the multicultural society of which they are a product. As in Régine Robin's texts, the multiple voices in his fiction echo urban polyphony and ethnic streams. The pastiche of *Hellman's Scrapbook* (1992) is a palimpsest of bilingual reportage interspersed with memories of the Holocaust. Competing voices in *Apikoros Sleuth* (forthcoming) recreate a palimpsest in Talmudic format: the central text narrates an urban detective mystery while marginal commentaries offer a range of Hebraic and Hellenic sources. The result is a postmodern 'second scroll': the quest for meaning resides in the reading process across subverted horizontal and vertical directions. Outside of the mainstream, Majzels' writing forms its own tributaries indicative of the 'new' Montreal signaled earlier in Leonard Cohen's *Beautiful Losers*.

Winnipeg (Ludwig, Waddington, Wiseman)

Canadian-Jewish literature has traditionally been a tale of two ghettoes—Montreal's Main, or St. Lawrence, area and the north end of Winnipeg (Cree, for 'muddy water'), where Jack Ludwig, Miriam

Waddington, and Adele Wiseman have accomplished for their prairie city what Klein, Richler, Cohen, and Layton have done for Montreal. From one perspective Montreal is a New York of the north with a Parisian twist, while Winnipeg is a northern version of Chicago with its Jewish-Ukrainian mix and Yiddish socialist background. As in Montreal, the Peretz School on the prairies provided the linguistic, literary, and political training for its writers. Geographically the center of Canada and the gateway to the west, Winnipeg offers an education that takes writers back to British roots: 'Even as children or grandchildren of immigrants, we proclaimed our loyalties not so much to Canada as to British North America.'[42] The writer remembers Armistice Day assemblies every November 11 at his Jewish day school in Winnipeg, where students saluted the Union Jack and honored the British Empire. Out of those competing English and Yiddish models, or two versions of the Old Country, Winnipeggers fashioned a vibrant culture through the middle of the twentieth century.

Jack Ludwig (b. 1922) left Manitoba near the end of World War II to pursue his career in the United States, and his writing, like Saul Bellow's, with whom he coedited the magazine *The Noble Savage*, is marked by a dual Canadian-American identity. Ludwig's first novel, *Confusions* (1963), opens with American exuberance characteristic of Saul Bellow's *Adventures of Augie March* (1953). 'I sing confusion, I, Joseph Gillis, myself confused, or, to put it another way, an American. Look at me, tall washed-out paleface with a father swarthy, squat, burning with Hasidic joy' (3). The novel's 'confusion' is not just between 'Doctor Gillis and Mister Galsky,' the title of the first chapter, which pits Ivy League Harvard against Hasidic roots, but also between energetic egoism and a more conservative self-reliance and a displaced American-Canadian confusion. Ludwig's conquest of America combines irony and allusiveness to ghettoize Harvard Yard. 'A ghetto! A *shtetl* like Pa's small Russian hometown, Krivoi Rog, that's what my Jewish bones recognized in Harvard Yard, a ghetto where everyone knew everyone else' (4). Just as New England turns to Old Russia in *Confusions*, so too does the chapter 'Thoreau in California' heighten those confusions by introducing Flamand, a Canadian Cree Indian, who wants to establish Walden in California with a Yiddish touch of Sholom Aleichem. Ludwig establishes confused identities in the North American melting pot.

'Take the Cree away from you and the Jew away from me and what's left is the same lousy one-hundred-percent American' (126). In this subtraction of hybrid identities, where '[m]y tribe, your tribe [are] defunct' (126), the residual all-American melting pot holds sway.

Ludwig's North American song of conquest recurs in his autobiographical second novel, *Above Ground* (1963), with its host of family characters from Winnipeg's north end before and after World War II. Uncle Bim, the protagonist's surrogate father and source of strength, combines the energy of Russian ancestors with biblical and classical sources. He and the peddler Bibul are among the novel's most memorable characters, and the award-winning short story 'Requiem for Bibul' forms part of the larger novel. As Bibul haggles in Yiddish over prices with the local women, Ludwig exposes the divisions of capitalism and communism during the 1930s and 1940s. With a degree of nostalgia he captures the mood and radical politics of his native city. As the protagonist's consciousness expands, he discovers more about his family, his city, and the world at large during the Second World War: '[M]y city is set where two rivers meet. Its two main streets hug the rivers, one better than the other. Often they wander off, but in time remember, and not much is lost' (74).

Describing Winnipeg's Red and Assiniboine Rivers, Ludwig concludes, '[O]ur familiar rivers become The River in our lives, undifferentiated in our imaginations from Shakespeare's Avon or Eliot's Thames or Joyce's Liffey—equally evocative, equally enigmatic, daring our puny imaginations to come up with a legend to match the truth of ice-break, thaw, or flooding.'[43] Not only is Ludwig's river an objective correlative for his creative imagination, connecting particulars to universals, but it assumes mythical and legendary proportions, transcending its immediate prairie source through an allusive network. Always, and never, going home again, writer and river of Jewish frontiers offer a way in and out of mindscapes. As with A. M. Klein, the Bible and James Joyce form two major influences on Ludwig, whose requiem puts Winnipeg's regional rivers on the map, only to be erased by the passing of a once vibrant immigrant community.

Adele Wiseman's (1928–1992) *Old Woman at Play* (1978) focuses on the creative life of the author's mother, who makes dolls out of buttons and scraps of cloth. From Winnipeg Wiseman tries to locate her mother's home in the Old Country: 'You went up from the edge of the prairie, over vague tracts of water, on a kind of wooden stepladder to a boardwalk in the sky, and there they were, the rickety wooden houses, the cows, the peasants, the rivers . . . my auxiliary world.'[44] Central to this auxiliary Chagallian world in Ukraine are two rivers—the Bug and the Sinyuha (blue river)—which meet and run briefly together. Her mother explains that these rivers are like brother and sister, or Siamese twins. A threshold for metamorphoses, it is a metaphor for human nature, flowing in all directions. Moreover, those two rivers may represent her two major novels, *The Sacrifice* and *Crackpot*: the first, a tragic family saga; the second, a comedy in a more experimental, free-flowing vein; and the two novels combine to create an overarching tragicomedy of Jewish immigration to Canada.

The Sacrifice (1956), which won the Governor General's Award, takes the patriarchs Abraham and Isaac to the New World after the pogroms of Eastern Europe. Abraham has lost two sons in the Old World and must begin anew. Wiseman captures the Yiddish rhythms of immigrant life on the prairies, exploitation in the clothing industry, and social snobbery. Through tragic circumstances Abraham blindly commits a murder. At the end of the novel his grandson, Moses, visits him at the asylum on Mad Mountain, a Sinai superimposed on flat Winnipeg, where a laying-on of hands between the generations suggests continuity in the midst of tragedy. Wiseman's epic saga is an act of translation from Yiddish to English, from persecution in Russia to gentler discriminations of immigrant Ukrainians and Scots in Winnipeg.

If *The Sacrifice*'s immigrant family succumbs to suffering, *Crackpot* (1974) surmounts the ordeals of immigration by shattering established Canadian structures and Jewish vessels. The protagonist, Hoda, transmutes Winnipeg's neo-Victorian motto on its city hall—COMMERCE, PRUDENCE, INDUSTRY—into a carnivalesque CONDOMS, PRURIENCE, INCESTRY. Her rebellious renaming constitutes an act of possession and formation of a new identity—a reformulation of Joyce's and Klein's silence, exile, and cunning. Wiseman domesticates the west through her comedy, cabalistic play, and Yiddish syntax, which goes hand in hand with her socialist background to combat injustices. She transforms Klein's tragic 'Break-up' into *Crackpot*'s comic spirit of restoration, and Melech

Davidson into Hoda's son David. Half-named Hoda stirs and tames the turbulent waters of Sambation and Winnipeg in her restorative vision and actions—songs of innocence and experience. With its cabalistic epigraph about creation and its concluding Cree allusion to Winnipeg's muddy waters, Wiseman's novel captures the spirit of Jewish life on the prairies through the first half of the twentieth century.

Miriam Waddington (b. 1917) is the third member of Winnipeg's radical troika who considers herself an outsider on the wintry Manitoba prairie, with her spiritual and cultural homes in eastern Europe and Jerusalem. Her second collection of poetry, *The Second Silence* (1955), seems to echo Klein's situation at that time. In her 1976 collection of poetry, *The Price of Gold*, Waddington, who has translated Yiddish writing into English, laments Klein's fallen grief in 'By the Sea: For A. M. Klein': 'He dropped a silver line / into the tides of verse.'[45] In her pioneering study of Klein she discusses the utopian kingdom of red Jews and its legendary river.[46] In 'Winnipeg' she praises the 'darling rivers, Red or Assiniboine,' and in one of her prose poems, 'Little Allegories of Canada,' she playfully joins Ottawa and Winnipeg: 'They turned into assiniboine frost and redriver gold' (399). Waddington shows her familiarity with the allegory of Sambation's red Jews and the irony of crossing her own Red River in Winnipeg.

Her Canadian focus expands to the rest of the world in 'My Travels' when she visits Bucharest, Moscow, Warsaw, Hamburg, and Jerusalem. By the end of the poem she no longer knows where home is. Similarly, in 'Disguises' she travels to the Moscow River, Tel Aviv, and New York and announces that she carries within her a dual identity of Lenin and a boisterous rabbi. After her travels through the Diaspora her journeys home and abroad are joined by rivers of personal identity:

(Don't shout
my name   whisper it
to the world's rivers)
I'm coming
Father Volga
wait for me
Mother Assiniboine[47]

West of Winnipeg: Eli Mandel and Henry Kreisel

Eli Mandel (1922–1992) pays homage to A. M. Klein, struggles with a Jewish-Victorian upbringing, and displaces authority in family romances. Mandel confronts an absence on the prairies, devoid of Jewish landmarks. Born in Estevan, Saskatchewan, where tiny, isolated agricultural Jewish communities settled early in the twentieth century, Mandel discovers poetry as a means of overcoming a sterile environment: 'I did not really descend from my Victorian Jewish bourgeois family, nor did I really belong to them, but in fact there on the prairies lived as the abandoned child of Martian royalty.'[48] He exaggerates class structures, for as one who experienced the Depression's poverty in his childhood he is as removed from bourgeois comforts as from extraterrestrial aristocracy. Mandel's family romance echoes his earlier comment about the duality of growing up Jewish on the prairie with a Yiddish-English bilingualism at home and school: 'Mentally, I was being brought up a genteel Victorian boy, with a quaint though serious touch of middle-European Yiddish gentility to boot.'[49] The suppressed savage in him works backward to uncover a lost childhood.

One substitute family appears in 'Snake Charmers,' a poem in memory of A. M. Klein. As the poet observes a snake charmer in Djemma el Fna's Moroccan marketplace, his Canadian childhood rises in that charmer's eyes. That rising childhood with its spices is a direct echo of Klein's memories of spices in 'Autobiographical'; and Mandel summons his family of poets: 'Abraham Klein, Irving, Leonard, / you and I could once have sung our songs' among Jews around the world. The strange loop of the serpent intertwines with the circle of Canadian-Jewish poets from Montreal to the west.

In one of the most complex Canadian Holocaust poems, 'On the 25th Anniversary of the Liberation of Auschwitz: Memorial Services, Toronto, January 25, 1970,' Mandel recounts his response to a ceremony held at Toronto's YMHA. Mandel's stuttering verse imitates the parade of survivors, German guttural sounds, and Gothic lettering on screen and hall platform. The 1970 service with its slides bleeds into the poet's prairie childhood in Estevan's Orpheum Theater (1930) before the war, and Mandel's presence in or absence from Europe during the war. He writes the poem after

January 25, 1970, and fourteen years later, in January 1984, he feels compelled to write an essay explaining the poem's composition and meaning. In his attempt at exorcism and (personal) liberation, he employs a series of negatives, using 'not-language' for his 'unsayable poem' (3). In 1970 Toronto and 1944 Europe he finds the Estevan of 1930, and these times and places are both causes and effects of fragmentation and disorientation. 'Its substitutions, the graves of the war dead, in Europe, for example, the place of the Jewish dead on the prairies, a father's grave' (8).

Mandel visits concentration camps in Europe and the Jewish dead on the prairies to come to terms with his own origins and identity. At the Souris River valley in rural Saskatchewan he rediscovers his biblical birth: 'birthmark' recounts how the poet's mother strikes her temple when she sees a mouse and remarks that the poet will be marked at birth.[50] That mouse and mark become the 'souris river' that the poet carries on his brow, 'the river / in my head' (along with phylacteries and the Holocaust). Mandel develops the mark of Cain in 'souris river': 'the mouse runs through passover and the harvest of matzoh' (17). With traditional influences from Klein and postmodern parallels to Cohen, Mandel combines biblical allusion and prairie riverscape, both underscoring forms of exile. The river runs through the 'province of poetry' (Saskatchewan and elsewhere) and speaks in 'Hebrew syntax' (countercurrent and undercurrent). This river of desire flows from an absent source before emptying into another absence. From the river of Babylon to Saskatchewan's Souris Mandel captures the course of exile. In the exchange between poet and prairie, headwater and backwater, Mandel registers the landscape and is in turn mapped into identity by it. His rural glyphs, like Richler's urban signs, are evidence of Jewish displacement within Canada; by highlighting these signs, writers rewrite history and landscape, restoring biblical origins to the New World.

Born in Vienna, Henry Kreisel (1922–1991) escaped from Austria before the *Anschluss* and arrived in England in 1938, but by 1940 he was placed in an English internment camp and soon transferred to another internment camp in Canada. After studying English and comparative literature in Toronto, he eventually became a professor and vice-president of the University of Alberta. While studying at the University of Toronto in 1942, Kreisel read A. M. Klein's collection of poetry, *Hath Not A Jew*, and discovered the importance of Klein's urban-Jewish voice in his own development as a writer. Kreisel's short story, 'The Almost Meeting,' is based upon a failed encounter between the two writers, because by the time Kreisel tried to meet Klein, the latter had already retreated into silence. Kreisel's fiction is preoccupied with 'almost meetings' between characters of different backgrounds—a theme emblematic not only of Kreisel's writing but of Canadian-Jewish literature in general.

In Kreisel's short story 'Chassidic Song' (1978), Arnold Weiss, a secular-Jewish Joycean scholar, finds himself seated on an airplane beside Josef Shemtov, a Chasidic Holocaust survivor. On the flight from Montreal to New York Weiss asks Shemtov if he is going to a *Farbrengen*, or Chasidic gathering, and Shemtov is surprised that Weiss knows that special word, which he must have learned from his Polish grandfather, Moses Drimmer, who died in Poland before the Holocaust. Shemtov's family, on the other hand, perished during the Shoah, but he is saved by a non-Jewish family. After the war he comes to Canada, having abandoned religion, but in Montreal one Friday evening he discovers the joys of Chasidism, which he conveys to Weiss. Joycean modernism almost meets Yiddish traditionalism in Kreisel's fiction.

A member of the Drimmer family also appears in 'Homecoming' (1959), a memory of Europe after the Holocaust. In search of any surviving members of his family after the war, Mordecai Drimmer returns to his Polish village, but only his uncle David Mantel remains. The avuncular role recurs in Kreisel's first novel, *The Rich Man* (1948), the first Holocaust novel written in Canada. In 1935 the protagonist, Jacob Grossman, leaves Toronto to visit his mother, his sisters, and their families in Vienna amid all the signs of a rising Nazism. A mere factory worker, Jacob pretends to be the rich Canadian relative, but the illusion serves to underscore the inability of the New World Jew to save his Old World family. With his two nephews, Jacob is exposed to the illusory delights of the Danube and the more realistic looming tragedy. By the end of the novel Jacob returns to Canada, abandoning his Viennese family to the fate of the Shoah, for the family reunion is little more than an almost meeting.

Kreisel's second novel, *The Betrayal* (1964), reverses the transatlantic theme, situating events in Edmonton after the war, replacing the not-so-blue Danube River with the frozen North Saskatchewan. European survivors appear in 'innocent' Edmonton to recount their tales of betrayal to the narrator, Mark Lerner, a Canadian-Jewish historian. Holocaust history intrudes in remote northwestern Canada as the novel concludes in the Arctic wilderness. In Kreisel's fictional world the Danube and North Saskatchewan almost meet across the Atlantic and across the great historical divide—the Shoah—pointing to Canada's failure to open its doors to Jewish refugees during the Second World War.

Ontario's Outsiders

Neither the spirit of individualism on the prairies nor the sense of communal creativity in Montreal finds similar expression in Toronto with its later wave of immigrants from different cultural backgrounds. Montreal's Yiddish renaissance, French connections, and major writers such as Klein, Layton, Cohen, and Richler have no counterpart in Toronto's Jewish community. In the absence of a usable past, Jewish writing in Ontario traditionally has been thin, compared to that of Montreal and Winnipeg. Instead of Richler's broad canvases, one finds the oblique views of the compressed novels and short stories of Helen Weinzweig (b. 1915), which portray the complexities of representing Jewish life in Ontario. Many of the stories in *A View from the Roof* (1989) dramatize the strains between members of Jewish families or the tensions between Jews and Gentiles. She undermines the myths and stereotypes of these relationships by introducing self-reflexive artists who defamiliarize realistic representation. The Toronto poet and science fiction writer Phyllis Gotlieb (b. 1926) combines a Chasidic past with children's schoolyard games in *Ordinary, Moving* (1969). The disjunctions between a European Jewish heritage and contemporary settings in Ontario in Gotlieb's and Weinzweig's writing are isolated examples of radical writers at odds with a conservative majority.

Norman Levine (b. 1923) grew up in the Yiddish ghetto of Ottawa's 'Lower Town' surrounded by a French community, but he has spent most of his adult writing life in rural England, composing realist fiction about his Canadian roots and English residence. Though Levine is known mainly for his short stories, his earliest publication is a collection of poetry, *The Tight-Rope Walker* (1950), whose title echoes Bellow's earlier *Dangling Man* (1944) and Richler's first novel, *The Acrobats* (1954)—all apprenticeship works about starting out in a state of limbo. For Levine, this looking for directions involves his bifurcation between his native Canada and England. The final poem, 'Letter from England,' demonstrates how Levine is split between two countries: 'Behind you left a long river, / With the only Saint you believed in; / (But Lawrence had his limitations).'[51] British, Canadian, and Jewish allusions alternate throughout the poem and throughout Levine's tripolar life: 'You added new things, but in translation / They dissolved into provinces: / Into Montreals, Torontos, and Ottawas' (29). The poem begins with a magnet pulling the poet in all directions and ends with his double exile from a Canadian past and an England without roots. The translation from Yiddish in Ottawa to a different accent in England is central to most of Levine's naturalistic fiction—minimalist lives depicted in the minimalist style of Chekhov or Hemingway.

Matt Cohen (1942–1999) also grew up in Ottawa, and his posthumous memoir, *Typing: A Life in 26 Keys* (2000), offers a glimpse into Canada's literary scene over the past several decades from the perspective of a Jewish outsider. Moreover, it is unique in explaining the problematics of Jewish writing in the conservative province of Ontario. Despite having published more than twenty-five books and won Canada's prestigious Governor General's Literary Award just before his death, Cohen complains in his memoir about neglect throughout his life. A self-proclaimed rootless Jew, who is mourned by his religious grandmother for marrying a non-Jew, Cohen frequents Toronto's YMHA, lives on Spadina Road (his 'cosmic spine' and once the heart of Toronto's Jewish community), and turns to Jewish subjects mainly in the second half of his writing career. An outsider to the Jewish community, he feels equally alienated from the Canadian mainstream, which he views as too conservative and Christian. What he finds in the international success of such Canadian writers as Robertson Davies, Timothy Findley, Margaret Laurence, Margaret Atwood, and Alice Munro is 'a conservative, small-town, restrained, Protestant tradition that found a tremendous echo of self-recognition across the country.'[52] Younger than these writers, offbeat, unconservative, and un-Protestant, Cohen nevertheless publishes a series of his 'Salem' novels about rural Ontario without any Jewish content. Growing up in the 1950s in Ottawa, he responds violently to antisemitic slurs, but stops attending synagogue after his bar mitzvah.

In the sixties in Toronto he becomes involved with left-wing politics and George Grant's philosophic critique of American imperialism and Canadian dependence on American ways. Although a mentor, 'Grant was part of what I saw as the British-Canadian ruling establishment, whose authoritarian nature and antisemitism had frequently rung extremely sour notes in my life' (39). Similarly, in the publishing world this self-proclaimed, self-hating Jew is equally mistrustful of poet and editor Dennis Lee—a Christian minister's son, 'a student of English literature and philosophy, wrapped up in codes of behavior that seemed to have come from fifties television serials I'd missed' (84–85). In the middle of the left-wing, anti-Vietnam, and drug-induced culture of the sixties, Cohen suddenly discovers two bookends from his aunt Reeva, who had settled on a socialist kibbutz in Israel. This talisman consists of different pieces of wood fitted together at bizarre angles, and its inside-out shape forms a 'cosmic geometry' (89) that ties in with the cosmic spine of Jewish Spadina Road. These bookends are emblematic of so many of Cohen's novels that alternate between experimental and traditional fiction with bizarre angles and points of view. They characterize Cohen's paradoxical career, his inside-out relationship as a Jew to mainstream Canadian writing.

By the 1980s Cohen turns away from agricultural Ontario regionalism to tap his Jewish roots. The process begins with a trip to Spain to research his historical novel, *The Spanish Doctor* (1984). Upon his arrival in Madrid he identifies with the country as the land of his ancestors, where he finally feels like an insider, in contrast to his outsider status in Canada. In Toledo he sees the present as a thin transparency covering the historical landscape of the Inquisition. This palimpsest of history provides a clue to Cohen's fiction over the past two decades and extends as well to other contemporary Jewish writers in Canada. Having arrived in Spain with a feeling of belonging, Cohen departs after two weeks in utter alienation. 'I was in the nightmare their ancestors and mine had shared, the nightmare that for some had ended in death and exile, for others in the beginnings of a new and dazzling empire' (200). Cohen is partly disappointed that his multicentury triptych of *The Spanish Doctor*, *Nadine* (1986), and *Emotional Arithmetic* (1990) has met with greater success in Europe than in Canada, and in the 1990s he spends considerable time in France and becomes increasingly involved with translating. *Typing* ends with Cohen identifying with the marginal lives of Joseph Roth, Kafka, and Walter Benjamin. Matt Cohen's memoir is a typing and translating of Jewish and Canadian writing as separate entities with different musical registers and keys to understanding. His aunt Reeva's bookends represent the Canadian mosaic, where Jewish wedges fit inside out at kaleidoscopic angles.

The Drift of New Voices

Matt Cohen's decades-long struggle with Ontario's conservative literary establishment epitomizes the differences between Jewish writing in Montreal and Toronto. For most of the century, Montreal—with the largest Jewish population in Canada, the most vibrant cultural institutions, and the most important writers, who drew on a heritage of irony and humor to counter the surrounding pressures of English and French—dominated the literary scene. In the past few decades, however, there has been an exodus from Montreal to Toronto in response to Quebec's threat of separation from the rest of Canada. Toronto now has the largest Jewish community in the country, and some younger writers have attempted to add their heritage to the multicultural complexion that has virtually overtaken the earlier WASP hierarchy. Playwright Jason Sherman was born in Montreal in 1962 and moved to Toronto in 1969: his play *Reading Hebron* (1997) struggles with the sense of Canadian-Jewish identity in light of the Israeli-Palestinian conflict. J. J. Steinfeld, the son of survivors, writes obsessively and surrealistically about the Shoah in his short stories, such as 'Dancing at the Club Holocaust' (1993), and has recently moved to the isolation of Prince Edward Island. Torontonian Cary Fagan goes to New York in search of Isaac Bashevis Singer in his novel *Felix Roth* (1999)—another attempt to capture a lost past.

The Toronto poet Anne Michaels achieved international recognition for her first novel, *Fugitive Pieces* (1996). Influenced by Michael Ondaatje, who in turn has drawn on Leonard Cohen's postmodernism and postcolonialism, Michaels creates a usable past for her Toronto fiction, where the Greek neighborhood borders the Jewish one. Athens and Toronto are 'way stations,' not simply because they are ports, but because they are the thresholds for immigrants or refugees. Privileging the underprivileged, Michaels captures the moment of transition between cultures, alternating between the solid buildings of established Toronto and the caravansary of the past. The hidden history of the city's ravines contrasts with the permanent architecture of neo-Victorianism or high modernism, such as the limestone of Union Station and the imposing Royal York Hotel. Bewildered by this urban onslaught, Jakob Beer arrives from Europe after the war and imagines that his father (who was killed by the Nazis) must have felt the same when he arrived in Warsaw with his own father for the first time. Immigrant history is layered and filtered through generations and different settings to add focus to blurred fugitive pieces. Way stations are sites of cultural exchange, ethnic mix, and synchronic intersections: 'Taverns, oasis, country inn on the king's highway. Way stations. Dostoyevsky and the charitable women in Tobol'sk. Akhmatova reading poetry to the wounded soldiers in Tashkent. Odysseus cared for by the Phaiakians on Scheria.'[53] Aftermath of war and rebirth of another life, the abandoned way station achieves greater permanence in a post-Holocaust new world. By the end of the century the Wandering Jew shares the fate of other groups in a global wandering that populates Toronto.

Michaels sifts through layers of underwater history from the drowned Polish city of Biskupin at the beginning of the novel to the waters of Greece at the center. River, history, and narrative intertwine: 'The invisible paths in Athos's stories: rivers following the inconsistencies of land' (51). Athos Roussos saves young Jakob Beer from the Holocaust by hiding him on the Greek island of Zakynthos during the war. The seven-year-old refugee describes his first view of Greece: 'I woke and saw signs in a fluid script that from a distance looked like Hebrew. Then Athos said we were at home, in Greece. When we got closer I saw the words were strange; I'd never seen Greek letters before' (14). This Hebraic-Hellenic conflation suggests a rebirth of civilization in a strange and familiar home away from home, a displacement that calls for translation: 'Above the bed, a broadsheet of "What Have You Done to Time," the Greek translation written in ink under the English, a shadow; the Hebrew translation written above, an emanation' (267). Athos and Jakob exchange languages, 'the ornate Greek script, like a twisting twin of Hebrew' (21).

Michaels's early poem 'Lake of Two Rivers' prepares for the international rivers of her novel: with her family on a summer vacation to Ontario's Lake of Two Rivers, she recalls the Lithuanian River Neman—her ancestors' river. Like Adele Wiseman's ancestral rivers of the imagination, these two rivers represent the bifurcation of Jewish writers in Canada, whose past belongs elsewhere. The second part of Michaels's novel opens with a description of Toronto's river: 'The Humber River flows southeast across the city. Even a generation ago, for most of its one-hundred-kilometre course it was still a rural river, meandering through outskirts' (201). The narrator measures the growth of a city by traveling upriver and uncovers cutlery in the river's sediment from the hurricane of 1954. Whether the Humber or the Don River, Toronto is a city of 'rerouted rivers' (101), like its immigrants. Through twinning, doubling, or seconding of languages, rivers, and identities, Michaels creates a usable past for Toronto's twisting, multicultural scene that differs from Montreal's earlier 'bilinguefact.'

The epigraphs to Aryeh Lev Stollman's and Michael Redhill's novels point to divergent directions for future Jewish fiction in Canada. Stollman's return to Jewish and Hebrew sources appears in the epigraphs from Proverbs and from *Children of the Flames: Dr. Josef Mengele and the Untold Story of the Twins of Auschwitz*. In Stollman's novel *The Far Euphrates* (1997), the Bible and the Shoah form the backdrops of history. The epigraphs to Redhill's novel *Martin Sloane* (2001), on the other hand, derive from non-Judaic sources—Euripides' *Alcestis* and Hugo von Hofmannsthal's *Lord Chandos Letter*. Upon second glance, however, Hofmannsthal had Jewish roots, and the passages from Euripides and Proverbs share 'rooms' as Hellenic and Hebraic overlap, the former hinting at life after death, the latter focusing on fulfillment in this world. The eponymous Martin Sloane is half

Jewish and half Irish, but the novel focuses only marginally on Jewish matters in its emphasis on crossing the Atlantic from Dublin to Bloomington, Indiana. Contemporary writers such as Michaels, Redhill, and Stollman chart 'the maze of migrant biographies that makes up their society.'[54]

If Michaels and Redhill telescope outward to Leonard Cohen by way of Michael Ondaatje's example, Stollman immerses himself directly in a Kleinian tradition, for his protagonist, Alexander, studies Genesis in Hebrew: 'the dotted vowels clustered like bees around the honeyed consonants.'[55] Stollman and Klein share the same itinerary and alphabet: Alexander's father visits Iraq because the Tigris and Euphrates Rivers are his lifelong passion; the Jew in Klein's drama in 'Gloss Dalid' of *The Second Scroll*'s heteroglossia seeks justice in Baghdad. Stollman brings the Euphrates and its freight of history closer to Canada and returns to Klein's dialectic between Zion and Diaspora: 'not Euphratic song nor praise of Tigris / Can steal my heart / Away from the banks of Jordan where it dreams.'[56]

Just as way stations are points of entry and departure in *Fugitive Pieces*, so border cities are transitional thresholds in *The Far Euphrates*. Driving over the Detroit River on the Ambassador Bridge between Canada and the United States, Alexander imagines himself first as a seagull, then as *Ruach Elohim* (the Spirit of God at Creation) hovering over the Nile (17). These transcendent metamorphoses highlight the instability of national boundaries for Jews of the Diaspora. Although most of the novel is set in Windsor, Ontario, with excursions to adjacent Detroit, Michigan, other locations such as the border city of Strasbourg, France, figure into the narrative to interrogate 'place' and create a multicultural dimension. The Strasbourg background—'an island between two arms of the same river, the Ill River' (53)—accounts for the characters' fluency in French and German. This questioning of place and identity forms part of Alexander's father's research into the history of the ancient Tigris and Euphrates. The rabbi tags the academic centers on a map on his wall, but he shifts these along the course of the river when he receives information from other scholars. 'Sometimes a river itself needed to be adjusted, as the courses of rivers changed over the millennia. Modern maps did not always reflect the ancient pathways' (41). This map forms a palimpsest in which modern history overlies the period of Babylonian Talmudic academies, and the rabbi's shifting flag pins indicate changes in unstable national boundaries. Similarly, the mixing of ancient languages recapitulates the modern linguistic mélange in the novel.

Just as border cities mark overlapping national identities, so twinning of personal identities is a central feature of *The Far Euphrates*. The narrator muses on his duplicated name, Aryeh Alexander, the Hebrew and Greek heritages from his great-grandfather who lived in Frankfurt. Another ethnic juxtaposition between Gypsies and Jews reappears in the novel from the proximity at Auschwitz of Gypsies and Jewish twins who were experimented on by Mengele. Identities are transformed as a result of these experiments, which in turn impinge on Alexander's post-Holocaust identity. Alexander visits a fortuneteller in Detroit (a maiden aunt or prophetess with Gypsy blood at the Ford estate, where Mrs. Ford is ironically *Die Italienerin*) and a rebbe in New York, who instructs him on the importance of the female *Shechinah* in Judaism. At the same time as Alexander comes to terms with his own sexual orientation, the sexual identity of Hannalore Seidengarn is revealed at her unveiling: Mengele had changed this twin, Elchanan ben David, into a woman. She is buried in a Jewish cemetery with a cross around her neck. Hannalore's fate points to the multiple, confused identities in the novel. Her name means 'silk yarn,' and Stollman's novel unravels this yarn, or lore, of shifting Jewish identities. At the culmination of his education, Alexander finds himself at McGill University, on 'an island set between two rivers'—like other settings and identities in *The Far Euphrates*. The river of Eden flows between borders of exile.

From neo-Victorian roots to postcolonial interrogations, Jewish writing in Canada reaches out to other marginal groups—from indigenous Indians to Quebecois to European immigrants in a multicultural society. This dialogue is often accompanied by rivers of the Diaspora and Canada that speak of home and exile. 'All rivers run to the sea; and the sea is never full; unto the place from whence the rivers come, thither they return again' (Ecclesiastes). By the waters of Montreal, A. M. Klein is both source and mouth of Jewish writing in Canada. His poem 'A Psalm Touching Genealogy' (1944) begins with his heritage—'Not sole was I born, but entire genesis'—and ends with his legacy: 'And there look generations through my eyes.' Klein's prophetic silence resonates in polyphonic heteroglossia: from Sambation, the Laurentian Shield, Babylon, and boreal regions, stones in water speak in words.

Notes

1. Mordecai Richler, ed., *Canadian Writing Today* (Harmondsworth, England: Penguin, 1970), 15.

2. Sacvan Bercovitch, *The Rites of Assent: Transformations in the Symbolic Construction of America* (New York: Routledge, 1993), p. 8. Among the distinctions Irving Abella draws between Canada and the United States is that no Canadian Jew could have written a panegyric to a Canadian river the way Jerome Kern rhapsodized the old Mississippi. 'Our great rivers, the Mackenzie, the St. Lawrence, the Fraser, have little resonance to Canadian Jewry' (Irving Abella, 'Canadian Jewry: Past, Present, and Future' [Toronto: York University Centre for Jewish Studies, Inaugural Lecture, 1998], p. 8). See also W. H. New, 'The Great-River Theory: Reading MacLennan and Mulgan,' *Essays on Canadian Writing* 56 (fall 1995): 162–82.

3. Northrop Frye, *The Bush Garden: Essays on the Canadian Imagination* (Toronto: Anansi, 1971), p. 217. See also Rachel Feldhay Brenner, 'Canadian Jews and Their Story: The Making of Canadian-Jewish Literature,' *Prooftexts* 18, no. 3 (September 1998): 283–97.

4. Northrop Frye, *Bush Garden*, p. 224.

5. James Atlas, *Bellow: A Biography* (New York: Random House, 2000), p. 15.

6. Leon Edel, 'Marginal *Keri* and Textual *Chetiv*: The Mystic Novel of A. M. Klein,' in *The A. M. Klein Symposium*, ed. Seymour Mayne (Ottawa: University of Ottawa Press, 1975), p. 18.

7. A. M. Klein, *Beyond Sambation: Selected Essays and Editorials, 1928–1955*, ed. M. W. Steinberg and Usher Caplan (Toronto: University of Toronto Press, 1982), p. 169.

8. Klein, *Beyond Sambation*, p. 169.

9. Chava Rosenfarb, *Bociany* (Syracuse, NY: University of Syracuse Press, 2000), p. 11. See Ira Robinson, Pierre Anctil, and Mervin Butovsky, eds., *An Everyday Miracle: Yiddish Culture in Montreal* (Montreal: Véhicule Press, 1990).

10. Robert Alter, *Defenses of the Imagination: Jewish Writers and Modern Historical Crisis* (Philadelphia: Jewish Publication Society, 1977), p. 157.

11. Ludwig Lewisohn, foreword to *Hath Not a Jew* (New York: Behrman House, 1940).

12. A. M. Klein, *The Second Scroll* (Toronto: McClelland and Stewart, 1961), p. 38.

13. A. M. Klein, *Beyond Sambation*, p. 470.

14. Leslie Fiedler, 'Some Notes on the Jewish Novel in English,' in *Mordecai Richler*, ed. G. David Sheps (Toronto: McGraw-Hill, 1971), p. 101. See also Bryan Cheyette, introduction to *Contemporary Jewish Writing in Britain and Ireland: An Anthology* (Lincoln: University of Nebraska Press, 1998), xxvi–xxviii.

15. See Michael Greenstein, 'Nobody Chasing Everyman,' *Jewish Book Annual*, vol. 51 (New York: Jewish Book Council, 1993–1994), pp. 42–54. Also see Michael Greenstein, *Third Solitudes: Tradition and Discontinuity in Canadian-Jewish Literature* (Montreal: McGill-Queen's University Press, 1989).

16. A. M. Klein, *The Rocking Chair and Other Poems* (Toronto: Ryerson, 1948), p. 25.

17. John Seelye, *Prophetic Waters: The River in Early American Life and Literature* (New York: Oxford University Press, 1977), p. 7.

18. Simon Schama, *Landscape and Memory* (New York: Knopf, 1995), p. 5.

19. Sander Gilman, ed., *Jewries at the Frontier: Accommodation, Identity, Conflict* (Urbana and Chicago: University of Illinois Press, 1999), pp. 15–21.

20. Quoted in William Kilbourn, ed., *Canada: A Guide to the Peaceable Kingdom* (Toronto: Macmillan, 1970), p. xviii.

21. Irving Layton, *The Pole-Vaulter* (Toronto: McClelland and Stewart, 1974), p. 32.

22. Irving Layton, *Engagements: The Prose of Irving Layton*, ed. Seymour Mayne (Toronto: McClelland and Stewart, 1972), p. 144.

23. For a detailed discussion of Cohen's archival material see Winfried Siemerling, *Discoveries of the Other: Alterity in the Work of Leonard Cohen, Hubert Aquin, Michael Ondaatje, and Nicole Brossard* (Toronto: University of Toronto Press, 1994), pp. 30–35.

24. Leonard Cohen, *The Spice-Box of Earth* (Toronto: McClelland and Stewart, 1961), quoted on back flyleaf.

25. Leonard Cohen, *Let Us Compare Mythologies* (Montreal: McGill Poetry Series, 1956), p. 18.

26. Leonard Cohen, *Beautiful Losers* (Toronto: McClelland and Stewart, 1966), p. 5. For a discussion of names and rivers see Sylvia Söderlind, *Margin/Alias: Language and Colonization in Canadian and Québec Fiction* (Toronto: University of Toronto Press, 1991), pp. 56–57.

27. Mordecai Richler, *Hunting Tigers under Glass* (London: Panther, 1971), p. 9.

28. Richler, *Hunting Tigers*, p. 9.

29. Mordecai Richler, 'Their Canada and Mine,' quoted in *The Spice Box*, ed. Gerri Sinclair and Morris Wolfe (Toronto: Lester and Orpen Dennys, 1981), p. 235.

30. Mordecai Richler, *Son of a Smaller Hero* (Toronto: McClelland and Stewart, 1966), p. 14.

31. Richler, *Son of a Smaller Hero*, p. 143.

32. Mordecai Richler, *Solomon Gursky Was Here* (New York: Knopf, 1990), p. 11.

33. Mordecai Richler, *Belling the Cat: Essays, Reports, and Opinions* (Toronto: Knopf Canada, 1998), p. 95.

34. Saul Bellow, *Dangling Man* (New York: Vanguard, 1944), p. 8.

35. Saul Bellow, *Herzog* (New York: Viking, 1964), p. 33.

36. Naïm Kattan, 'A. M. Klein: Modernité et loyauté,' *Journal of Canadian Studies* 19, no. 2 (1984): 25.

37. Régine Robin, *The Wanderer*, trans. Phyllis Aronoff (Montreal: Alter Ego Editions, 1997), p. 113.

38. Monique Bosco, *Babel-Opéra* (Laval PQ: Editions Trois, 1989), p. 58.

39. Naïm Kattan, *Paris Interlude*, trans. Sheila Fischman (Toronto: McClelland and Stewart, 1979), p. 208.

40. Naïm Kattan, 'Montreal Comes of Age,' in *Canada: A Guide to the Peaceable Kingdom*, p. 109.

41. Kattan, 'Montreal,' p. 110.

42. Robert Schwartzwald, 'an / other Canada, another Canada? other Canadas,' *The Massachusetts Review* 31 (spring–summer 1990): 15.

43. Jack Ludwig, 'You Always Go Home Again,' *Mosaic* 3, no. 3 (1970): 108.

44. Adele Wiseman, *Old Woman at Play* (Toronto: Clarke, Irwin, 1978), p. 54.

45. Miriam Waddington, *Collected Poems* (Toronto: Oxford University Press, 1986), p. 246.

46. Miriam Waddington, *A. M. Klein* (Toronto: Copp Clark, 1970), p. 25.

47. Miriam Waddington, *Say Yes* (Toronto: Oxford University Press, 1969), p. 68.

48. Eli Mandel, *The Family Romance* (Winnipeg: Turnstone, 1986), p. ix.

49. Eli Mandel, *Another Time* (Erin ON: Press Porcépic, 1977), p. 73.

50. Eli Mandel, *Out of Place* (Erin ON: Press Porcépic, 1977), p. 16.

51. Norman Levine, *The Tight-Rope Walker* (London: Totem, 1950), p. 28.

52. Matt Cohen, *Typing: A Life in 26 Keys* (Toronto: Random House, 2000), pp. 157–58.

53. Anne Michaels, *Fugitive Pieces* (Toronto: McClelland and Stewart, 1996), p. 290.

54. Elleke Boehmer, *Colonial and Postcolonial Literature* (New York: Oxford University Press, 1995), p. 220.

55. Aryeh Lev Stollman, *The Far Euphrates* (New York: Riverhead, 1997), p. 3.

56. Klein, *Second Scroll*, p. 134.

Leonard Cohen

Leonard Cohen was born in Westmount, an affluent district of Montreal, in 1934. Shortly after graduating from McGill University, he published his first book of poetry, *Let Us Compare Mythologies* (1956). In the next few years he attempted graduate study at Columbia University and worked in his family's clothing business. After publishing a second book of poetry, *The Spice Box of Earth* (1961), he published his first novel, *The Favorite Game* (1963), which is currently being made into a movie. In 1966 he published his second novel, *Beautiful Losers*, and won the Governor General's Award for his *Selected Poems* (1968). Since completing his six collections of poetry, Cohen has turned to composing and recording songs and has lived on the Greek island of Hydra as well as in a Zen retreat in California. Excerpts from his first, autobiographical novel are in a realistic mode, depicting Montreal in the 1950s, whereas his second novel belongs to a more experimental style that combines indigenous Canadian myths and history with contemporary political events of the 1960s. Both novels have shocked readers because of their abrupt allusions to the Holocaust, featured in his poetry collection *Flowers for Hitler* (1964).

Leonard Cohen

EXCERPTS FROM *The Favourite Game*

The Breavmans founded and presided over most of the institutions which make the Montreal Jewish community one of the most powerful in the world today.

The joke around the city is: The Jews are the conscience of the world and the Breavmans are the conscience of the Jews. 'And I am the conscience of the Breavmans,' adds Lawrence Breavman. 'Actually we are the only Jews left; that is, super-Christians, first citizens with cut prongs.'

The feeling today, if anyone troubles himself to articulate it, is that the Breavmans are in a decline. 'Be careful,' Lawrence Breavman warns his executive cousins, 'or your children will speak with accents.'

Ten years ago Breavman compiled the Code of Breavman:

We are Victorian gentlemen of Hebraic persuasion.

We cannot be positive, but we are fairly certain that any other Jews with money got it on the black market.

We do not wish to join Christian clubs or weaken our blood through inter-marriage. We wish to be regarded as peers, united by class, education, power, differentiated by home rituals.

We refuse to pass the circumcision line.

We were civilized first and drink less, you lousy bunch of bloodthirsty drunks. [. . .]

The Japs and Germans were beautiful enemies. They had buck teeth or cruel monocles and commanded in crude English with much saliva. They started the war because of their nature.

Red Cross ships must be bombed, all parachutists machine-gunned. Their uniforms were stiff and decorated with skulls. They kept right on eating and laughed at appeals for mercy.

They did nothing warlike without a close-up of perverted glee.

Best of all, they tortured. To get secrets, to make soap, to set examples to towns of heroes. But mostly they tortured for fun, because of their nature.

Comic books, movies, radio programmes centred their entertainment around the fact of torture. Nothing fascinates a child like a tale of torture. With the clearest of consciences, with a patriotic intensity, children dreamed, talked, acted orgies of physical abuse. Imaginations were released to wander on a reconnaissance mission from Calvary to Dachau.

European children starved and watched their parents scheme and die. Here we grew up with toy whips. Early warning against our future leaders, the war babies. [. . .]

At night the park was his domain.

He covered all the playing fields and hills like a paranoiac squire hunting for poachers. The flower-beds, the terraces of grass had an aspect of formality they did not have by daylight. The trees were taller and older. The high-fenced tennis court looked like a cage for huge wingless creatures which had somehow got away. The ponds were calm and deadly black. Lamps floated in them like multiple moons.

Walking past the Chalet he remembered the masculine smell of hockey equipment and underwear, the thud of skates on wooden planks.

The empty baseball diamond was blurred with spectacular sliding ghosts. He could hear the absence of cheers. With no bikes leaning against them the chestnut tree and wire backstop seemed strangely isolated.

How many leaves have to scrape together to record the rustle of the wind? He tried to distinguish the sound of acacia from the sound of maple.

Just beyond the green rose the large stone houses of Westmount Avenue. In them the baseball players were growing their bodies with sleep, resting their voices. He imagined that he could see them dimly through the walls of the upper storeys, or rather the sheets they were wrapped in, floating row upon row over the street, like a colony of cocoons in a moonlit tree. The young men of his age, Christian and blond, dreaming of Jewish sex and bank careers.

The park nourished all the sleepers in the surrounding houses. It was the green heart. It gave the children dangerous bushes and heroic landscapes so they could imagine bravery. It gave the nurses and maids winding walks so they could imagine beauty. It gave the young merchant-princes leaf-hid necking benches, views of factories so they could imagine power. It gave the retired brokers vignettes of Scottish lanes where loving couples walked, so they could lean on their canes and imagine poetry. It was the best part of everyone's life. Nobody comes into a park for mean purposes except perhaps a sex maniac and who is to say he isn't thinking of eternal roses as he unzips before the skipping-rope Beatrice?

He visited the Japanese pond to ensure the safety of the goldfish. He climbed through the prickly bushes and over the wall to inspect the miniature waterfall. Lisa was not there. He somersaulted down the hill to see if it was still steep enough. Wouldn't it be funny if Lisa of all people should be waiting at the bottom? He sifted a handful in the sand-box to guard against polio. He did a test run on the slide, surprised that it squeezed him. He looked gravely from the lookout to guarantee the view.

'My city, my river, my bridges, shit on you, no I didn't mean it.'

The bases had to be run, the upper ponds examined for sail-boat wrecks or abandoned babies or raped white nurses. Touch the tree trunks to encourage them.

He had his duty to the community, to the nation.

At any moment a girl is going to step out of one of the flower-beds. She will look as though she has just been swimming and she'll know all about my dedication.

He lay under the lilacs. The flowers were almost gone, they looked like molecular diagrams. Sky was immense. Cover me with black fire. Uncles, why do you look so confident when you pray? Is it because you know the words? When the curtains of the Holy Ark are drawn apart and gold-crowned Torah scrolls revealed, and all the men of the altar wear white clothes, why don't your eyes let go of the ritual, why don't you succumb to raving epilepsy? Why are your confessions so easy?

He hated the men floating in sleep in the big stone houses. Because their lives were ordered and their rooms tidy. Because they got up every morning and did their public work. Because they were going to dynamite their factories and have naked parties in the fire.

There were lights on the St. Lawrence the size of stars, and an impatient stillness in the air. Trees as fragile as the legs of listening deer. At any minute the sun would come crashing out of the roofs like a clenched fist, driving out determined workers and one-way cars to jam the streets. He hoped he wouldn't have to see the herds of traffic on Westmount Avenue. Turning night into day. [. . .]

Among certain commercial Jews he was considered a mild traitor who could not be condemned outright. They were dismayed by the possibility that he might make a financial success out of what he was doing. This their ulcers resented. His name was in the newspapers. He might not be an ideal member of the community but neither was Disraeli or Mendelssohn, whose apostasies the Jewish regard for attainment has always overlooked. Also, writing is an essential part of the Jewish tradition and even the degraded contemporary situation cannot suppress it. A respect for books and artistry will persist for another generation or two. It can't go on forever without being reconsecrated.

Among certain Gentiles he was suspect for other reasons. His Semitic barbarity hidden under the cloak of Art, he was intruding on their cocktail rituals. They were pledged to Culture (like all good Canadians) but he was threatening the blood purity of their daughters. They made him feel as vital as a Negro. He engaged stockbrokers in long conversations about over-breeding and the loss of creative vitality. He punctuated his speech with Yiddish expressions which he never thought of using anywhere else. In their livingrooms, for no reason at all, he often broke into little Hasidic dances around the tea table.

He incorporated Sherbrooke Street into his general domain. He believed he understood its elegant sadness better than anyone else in the city. Whenever he went into one of the stores he always remembered that he was standing in what was once the drawingroom of a smart town house. He breathed a historical sigh for the mansions become brewery and insurance head offices. He sat on the steps of the museum and watched the chic women float into dress shops or walk their rich dogs in front of the Ritz. He watched people line up for buses, board, and zoom away. He always found that a mystery. He walked into lavatory-like new banks and wondered what everyone was doing there. He stared at pediments or carved grapevines. Gargoyles on the brown stone church. Intricate wooden balconies just east of Park. [. . .]

He had no plans for the future. [. . .]

Some say that no one ever leaves Montreal, for that city, like Canada itself, is designed to preserve the past, a past that happened somewhere else.

This past is not preserved in the buildings or monuments, which fall easily to profit, but in the minds of her citizens. The clothes they wear, the jobs they perform are only the disguises of fashion. Each man speaks with his father's tongue.

Just as there are no Canadians, there are no Montrealers. Ask a man who he is and he names a race.

So the streets change swiftly, the skyscrapers climb into silhouettes against the St. Lawrence, but it is somehow unreal and no one believes it, because in Montreal there is no present tense, there is only the past claiming victories.

Breavman fled the city. [. . .]

No, his uncles were not grave enough. They were strict, not grave. They did not seem to realize how fragile the ceremony was. They participated in it blindly, as if it would last forever. They did not seem to realize how important they were, not self-important, but important to the incantation, the altar, the ritual. They were ignorant of the craft of devotion. They were merely devoted. They never thought how close the ceremony was to chaos. Their nobility was insecure because it rested on inheritance and not moment-to-moment creation in the face of annihilation.

In the most solemn or joyous part of the ritual Breavman knew the whole procedure could revert in a second to desolation. The cantor, the rabbi, the chosen laymen stood before the open Ark, cradling the Torah scrolls, which looked like stiff-necked royal children, and returned them one by one to their golden stall. The beautiful melody soared, which proclaimed that the Law was a tree of life and a path of peace. Couldn't they see how it had to be nourished? And all these men who bowed, who performed the customary motions, they were unaware that other men had written the sacred tune, other men had developed the seemingly eternal gestures out of clumsy confusion. They took for granted what was dying in their hands.

But why should he care? He wasn't Isaiah, and the people claimed nothing. He didn't even like the people or the god of their cult. He had no rights in the matter.

He didn't want to blame anyone. Why should he feel that they had bred him to a disappointment? He was bitter because he couldn't inherit the glory they unwittingly advertised. He couldn't be part of their brotherhood but he wanted to be among them. A nostalgia for solidarity. Why was his father's pain involved?

He turned away from the city. He had abused the streets with praise. He had expected too much from certain cast-iron fences, special absurd turrets, staircases to the mountain, early-morning views of bridges on the St. Lawrence. He was tired of the mystery he had tried to impute to public squares and gardens.

Mordecai Richler

Mordecai Richler was born in the working-class Jewish neighborhood of Montreal in 1931 and attended Baron Byng, the predominantly Jewish high school. In 1951 he left for Spain and Paris, where he remained for two years. He then returned to Canada, moved to England in 1959, and returned to Canada permanently in 1972. He died in Montreal in 2001. The author of several books of nonfiction and children's books, he is known mostly for his ten novels, two of which have won the Governor General's Award for fiction—*Cocksure* (1968) and *St. Urbain's Horseman* (1971). Two other novels—*The Apprenticeship of Duddy Kravitz* (1959) and *Joshua Then and Now* (1980)—have been made into films. The excerpt from his last novel, *Barney's Version* (1997), which has gone through six printings in Italy, exemplifies his fast-paced dialogue and irreverent satire of the nouveaux riches of Montreal's Jewish community.

Mordecai Richler

EXCERPT FROM *Barney's Version*

As for me, following my retreat from Paris and the artistic wankers I had wasted my time with there, I resolved to make a fresh start in life. What was it Clara had once said? 'When you go home, it will be to make money, which is inevitable, given your character, and you'll marry a nice Jewish girl, somebody who shops . . .' Well, I'll satisfy her ghost, I thought. From now on, it was going to be the bourgeois life for Barney Panofsky. Country club. Cartoons scissored out of *The New Yorker* pasted up on my bathroom walls. *Time* magazine subscription. American Express card. Synagogue membership. Attaché case with combination lock. Et cetera et cetera.

Four years had passed, and I had graduated from dealing in cheese, olive oil, antiquated DC-3s, and stolen Egyptian artifacts, but was still brooding about Clara, guilt-ridden one day, defiant the next. I went out and bought myself a house in the Montreal suburb of Hampstead. It was perfection. Replete with living-room conversation pit, fieldstone fireplace, eye-level kitchen oven, indirect lighting, air-conditioning, heated toilet seats and towel racks, basement wet bar, aluminum siding, attached two-car garage, and living-room picture window. Admiring my acquisition from the outside, satisfied that it would make Clara spin in her grave, I saw what was wrong, and immediately went out and bought a basketball net and screwed it into place over the garage double doors. Now all that was missing was a wifey and a dog called Rover. By this juncture, sitting on $250,000 in the bank, I sold off my agencies, netting even more *mazuma*, registered the name Totally Unnecessary Productions Ltd., and rented offices downtown. Then I set out in quest of the missing piece in my spiteful middle-class equation, the jewel in Reb Barney's crown, so to speak. After all, it is a truth universally acknowledged that a single man in possession of a good fortune must be in want of a wife. Yes. But, in order to acquire Mrs. Right, I had first of all to prove myself a straight arrow.

So I decided to infiltrate the Jewish establishment, set on qualifying as a pillar or at least a cornice. For openers, I volunteered to work as a fund-raiser for United Jewish Appeal, which explains how late one afternoon I actually found myself sitting in the office of a suspicious but hot-to-trot clothing manufacturer. Certainly I had come to the right place. A Man-of-the-Year plaque hung on the wall behind tubby, good-natured Irv Nussbaum's desk. So did a pair of bronzed baby shoes. There was an inscribed photograph of Golda Meir. In another photograph Irv was shown presenting a Doctor of Letters scroll to Mr. Bernard Gursky on behalf of the Friends of the Ben-Gurion University of the Negev. A model of an eighteen-foot yacht that Irv maintained in Florida was mounted on a pedestal: the good ship *Queen Esther*, after Irv's wife, not the biblical Miss Persia. And photographs of Irv's obnoxious children were here, there, and everywhere. 'You're kind of young for this,' said Irv. 'Usually our fund-raisers are, well, you know, more mature men.'

'A guy can't be too young to want to do his bit for Israel.'

'Care for a drink?'

'A Coke would be nice. Or a soda water.'

'How about a Scotch?'

'Darn it. It's too early in the day for me, but you go right ahead, please.'

Irv grinned. Obviously, contrary to reports, I wasn't a boozer. I had passed a test. So now I submitted to a crash course of dos and don'ts.

'I'm going to trust you with just a few cards to begin with,' said Irv. 'But listen up. Rules of the game. You must never visit your target in his office, where he is king shit and you're just another *shmuck* looking for a handout. If you run into him in the synagogue, you can butter him up with Israel's needs, but it's no good putting the touch on him there. Bad taste. Money-changers in the temple. Use the phone to schedule a meeting, but the time of day you get together is of the utmost importance. Breakfasts are out, because maybe his wife wouldn't let him bang her last night, or he didn't sleep because of heartburn. The ideal time is lunch. Pick a small restaurant. Tables far apart. Some place you don't have to shout.

Make it eyeball to eyeball. Shit. We've got a problem this year. There's been a decline in the number of anti-Semitic outrages.'

'Yeah. Isn't that a shame,' I said.

'Don't get me wrong. I'm against anti-Semitism. But every time some asshole daubs a swastika on a synagogue wall or knocks over a stone in one of our cemeteries, our guys get so nervous they phone me with pledges. So, things being how they are this year, what you've got to do is slam-dunk your target about the Holocaust. Shove Auschwitz at him. Buchenwald. War criminals thriving in Canada to this day. Tell him,'Can you be sure it won't happen again, even here, and then where will you go?' Israel is your insurance policy, you say.

'We will provide you with the inside info on your target's annual income, and if he starts to cry, saying he's had a bad year, you say bullshit and read him numbers. Not the numbers on his tax returns. The real numbers. You tell him now that we've got that fucker Nasser to contend with, his pledge has to be bigger this year. And if he turns out to be a hard nut, a *kvetcher*, you slip in that everybody at Elmridge, or whatever country club he belongs to, will know exactly how much he pledged, and that his order books could suffer if he turns out a piker. Hey, I understand you've gone into television production. You need help with casting, Irv's your man.'

Help with casting? A babe in the show-biz woods that swarmed with ferrets, conmen, and poisonous snakes, I even needed help tying my shoelaces in those days. I was bleeding, no, haemorrhaging money. My first pilot, the idea sold to me by a hustler who claimed he had a co-credit on a *Perry Mason* episode, was for a projected series about a private eye 'with his own code of honour.' A sort of Canadian son of Sam Spade. The pilot, directed by a National Film Board hack, starred a Toronto actor (our Olivier, his agent said, who turned down Hollywood offers on principle) who could be counted on to be drunk before breakfast, while the woman cast as his Girl Friday was, unbeknownst to me, a former mistress of his who broke into sobs whenever they had to do a scene together. The result was so unbelievably awful I didn't dare show it to anybody, but I've got it on a cassette now and play it back for laughs whenever I'm feeling depressed.

I proved to be such an adroit fund-raiser that Irv invited me to his twenty-fifth wedding anniversary party, a dinner dance for the quality held in private rooms at Ruby Foo's, black tie, everybody there except me good for a minimum twenty-thousand-dollars-a-year UJA bite, never mind the bond drive, and other community appeals for vigorish. And that's where I met the virago who would become my second wife. Damn damn damn. Here I am, sixty-seven years old, a shrinking man with a cock that trickles, and I still don't know how to account for my second marriage, which now sets me back ten thousand dollars a month before adjustments for inflation, and to think that her father, that pompous old bore, once feared *me* as the fortune-hunter. Looking back, in search of anything that would justify my idiocy, pardon my sins, I must say I was not the real me in those days but an impersonator. Pretending to be the go-getter Clara had damned. Guilt-ridden. Drinking alone in the early-morning hours, fearful of sleep, which was invaded by visions of Clara in her coffin. The coffin, as ordained by Jewish law, was made of pine, holes drilled into it, so that the worms might fatten on that too-young corpse as soon as possible. Six feet under. Her breasts rotting. '. . . you'll be able to entertain guys at the United Jewish Appeal dinner with stories about the days you lived with the outrageous Clara.' Bingeing on respectability, I was now determined to prove to Clara's ghost that I could play the nice middleclass Jewish boy better than she had ever dreamed. Hey, I used to stand back, observing myself, as it were, sometimes tempted to burst into applause in celebration of my own hypocrisy. There was the night, for instance, when I was still caught up in the lightning one-month courtship of the time-bomb who would become The Second Mrs. Panofsky, taking her to dinner at the Ritz, drinking far too much as she continued to yammer about how she would do up my Hampstead respectability trap with the help of an interior decorator she knew. 'Will you be able to drive me home,' she asked, '. . . in your condition?'

'Why,' I said, bussing her on the cheek, and improvising on a script that could only have been produced by Totally Unnecessary Productions Ltd., I could never forgive myself if you were hurt in an accident, because of my 'condition.' You're far too precious to me. We'll leave my car here and take a taxi.'

'Oh, Barney,' she gushed.

I shouldn't have written ' "Oh, Barney," she gushed.' That was rotten of me. A lie. The truth is I was an emotional cripple when I met her, drunk more often than not, punishing myself for doing things that went against my nature, but The Second Mrs. Panofsky had sufficient vitality for the two of us, and a comedic flair, or sparkle, all her own. Like that old whore Hymie Mintzbaum of blessed memory, she possessed that quality I most admire in other people—an appetite for life. No, more. In those days a determination to devour all matters cultural, even as she could now wolf her way through the counter in the Brown Derby without pause. The Second Mrs. Panofsky didn't read for pleasure, but to keep up. Sunday mornings she sat down to *The New York Times Book Review*, as though to an exam that had been set for her, noting only those books likely to be discussed at dinner parties, ordering them promptly, and careering through them at breakneck speed: *Dr. Zhivago*, *The Affluent Society*, *The Assistant*, *By Love Possessed*. The deadliest sin, so far as she was concerned, was time-wasting, and I was accused of it again and again, squandering hours on nobodys encountered in bars. Shooting the breeze with superannuated hockey players, boozy sports columnists, and smalltime conmen.

On a three-day junket to New York we stayed at the Algonquin, booked into separate bedrooms, which I insisted on, eager to play by what I took to be the rules. I could have happily passed that interlude wandering aimlessly, drifting in and out of bookshops and bars, but she was locked into a schedule that would have required a fortnight for a normal person to fill. Plays to be monitored afternoon and evening: *Two for the Seesaw*, *Sunrise at Campobello*, *The World of Suzie Wong*, *The Entertainer*. Between times her check-list included forced marches to out-of-the-way craft shops and jewellery designers recommended by *Vogue*. Footsore, she was still among the first through the doors of Bergdorf Goodman when it opened in the morning, hurrying on to Saks, and those places on Canal Street, known only to the *cognoscenti*, where Givenchy's new 'bag' dresses could be bought on the cheap. Flying down to New York, she wore an old outfit that could be dumped into her hotel-room wastepaper basket as soon as she acquired her first new one. Then, on the morning of our scheduled flight home, she tore up incriminating sales receipts, retaining only those that obliging salesladies had fabricated for her, say a bill for $39.99 for a $150 sweater. Boarding the plane, she wore only God knows how many sets of underwear, and one blouse over another, and then she clowned her passage past the Montreal customs inspector, flirting with him *en français*.

Yes, The Second Mrs. Panofsky was an exemplar of that much-maligned phenomenon, the Jewish-American Princess, but she succeeded in fanning my then-dying embers into something resembling life. When we met she had already served a season on a kibbutz and graduated from McGill, majoring in psychology, and was working with disturbed children at the Jewish General Hospital. They adored her. She made them laugh. The Second Mrs. Panofsky was not a bad person. Had she not fallen into my hands but instead married a real, rather than a pretend, straight arrow, she would be a model wife and mother today. She would not be an embittered, grossly overweight hag, given to diddling with New Age crystals and consulting trance-channellers. Miriam once said to me, Krishna was licensed to destroy, but not you, Barney. Okay, okay. The truth, then.

'You're far too precious to me,' I gushed. 'We'll leave my car here and take a taxi.'

'Oh, Barney,' she said, 'are you ever full of shit tonight.'

Oh, Barney, you bastard. When I try to reconstruct those days, failing memory is an enormous blessing. Vignettes wash over me. Embarrassing incidents. Twinges of regret. Boogie flew in from Las Vegas, moderately successful at the tables for once, to be my best man. He met my bride a couple of days before the ceremony was to take place and the two of us went out to dinner, on a night I should have been at Maple Leaf Gardens in Toronto, watching the Canadiens beat the Leafs 3–2, taking a 3–1 lead in the Stanley Cup Finals. Some game I missed. Down one-zip going into the third period, the *bleu, blanc, et rouge* potted three goals in just over six minutes: Backstrom, McDonald, and Geoffrion.

'Don't go through with it, Barney, please,' said Boogie. 'We could drive to the airport as soon as we finish our cognacs and catch the first plane to Mexico or Spain or wherever.'

'Aw, come on,' I said.

'I can see that she's attractive. A luscious lady. Have an affair. We could be in Madrid tomorrow. Tapas on those narrow streets running off the Plaza Mayor. *Cochinillo asado* at Casa Botin.'

'Goddamn it, Boogie, I can't leave town during the Stanley Cup Finals.' And, with a heavy heart, I went on to show him my two tickets in the reds for the next game in Montreal. The game that was being played on my wedding night. If the Canadiens won, it would mean our fourth straight Stanley Cup, and, just this once, I was hoping that they'd lose, so that I could postpone our honeymoon and take in what would surely be the final and winning game. 'Do you think she'd mind,' I asked, 'if, after the dinner, I slipped out for an hour and maybe caught the third period in the Forum?'

'Brides tend to be touchy about things like that,' he said.

'Yeah, I guess so. My luck, eh?'

Irv Nussbaum had radiated joy at his anniversary-dinner dance.

'Seen this morning's *Gazette*? Some guys shat on the front steps of the B'nai Jacob synagogue. My phone's been ringing all day. Terrific, eh?' This was followed by a wink and an elbow nudge. 'You dance any closer with her and I'm going to have to book you a room here.'

Saucy, voluptuous, smelling of everything nice, my future bride did not withdraw from my embrace on the dance floor. Instead, she said, 'My father is watching us,' pressing even harder against me.

Seemingly polished bald head. Waxed moustache. Gold-rimmed glasses. Bushy eyebrows. Small beady brown eyes. Jowly. Cummerbund squeezing prosperity belly. Foolish rosebud mouth. And no warmth in that measured smile as he descended on our table. He was a property developer. A builder of biscuit-box office blocks and beehive apartment buildings, owner of an engineering degree from McGill. 'We haven't met,' he said.

'His name's Barney Panofsky, Daddy.'

I accepted the offer of a damp, limp little hand. 'Panofsky? Panofsky? Do I know your father?'

'Not unless you've ever been booked for anything, Daddy, and didn't tell me.'

'My father's a detective-inspector.'

'I say. Is he, indeed? And how do you earn your daily bread?'

'I'm in television production.'

'You know that commercial for Molson's beer, it's such a scream? The one that makes you laugh? Barney produced it.'

'Well, well, well. Mr. Bernard's son is sitting with us, and he would like to dance with you, precious, but he's too shy to ask,' he said, taking her firmly by the arm. 'Do you know the Gurskys, Mr. . . . ?'

'Panofsky.'

'We're good friends of theirs. Come, my sweet.'

'No,' she said, yanking her arm free, tugging me out of my chair, and leading me back onto the dance floor.

You've heard of mock turtle soup? Well, the father of the bride turned out to be the ultimate mock WASP Jew. From the points of his waxed moustache to the toes of his Oxford wingtip shoes. Most days he fancied a pinstripe suit, his canary-yellow waistcoat enhanced by a gold pocket-watch chain and fob. For sojourns in the countryside, he carried a malacca walking stick and, out for an afternoon of golf with Harvey Schwartz, he wore plus-fours. But for dinner parties at his Westmount manse, he favoured a magenta velvet smoking-jacket with matching slippers, and was forever stroking his wet lips with his forefinger, as if lost in contemplation of weighty philosophical problems. His insufferable wife, who wore pince-nez, jiggled a tiny bell each time the company was ready for another course. The first time I dined there, she corrected the way I wielded my soup spoon. Demonstrating the proper manner, she said, 'Ships sail out to sea.'

Naturally the ladies took their coffee in the living room, while the chaps, lingering at the table, were offered port, the decanter passed to the left, as Mr. Mock WASP announced a subject worthy of debate: 'George Bernard Shaw once said . . .' or 'H. G. Wells would have us believe . . . Now what do you say to that, gentlemen?'

The old fool objected to me, of course. But, to be fair, he was one of those possessive fathers who would have been outraged by the thought of even a Gursky screwing Daddy's girl, not that we had gone that far yet. Complaining to her, he said, 'He talks with his hands.' An attribute he considered compromising. *Très* Jewy. 'I don't want you to see him again.'

'Oh, yeah? Well in that case I'm moving out. I'm going to rent an apartment.'

Where, in his mind's eye, the poor man visualized his precious one being ravished morning, noon, and night. 'No,' he protested. 'You will not move out. I won't stop you seeing him. But it is my fatherly duty to warn you that you are making a bad mistake. He comes from another *monde*.'

As things turned out, he was right to object to his daughter marrying such a scamp, but he did not intervene, for fear of losing her entirely. Summoning me into his library, he said, 'I can't pretend this match delights me. You come from no family, you have no education, and you are engaged in a vulgar business. But once the two of you are wed it will be contingent upon my good wife and me to accept you as one of our own, if only for the sake of our beloved daughter.'

'Why, you couldn't have put it more graciously,' I said.

'Be that as it may, I do have one request. My good wife, as you know, was one of the first Jewish women to graduate from McGill. Class of '22. She is a past president of Hadassah and has had her name entered in the mayor's Golden Book. She has been commended by our prime minister for the work she did with British children who were evacuated here during the last global conflict—'

Yes, but only after he had written to the prime minister's office, pleading for that letter of appreciation, which was now framed and hung in their living room.

'—She is a most fastidious lady, and I would be grateful if, in the future, you would refrain from garnishing your conversation with expletives at our dining-room table. Surely this is not too large an imposition to impose on your good self.'

With hindsight, there were things to be said in the old boy's favour. He had served in the Tank Corps during the Second World War, a captain twice mentioned in dispatches. Look at it this way. The sour truth is that many people whom liberals like me poke fun at—army colonels, dim private-school boys, suburban golfers, banal-tongued mediocrities, tiresome stuffed shirts—were the ones who went to war in 1939 and saved Western civilization, while Auden, ostensibly an anti-Fascist commando, fled to America when the barbarians were at the gate.

My father-in-law's business reputation was impeccable. He was a constant husband, and a loving father to The Second Mrs. Panofsky. Stricken with cancer only a year after we married, he behaved with dignity during his last wasting months, as stoic as any of the G. A. Henty heroes he so admired. Unfortunately, my relationship with both Mr. and Mrs. Mock WASP got off to a rocky start. There was, for instance, my first meeting with my future mother-in-law, a lunch *à trois* in the Ritz Gardens, arranged by my apprehensive bride who coached me for hours the night before. 'You are not to order more than one drink at the table before lunch.'

'Right.'

'And, whatever you do, no whistling at the table. Absolutely no whistling at the table. She can't stand it.'

'But I've never whistled at the table in my life.'

Things started badly, Mrs. Mock WASP disapproving of our table. 'I should have had my husband make the reservation,' she said.

It was an effort to begin with, the conversation halting, Mrs. Mock WASP infuriating me by demanding answers to direct questions about my family background, my past, my health, and my prospects, before I eased us into safer territory: the death of Cecil B. DeMille, how enjoyable Cary Grant was in *North by Northwest*, and the coming Bolshoi Ballet tour. In fact, my behaviour was four-star exemplary until she told me how she had adored *Exodus*, by Leon Uris, and, all at once, I began to whistle 'Dixie.'

'*He's whistling at the table.*'

'Who?' I asked.

'You.'

'But I never. Shit, was I?'

'He didn't mean to, Mother.'

'I apologize,' I said, but when the coffee came I was so nervous I found myself suddenly whistling 'Lipstick on Your Collar,' one of that year's hit numbers, stopping abruptly. 'I don't know what's got into me.'

'I would like to contribute my share of the bill,' said my future mother-in-law, rising from the table.

'Barney wouldn't hear of it.'

'We come here often. They know us. My husband always tips twelve and a half per-cent.'

Next there came the dreaded day I was obliged to introduce my father to my future in-laws. My mother was already out of it by this time (not that she was ever deeply into it), wasting in a nursing home, her mind adrift. The walls of her bedroom were plastered with signed photographs of George Jessel, Ishkabibble, Walter

Winchell, Jack Benny, Charlie McCarthy, Milton Berle, and the Marx Brothers: Groucho, Harpo, and, you know, the other one. It's on the tip of my tongue. Never mind. The last time I had been to see my mother she had told me that a male orderly had tried to rape her. She called me Shloime, her dead brother's name, and I fed her chocolate ice cream out of a tub, her favourite, assuring her that it wasn't poisoned. Dr. Bernstein said she was suffering from Alzheimer's, but I mustn't worry, it needn't be hereditary.

In preparation for the visit of Mr. and Mrs. Mock WASP to my house, I drew a 'W' with a ballpoint on my right hand, a reminder not to whistle. I purchased appropriate books and left them lying about: the latest Harry Golden, a biography of Herzl, the new Herman Wouk, a photo book on Israel. I bought a chocolate cake at Aux Délices. Filled the fruit bowl. Hid the liquor. Unpacked a box of hideous china cups and saucers I had acquired only that morning and set five places with linen napkins. I vacuumed. Plumped up the sofa cushions. And anticipating that her mother would find an excuse to look into my bedroom, I checked it out inch by inch for hairs that did not belong to me. Then I brushed my teeth for the third time, hoping to kill the Scotch smell. Mr. and Mrs. Mock WASP, as well as their daughter, were already seated in the living room when my father finally arrived. Izzy was impeccably dressed in the clothes I had chosen for him at Holt Renfrew, but, as a small act of rebellion, he had added a touch distinctively his own. He was wearing his snappy soft felt fedora with that ridiculous, multicoloured brush in the brim large enough to serve as a duster. He also reeked of Old Spice and was in a mood to reminisce about his old days on the beat in Chinatown. 'We was young fellers, pretty smart, and we soon learned us a few words of China. We watched from the rooftops when they made their trades. Then you could tell if they was smoking, because they always hung wet blankets on the street, due to the smell. Barney, would you pour me a Scotch, please,' he said, pushing away his teacup.

'I don't know if I have any,' I hissed, glaring at him.

'Yeah, and there's no coal in Newcastle,' he said, pronouncing the 't,' 'or snow in the Yukon.'

So I fetched him a bottle and a glass.

'What about you? Aren't you drinking this afternoon?'

'No.'

'*L'chaim*,' said Izzy, belting one down, my own throat dry. 'There was girls involved, you know. Oh yes, it was—Christ—now you take the average French-Canadian family, I don't know about today but years ago they had ten or fifteen kids, so you know, they had nothing to eat, so they used to send the girls down there and one would bring another and you come in, you raid some place, you know, and you found four-five Chinamen with four-five girls, Christ, they'd even give them dope, you know. There was a lot of opium then. I'm talking 1932, when, you know, our entire detective force had only one automobile, a two-seater Ford.' Izzy paused to slap his knee. 'If we catch us two crooks, you know, we'd just throw them across the hood and put the handcuffs on, and vroom-vroom, off we go. They'd be laying there like deer, you know, when you go hunting, they just lay on the hood.'

'But the engine was under it,' said my future bride. 'Wasn't it hot?'

'We weren't going very far. Just to headquarters. And anyways I didn't feel it,' said Izzy, chuckling. '*They* was on there.'

'On second thought,' I said, not daring to look at my future in-laws, 'I just might have a wee drink myself.' And I reached for the bottle.

'Are you sure, darling?'

'I feel a cold coming on.'

Izzy now cleared his throat, and shot a wad of snot into one of my new linen napkins. Bull's-eye. I sneaked a glance at my future mother-in-law, attracted by her rattling teacup.

'We'd arrest a guy, we'd take him downstairs to open him up, if you know what I mean?'

'You weren't gratuitously violent with suspected felons, were you, Inspector Panofsky?'

Izzy looked pained. 'Gratuitously?'

'Unnecessarily,' I said.

'No fucken way, mister. I condoned it. Absolutely. But, you know, it's human nature, when a feller is young, you give him authority, he likes to push people around. But when I was young I didn't, because I knew my name was Panofsky.'

'But how did *you* get suspects to talk, Inspector?' asked my future father-in-law, looking directly at his daughter, as if to say, are you prepared to marry into such a family?

'I got my ways and means how.'

'How time flies,' I said, glancing pointedly at my wristwatch. 'It's almost six o'clock.'

'You lay down the law to them. They don't want to talk, you take them down below.'

'Then what transpires, Inspector?'

'Well, we get this feller in the room, we slam the bloody door and then we start to throw chairs around. You know, scare the shit out of them. Maybe I step on his toes. Come clean, I shout.'

'What happens if, perchance, it's a woman you take downstairs?'

'Well I never remember—I'm sincere when I tell you about this—I never remember beating a woman, we never had occasion to, but if you get a tough guy, in many instances I could tell you . . .'

'Dad, may I have the bottle back, please?'

'Darling, should you?'

'Let me give you another for instance. In 1951 this was, I found those bearded rabbinical students were being beaten up outside their school on Park Avenue by all those punks. Just because they were Jews. Well, those punks they see you and I, well they doubt a little bit because we may not look too much like Jews, and we don't act it, but when they see a guy all dressed up, you know . . . Anyways their leader, this Hungarian roughneck, just off the boat, was caught, and I drove him to Station 17 to have a look at him. He's got those boots on, you know those big boots, rough as hell, I shut the door. What's your name, I says? I don't care about anybody, he says in that accent they have. His English is terrible. So I slammed him good, mister. Down he goes. He passes out. Jesus Christ. I thought he would die. I tried to give him first aid. You know what passed through my mind? Just imagine . . . JEW POLICE OFFICER KILLS . . . if the guy died. So I rushed up an ambulance and we get him to come to. . . .'

Then, even as Izzy wiped his mouth with the back of his hand, and was about to embark on another for instance, I was driven to take a desperate measure. I started to whistle. But this time, in deference to my future mother-in-law, something cultural, the 'La donna è mobile' aria from *Rigoletto*. That succeeded in clearing the house of both my future in-laws and my bride. Following their hasty departure, Izzy said, 'Hey, congrats. They're very nice people. Warm. Intelligent. I enjoyed talking to them. How'd I do?'

'I think you made an unforgettable impression.'

'I'm glad you brought me here to look them over. I'm not a cop all these years for nothing. They're loaded. I could tell. Demand a dowry, kid.'

David Solway

David Solway (b. 1941) is a native of Montreal, where he teaches at John Abbott College, and served as writer-in-residence at Concordia University. He is the author of several award-winning books of poetry and controversial books of criticism denouncing postmodern trends in education. He does much of his writing in Greece, where he has also translated Greek poetry. His style is marked by neologisms that lead ultimately to the invention of a persona. The following excerpt links him to his renowned fellow poet Irving Layton, who, like so many other Canadian-Jewish writers, has been inspired by the Greek way of life. Layton was born in Romania in 1912 and came to Montreal with his family at the age of one; he has published numerous collections of poetry, and in 1959 he won the Governor General's Award for *A Red Carpet for the Sun*. He has been outspoken in his critique of Canadian society as he assumes the role of Nietzschean prophet, attacking the shortcomings of Jews and Canadians alike for their materialism, bigotry, and prudishness. 'Framing Layton' is taken from Solway's *Random Walks: Essays in Elective Criticism*.

David Solway

EXCERPT FROM 'Framing Layton'

Panel I

So much has by now been written about, against, around, on behalf of, in reaction to, in gratitude for, and in displacement from the doyen of Canadian poetry that anyone starting to write an article on Irving Layton must quickly approach a state of prepositional collapse. Doubting that much remains to be said, I almost regret having undertaken to add yet another affidavit to the towering stack of analysis, reminiscence, and obfuscation that constitutes the Canadian mini-industry of Layton scholarship. All I can do, I'm afraid, is hazard a small, tentative, perspectival account, a personal footnote to the Britannica as an apophradic tribute to the man who stands to me and to so many other younger poets as friend, mentor, benefactor, example, and, at times, as monumental Bloomian impediment. For any writer who has been influenced *in any way* by Layton must recognize the accursed precursor-ephebe dialectic that accounts for the peculiar mix of resentment and gratitude one feels for the greatest of our poets. I should confess at the outset that what I feel is mainly gratitude, though honesty compels me to acknowledge those disturbing moments when I could wish that Layton's shadow were not quite so long and so encompassing.

The problem remains. To write about Layton means initiating a series of endlessly deferred beginnings (a bit like Hesiod who has to crank up three separate starts before getting into the *Theogony*), since no end, no final understanding or definitive summation is possible. The analysis of the poems has been long undertaken by a host of perceptive critics. The novel has been written (Aviva Layton's *Nobody's Daughter*). The biography, skewed and controversial, has generated the predictable flap—for three transgressions and for four, there's little point in pummelling Elspeth Cameron any further, and Layton's autobiography, *Waiting for the Messiah*, compensates more than adequately while contributing to the memorial parallax that bedevils the 'Life' of any great writer, turning it into a sequence of perpetual adjustments. The Encyclopedia has accomplished its work of canonization. Nobel nominations have added to the reputation. An arsenal of revisionary estimates will be massively deployed in the coming years as time performs its work of editorial sifting, disengaging the core of truly remarkable work from the forty to fifty volumes of Layton's prolific output. And the analyses, critiques, and recapitulations will begin all over again, with the inevitable result of replacing one legend with another, presumably more authoritative, more considered, more definitive, yet I suspect no less a collective fiction, the signal of greatness. (Will we ever find out who really issued the challenge to the famous handball game?) When little remains to be said while the commentaries continue to ramify and proliferate, we know we are in the company of genius, which, being not so much a 'life' as a crowd of assumed identities, explains the analogy of plenitude between the creative source and the expository apparatus.

Take three: let me begin anecdotally. I first heard of Irving Layton when I was fourteen, chugging on Lac de Sable (in my hometown of Ste Agathe) in Henry Moscovitch's three-horsepower chaloupe. Henry, a precocious and talented protégé of Layton's, used to spend his summer vacations in the Laurentians. At this time he was preparing his first slim volume of bourgeois-bashing poetry (*The Serpent Ink*), and would regularly putter me out to the middle of the lake, turn off the motor, and read interminably from a blackbound portfolio of terse vituperations that he called poems—he had Layton's crisp accents down pat. Occasionally he interspersed these pieces with resonating verse proclamations of his sexual exploits, testimony to the power of the poetic imagination and to his fidelity as Layton's amanuensis.

I must admit that my complicity was motivated by other concerns, namely the hope that Henry, the scion of a wealthy bourgeois family, might from time to time relent, swing the megapower inboard out of the boathouse, and take me water skiing. But I paid exorbitantly for these brief episodes of genuine fun by a summerful of becalmed, lacustrine recitations which constituted my first exposure to the muse. I discovered that poets were privileged beings, feared by society, honoured by posterity, anointed by God, indefatigably potent, and overwhelmed by the adulterous ministrations of bored, lascivious, middle-class wives. It was at that point that I first began meditating a career as a poet, learning at second hand from Henry what he assured me he had absorbed from the master himself. As further corroboration he quoted prodigiously from the sybilline texts Layton had regularly schlepped into class, the works of the Romantic triumvirate who justified the splendour and necessity of imaginative commitment—Blake, Nietzsche, and Lawrence, none of whom, as a country-school hooky player, I had ever heard of. But the gap in my education was amply filled by Henry's motorboat tutorials and the loan of Layton's early books. And in fact the very first poem I ever committed *voluntarily* to memory was Layton's 'The Cold Green Element' which, as Henry's captive if not entirely captivated audience, sweating under the hot sun in the middle of the lake while my tormentor read endlessly from his bulging folder, wanting nothing more than to dive into the water, I would recite inwardly to myself, especially the conclusion:

And misled by the cries of young boys
I am again
A breathless swimmer in that cold green element.

Four years later, as a student living in Montreal, I attended one of Layton's night classes at Sir George Williams University. I was no longer the country neophyte inhabiting that ambiguous region between awe and boredom into which poetry had inducted me, but a practising poetaster in my own right, bristling with convictions and a sense of adolescent infallibility. Moreover, as a student of Louis Dudek, I had become aware of the hothouse conflict between Dudek and Layton which divided the aspirant community of young poets into roving partisan bands doing battle in the cloakroom of Redpath Library and in the pages of the *McGill Daily*. I was at the time a loyal Dudekin, arrogant with sceptical modesty, heaping scorn and animadversion on the company of mad Laytonians who were immediately conspicuous by the fact that they all affected Layton's clipped, oddly British pronunciation, were 'Fanatic in belief some rival / Mode of metaphor lacks wit and style,' chewed garlic and onions with revolutionary ardour, and slathered their conversation with the names of Blake, Nietzsche, and Lawrence. I decided it was high time to check out the fire-breathing Moloch who devoured young poets for breakfast or turned them into diminutive clones of his own fulminating presence.

What I encountered was totally unexpected. There, holding forth at the head of the class, short, built like a wedge, resembling a boxer, strode a veritable pedagogic titan. A lordly, megaphonic rhetoric with the 'wonderful claiming power' of Sara Jeannette Duncan's Dr Drummond carried across the entire room, so that, sitting in the back row, I felt catapulted to the front, vulnerable, stripped of saving anonymity. But it was the *subtlety*, the fine distinctions he so adroitly manipulated within the protagonistic delivery, that extorted unwilling respect and admiration. The poem under discussion was Randall Jarrell's 'The Death of the Ball-Turret Gunner,' which I had read with much appreciation and little understanding. Layton proceeded to analyse the poem with such delicacy of insight, probing carefully and lovingly to its metaphoric core (which had escaped me entirely), that I had the uncanny feeling of listening in to the author's own thought processes, as if I were present at the act of composition itself. This was not criticism but telepathy, a transferring of the self into the privacy of another mind, which only the very greatest of teachers is capable of performing. And I was aware even then of the irony tacit in the performance, considering the notoriety of Layton's robust, basilican, and narcissistic poetic ego. I had (and have) seldom observed so gracious and productive a deference of self to the work of another. I learned many things in that class. I learned more about the complex operations of metaphor in an hour than I had in years of reading—I continue to bring Jarrell's poem as an illustration of the metaphoric principle to the attention of my own students to this day. But perhaps most importantly, I learned that love of life-and-literature has many forms and is by no means cancelled or compromised by the driving, aggressive, flamboyant manifestation of self associated with the poetic ego in need of confirmation. Not that Layton's really needed it. Jarrell has said that if a poet is struck by lightning six times, he is a genius. Layton has been *charred* by lightning innumerable times—even a dubious Elspeth Cameron gives him fifteen 'world-class poems,' and an ambivalent George Woodcock thirty-five 'first-rate poems'—so that he bears a metaphorical resemblance to the tree in 'The Cold Green Element' 'for whom the lightning was too much / and grew a brilliant / hunchback with a crown of leaves.' (However, all this notwithstanding, I did not return for the second part of the class, sensing the danger inherent in prolonged exposure to so powerful and *vortical* a personality.)

I finally got around to meeting this strange, promethean hybrid, this nemesis/benefactor, quite by accident some three or four years later, halfway around the world. I had rented a villa for the summer on the island of Mallorca, in a tiny hamlet called Fornalutx tucked away in the mountains to the northeast. Now in my early twenties, I had come to the conclusion that one could do nothing great in Canada (forgetting Layton's example), and that for an aspiring young Canadian writer, expatriation was the only solution to citizenship. After six weeks or so, I reluctantly admitted to myself that not only was I doing nothing great, I was doing nothing at all, with the result that I spent most of my time sitting outside the village café drinking brandy and coffee and at least feeling like a writer if not being one. It was during one of these daily, unproductive sessions that I noticed a taxi pull up across the street and disgorge three uncomfortable passengers, one of whom I seemed to recognize: a short, bullish man addressing everyone in his immediate vicinity in a huge, oratorical voice, pounding away like a Mobilfacta compressor on an Ikea display platform, commenting on the heat, the dust, the glazed enamel of the sky, the remoteness of the village, and didn't Robert Graves live around here, a fine poet and mythographer but somewhat lacking as a novelist, and where was the house he had been promised, why was there nobody to meet him, could that be construed as neglect? 'Let's ask *him*,' said Bill Goodwin, Layton's nephew, pointing in my direction, and Aviva Layton inquired as to the condition of my English.

My first encounter with Layton and his party did not begin auspiciously. I could not help him immediately locate the house which had been put at his disposal, and Bill considered that they should perhaps backtrack to Soller, the nearest large town. How far was Soller from here, Bill wanted to know. About six miles as the crow flies, I replied. 'Well, we don't intend to fly,' Bill remarked witheringly, and Layton grunted in approval.

Smarting under the rebuke, feeling more and more like a Canadian and less and less like a writer, intimidated by the proximity of greatness, I left the table and scampered around the village like Carroll's unicorn, asking everyone I met about a mysterious empty house awaiting visitors. This, I realized, was a crucial moment in my development as a poet, once again, as if 'to the clanging tunes of appetite and chance,' implicated with Layton's charismatic presence, and if I were to fail in my quest—the phrase 'triumph of accommodation' ran through my head—I might as well turn in my ambitions and become rich. Fate intervened in the guise of the local blacksmith, who had been informed by the owner of the house and was able to give me precise directions. And so it was that I led the great poet in a triumph of accommodation to the door of his sanctum, receiving in return the benediction of his 'good work' and a remark about the appropriateness of the blacksmith—Blake's Urthona, Joyce's forging Dedalus—as a metaphor of the poet. (Layton's comment in his poem 'Fornalutx' was untypically laconic: 'The house, of course, was decent enough.' The town, however, he situated in one of Dante's bituminous circles.)

Later in the afternoon we gathered at the reservoir for a swim. This concrete rectangle, filled with weedy, brackish water, sat in a kind of coulee or arroyo about a kilometre out of town in the direction of Deya where Robert Graves held court. I had heard that Graves was throwing a party that evening for friends and members of the local intelligentsia, but neither Layton nor I had been invited. 'One must be magnanimous,' Layton observed. 'He probably doesn't know I'm here.' This led to a discussion of Graves and his work—'a considerable poet,' Layton conceded. Across the valley from the reservoir rose the grey mass of the highest mountain in the northern chain, which Layton speculated was the source of one of Graves's most celebrated poems, 'Rocky Acres,' a meticulously descriptive work, a piece of mood-painting. I suggested rather timorously that the descriptive aspect of the poem was entirely pretextual, that the mountain could only be regarded as inadvertent, and that what Graves was actually providing was a detailed mindscape, a pictorial representation of the spiritual dimension in which he lived, somewhat like Hopkins's sonnet, 'No worst, there is none . . . ' (To credit Katherine Snipes's account in her *Robert Graves*, we were both wrong. The poem is, apparently, a 'stark description of the Welsh countryside.') I went on at some length, recalling Layton's own exegesis of Jarrell, and was gratified and relieved by his willingness to listen and his approval of my hermeneutic efforts. I have never forgotten that day in Fornalutx, partly because it was the day on which I first began to feel a preliminary sense of confirmation in that elusive adequacy of self which underlies all the madness and ostentation of the persona. I was never a student, a disciple, or a protégé of Layton's, but I benefited enormously from the mere generosity of his presence—despite the evident dangers. The inveterate talker was also the most stringent and encouraging of listeners—if, that is, you had something to say.

Ten years elapsed before I saw Layton again, this time in another small village on another remote island, as if our encounters had somehow been ordained to be fleeting and insular, intersections, really, rather than meetings. Layton was spending the summer of 1973 in Molibos (not an island, as Elspeth Cameron assumes, but a village) on the island of Lesbos where I had also rented a house, about five kilometres outside the town in a gaggle of dwellings dignified by the name of Eftalou (Seven Hills). To add to the strangeness of the time, Bill and Aviva were also there, so that the summer we spent in one another's company had a weird, orchestrated air, like something scripted, revised, and polished by an unknown hand. I can't explain how these peculiar things happen except to suggest that certain places tend obscurely to attract certain writers at certain moments in their careers by a kind of coordinate magnetism. In the short time I spent on Lesbos (actually, in Eftalou), I met the Greek novelist Nasos Theophilos, was introduced to the Danish poet Henrik Nordtbrand, entertained Andy Wainwright on my front porch, drank with Harry Sarr and crossed paths if not swords with Peter Green. In the serendipitous light of these occasions, the fact that Layton and I should have found ourselves once more within hailing distance in faraway places should have been entirely predictable.

Miriam Waddington

Born in Winnipeg in 1917, Miriam Waddington attended high school in Ottawa, graduated from the University of Toronto, and studied social work in Philadelphia. She joined the English faculty at York University in 1964 and retired as a professor in 1983. She now lives in Vancouver. Waddington has published eleven books of poetry, and her *Collected Poems* appeared in 1986. In addition, she has published a collection of short stories, a critical study of A. M. Klein, and *Apartment Seven: Essays Selected and New* (1989), from which 'Mrs Maza's Salon' is taken. The essay is characteristic of her keen interest in Yiddish literature (which she has translated), her empathy for the human subject, and a direct, lyrical style that pervades most of her poetry.

Miriam Waddington

Mrs Maza's Salon

In the fall of 1930, when I was twelve, my family moved to Ottawa from Winnipeg. The reason was this: my father had lost his small sausage-making and meat-curing factory to a partner in a lawsuit. The world was then in the grip of the great Depression, and the west had been especially hard hit. My father had the idea of starting a small sausage factory in Ottawa, and since there seemed nothing else to do, my parents rented out our Winnipeg house, sold the piano, packed us children into the car, and set out.

The whole family was unhappy about the move. My parents had come to Canada before the First World War. They had met and married in Winnipeg and once there became firmly integrated in a circle of secular Jews who had founded a Yiddish day school and named it after the famous Yiddish writer I. L. Peretz. They had many close friends and led a busy social life of meetings, lectures, and family-friend dinners in winter, and picnics or camping with other families in summer.

In Ottawa it was a different story. There were very few non-observant Jews and even fewer Jews who had, like my parents, made Yiddish language and culture their home and community. It took them some months to find congenial friends, especially since their energies were absorbed by the task of finding a place to live and settling us four children—all under the age of fourteen—into a new school environment.

Their problems in adjusting to this strange and unfamiliar Ottawa community must have affected us children. I know that I mourned the loss of my two best friends until I found a new one with whom I could walk to school, go to the movies, and share my innermost thoughts and feelings. Also, Ottawa in 1930 was still a small city, which with its population of 80,000 seemed like a village compared to Winnipeg. There was some compensation in the fact that Montreal was so close—only 120 miles away, with frequent two-dollar weekend train excursions. After a year or so, my parents discovered the Jewish community in Montreal, and we came to know a number of families whom we could visit.

Among them was a Yiddish poet, Ida Maza. She had published several volumes of poetry and knew all the Yiddish writers and painters in Montreal and New York. Her husband was an agent who represented several manufacturers of men's haberdashery—mostly shirts and ties. His route took him through the small towns between Ottawa and Montreal, and also past Lachute up into the Laurentians. Whenever he was in Ottawa he stayed with us, and he often took me back with him at times when I had no school.

It is hard to describe Mrs Maza and what I have come to think of as her salon without placing her in the social context that I remember from my childhood. For example, my parents and their friends spoke Yiddish among themselves and regularly addressed one another by their surnames. If it was a man, he would be addressed simply as 'Maza,' and if it was a woman, it would be 'Mrs Maza.' First names were rare and reserved for close relatives. Similarly, when speaking Yiddish—which is an inflected language—they used the polite form of 'you,' never the intimate 'thou.'

Mrs Maza was what is called a *jolie laide*. She looked Japanese and emphasized her oriental exoticism with her carriage, her way of walking and dressing, and her hairdo. She had thick black hair which she piled up around her face in interesting twists and turns like doughnuts and buns. Her colouring was that of the native girls in Gauguin's paintings, and like theirs, her cheekbones were wide apart and prominent. Her eyes were large and dark and Mongolian in feeling. She was short in stature and slight in build, and always wore long kimono-like dresses with sashes and wide sleeves into which she would tuck her hands. Her shoes were simple low-heeled slipper affairs, and she walked with small shuffling steps, for all the world as if her feet had been bound. She had a beautiful low voice, full of dark rich tones, and a chanting, trance-like way of talking. Most of the time she was serious and melancholy in mood, but every now and again she would break into short little bursts of soft chuckling laughter. This was usually when she was with her husband, whom she always treated with tender affection. She liked to tease and jolly him because he took everything to heart with a childlike seriousness.

Looking back I realize she was not only a very intelligent woman, but full of cleverness and wisdom. She had been born in a village in White Russia and been brought to Montreal while she was still a child. Since she had lived most of her life in Montreal, she spoke English with only a slight accent.

I met Mrs Maza when I was fourteen. I had been writing poetry for about four years, and my mother must have mentioned it, because Mrs Maza at once offered to read my work. I showed it to her hesitatingly, and with fear, because she was not just a teacher but a real writer. She praised it and at once took charge of my reading, urging me to Emily Dickinson, Edna St Vincent Millay, Sara Teasdale, Vachel Lindsay, Conrad Aiken, and Yeats. Occasionally she would read me one of her own Yiddish poems. I listened but I confess that I didn't give her poems my fullest attention. Most of them were children's poems, playful and tender; or else they dealt with the relationship between mothers and children, not a subject of great interest to an adolescent girl. I have since gone back to read Ida Maza's poems with an adult eye, and find them full of warmth and a lyrical charm that manages to shine through even a rough translation.

In the next two or three years I often stayed with the Mazas during my Christmas and Easter holidays. They lived in a third-floor walk-up on Esplanade. The building was old and resembled a tenement. It contained a buzzing hive of small apartments that you entered through an enclosed courtyard. It faced east and looked across a small park to the Jewish Old People's Home, and just down the street, also on Esplanade, was the Jewish People's Library, which served as a lively community centre for lectures and educational programs.

The staircase leading up to the Maza apartment was narrow and dark. Once inside, however, the front room was bright and colourful, the walls covered with paintings and the furniture draped in Eastern European embroideries and weavings. The furniture consisted of a small sofa and two mission-style oak chairs sternly upholstered in brown leather. There was a matching oak library table loaded with books, and more books were encased in glass on the shelves of an oak bookcase. A long skinny hallway led from the front room to the kitchen past two bedrooms that branched off to one side. On the way to the kitchen, and before you reached it, there was a dining room with a round table in the middle, surrounded by chairs. There was also a sideboard, and what was probably the most important and most used piece of furniture in the house, something called a Winnipeg couch—but by Mrs Maza and her friends it was referred to as a lounge, and pronounced *lontch*. On this couch her husband took his Sunday afternoon naps, and in the evenings visiting poets and painters sat on it two or three abreast, listening to poetry being read out loud by one of them or, on occasion, trying out new ideas for publishing a magazine or a manifesto. Or else they discussed new books and gossiped. The reason they sat in the dining room instead of the front sitting room, I now realize, was that it was close to the kitchen, that universal, nonpareil source of food.

To these artists, most of them middle-aged and impecunious, and all of them immigrants, Mrs Maza was the eternal mother—the foodgiver and nourisher, the listener and solacer, the mediator between them and the world. There she would sit with hands folded into her sleeves, her face brooding and meditative, listening intently with all her body. As she listened she rocked back and forth, and, as it then seemed to me, she did so in time to the rhythm of the poem being read.

She gave herself entirely and attentively to the poem; she fed the spiritual hunger and yearning of these oddly assorted Yiddish writers whenever they needed her; but not only that. She also fed them real food, and not just once a week, but every day. She served endless cups of tea with lemon, jam, and sugar lumps, plates of fresh fruit, Jewish egg-cookies, homemade walnut strudel, and delicately veined marble cake. And for the really hungry there were bowls of barley soup, slices of rye bread thickly buttered, and eggs—countless eggs—boiled, omeletted, and scrambled. I never knew her to serve anyone, including her family, a conventional meal from beginning to end; but she was always making someone an egg or opening a can of salmon or slicing a tomato to go with a plate of pickled herring.

Who were these Yiddish writers and painters? Some were occasional visitors brought from New York or Israel to give a lecture in Montreal. If I ever knew their names I have forgotten most of them, but there is one writer I remember well. She was Kadya Molodovsky, a Yiddish poet from Warsaw living in New York. One of her poems, *Der Mantel* (The coat) was read and loved by Jewish children everywhere. She had a mild European face that shone with blessedness.

One occasion I remember is Louis Muhlstock's coming to Mrs Maza's apartment to draw Kadya's portrait. He was very tall and thin with a mop of dark hair and an animated rosy face. He was a well-known painter even then, although he couldn't have been more than twenty-three or -four. He set up his easel in the front room, unrolled his paper, tacked it up, and in the most relaxed way began to draw and talk, talk and draw. Kadya talked too, and laughed, and told funny stories—and neither of them minded the awkward fifteen-year-old girl who sat there watching.

Of the poets who lived in Montreal and frequented Mrs Maza's salon, J. I. Segal was the most outstanding. He was a prolific writer, well known in the Yiddish literary world, and had already published many books. At the time I stayed with the Mazas, Segal was on the staff of the Yiddish newspaper *Der Kanader Adler* (The Canadian Eagle) and was also giving Yiddish lessons to children. A number of other poets also frequented Mrs Maza's. Moshe Shaffir, Shabsi Perl, Esther Segal—the sister of J. I. Segal—N. I. Gottlieb, Yudika (Judith Tzik), and one or two other women poets. Some of the writers worked in factories and lived lonely lives in rooming houses. One of them wrote a poem with an image that has stayed with me to this day. He likened his heart to the jumbled untidiness of an unmade bed. At the time I thought the metaphor with its image of the unmade bed was so weird that I remembered it for its absurdity. But since it has stayed in my mind for more than fifty years it can't really have been so absurd. The more I think about it, the more it seems to epitomize and sum up the essence of poverty with all its disorder and loneliness.

The image must have also touched a sensitive spot in my own unconscious, and that was my ambivalence about my parents' generation of immigrant Jews. At that time I bitterly resented my difference from my Canadian friends whose parents had been born in

Canada of English background, and who spoke without an accent. How could it have been otherwise? Canadian society during the twenties and thirties brainwashed every schoolchild with British Empire slogans, and promoted a negative stereotype of all Eastern European immigrants, but especially of Jews. Moreover, during all my primary-school years, the phrase 'dirty Jew' had regularly been hurled at me from the street corners and back alleys of North Winnipeg. Later, when I attended Lisgar Collegiate in Ottawa, I also sensed a certain disdain directed towards Jews, a disdain equalled only by that felt for French Canadians in those days. Perhaps it was no accident that the girl who became my bosom friend was French. She was also from a minority within her social group because her parents were that rare thing, French-speaking Protestants. Her mother came from an old clerical Huguenot family in France and her father was the son of a well-to-do converted Catholic who had quarrelled with the priest in his small Quebec village.

I was not very conscious in those adolescent years of the nature and source of my ambivalences and conflicts—but they manifested themselves in vague feelings of uneasiness and guilt and an awkward sense of always being a stranger in both worlds and not belonging fully to either. Ambivalence, I now realize, also tinged my admiration and fondness for Mrs Maza and her circle. I often felt uneasy at what I thought of as their exaggerated feelings, or at any rate, their exaggerated expression of those feelings.

I didn't see Mrs Maza only when I visited Montreal on school holidays. For several years our families spent part of each summer together near St Sauveur in the Laurentians. The Mazas would rent an old farmhouse, and my parents would camp somewhere not far away. Mrs Maza loved the gentle contours of the mountains and the way the changing light continually moved up and down their slopes. And there was always a little river—hardly more than a creek—in the neighbourhood of her house. It was good for wading in the shallows, but we children wanted to be near a lake where we could swim. Failing that, we had to amuse ourselves by hunting for mushroom puffballs in the farmer's pasture or climbing up the mountain to pick raspberries.

Sometimes I would wander over to the Mazas' house at four o'clock when the humming heat hung over the afternoon, and would find Mrs Maza sitting alone on the veranda, her hands folded into her sleeves—she always wore long sleeves, even in summer—rocking back and forth and looking sad. I remember asking her once why she was so sad. She answered in her slow, musical voice, making every word count, that today was the anniversary of Jacob Wasserman's death. Thanks to her I already knew who he was, and under her tutelage had read *The Maurizius Case*, *The Goose Girl*, and *Dr Kerkhoven's Third Existence*. There wasn't much I could say, so I sat there dumb as a stone, watching the bees alight on the blue chicory flowers beside the veranda, listening to her as she dramatized Wasserman's unhappy life and mourned for him in sad funereal tones.

And he wasn't the only writer whose anniversary of death she observed; there was Edna St Vincent Millay, Elinor Wylie, Sara Teasdale, and a long roll call of dead Yiddish writers. She mourned them all, and recounted their tragic lives as well as their artistic triumphs in spite of adversity. She would often read me passages from their work, and sometimes she would ask to see my poems and read them back to me, analyzing and praising and prophesying a good future.

When I think back to those summer afternoons on her veranda—actually it was a low open balcony in the French-Canadian style—I can still picture her rocking and keening. She radiated a sybilline and mystical quality, and possibly that was the secret of the magnetism that drew so many artists to her Esplanade apartment.

My parents, in spite of their unquestionable identification with Jewishness, were not observant of rituals and never went to synagogue. When it came time for the high holidays, Rosh Hashonah and Yom Kippur, my parents, the Mazas, and two or three other families all converged upon a farmer's house near St Sauveur—the Lamoureux place. There we stayed for a week or ten days enjoying continual harvest pleasures. Mme Lamoureux set a long table with huge bowls of food: soup, chicken, beef, vegetables—raw and cooked—apple and blueberry pies, and home-grown Lamoureux pears, apples, and plums. Everyone heaped his or her own plate at these country feasts. And I have no doubt that the grownups, as they strolled along the gravel roads, gave thought in their own way to the year past and the year still to come.

The Lamoureux are long dead and their farm is no longer a

landmark. It was long ago absorbed by modernism and the autoroute to the Laurentians. And Mrs Maza is no longer alive to mark and mourn the anniversaries of the death of her favourite writers or the loss of the Lamoureux farm with its harvest bounties that were so happily shared by a group of friends. But they are still alive and present in my mind, and they keep me company whenever I watch the light change on mountains or pick wild raspberries in some overgrown ditch. Somewhere Mrs Maza is still urging hungry poets to have a bite to eat, and turning on the light in her dining room to illuminate a crowd of displaced Yiddish writers. And behind them stretches a larger crowd, the long procession of every writer who ever wrote in whatever language. No matter. Each one paid his individual tribute to the love of language and to its inexhaustible resources. And their traces still linger, marking out the path for all writers still to come.

Chava Rosenfarb

Born in Lodz, Poland, in 1923, Chava Rosenfarb attended a Yiddish secular school and Polish High School from 1940 to 1944. She lived and taught in a Jewish primary school in the Lodz ghetto and was sent to Auschwitz and Belsen. She emigrated to Montreal in 1950 and has lived in Toronto for the past several years. Her three-volume work *Der Boim vun Leben* (The tree of life) was published in Tel Aviv in 1972 and won the Israeli Lamed Prize for literature. She has recently won the John Glassco Prize for translation from Yiddish to English of her two novels, *Bociany* and *Of Lodz and Love*, which were originally published in Tel Aviv in 1983 and in the United States in 2000. The story that follows chronicles her memories of suffering in a post-Holocaust world and has been translated from the Yiddish by her daughter, Goldie Morgentaler, who teaches English at the University of Lethbridge, Alberta.

Chava Rosenfarb

A Friday in the Life of Sarah Zonabend

Before she went to the hospital for her operation, Sarah had thrown all the pages of her latest diary into the incinerator. This was not the first time that she had destroyed her personal notes, which she had been keeping on and off throughout most of her literate life. Somehow she had always felt like jotting down a few more or less sincere accounts of happenings and feelings—yet had always been careful not to leave such intimate documents behind.

She hardly knew why she was writing those pages. She justified the habit to herself, using her bad memory as an excuse: she was having difficulties recalling what had happened a year or two ago. Only her concentration camp memories stood out in her mind like an island of sharp, blistering clarity amid a sea of forgetfulness. But as far as the rest of her life was concerned, the past had turned into a terrifying blank, which slipped through her fingers, as if all the living she had ever done had occurred in her childhood and youth and in that surrogate 'life' she had endured in the concentration camp. She told herself that by making notes she would feel more alive; she would supply herself with the tangible proof that something—no matter how meaningless and insignificant that something was—had actually happened to her.

Although in her diary entries she mostly gave an account of her suffering as a lonely wife, or of the illnesses and problems of her children, or of the loss of loved ones, she always hoped, while writing, that in the future she would be able to detect between the lines a reflection of that other form of life, that elusive inner life of the soul, whose exact nature she found impossible to describe. As a matter of fact, she seldom reread her journal entries, and when she did, it was with a sort of dread.

Occasionally she told herself that she was writing these diaries with a dedication in mind—a dedication to her children who might read them one day and learn of her experiences and so come to know her better as the person she really was, although in her heart of hearts she knew perfectly well that nobody learns from someone else's experiences, that her children would never be able to see her in the same light as she saw herself, that there was no other way for children to know their mother than by watching her with their own eyes, by being exposed to her through daily contact. She also knew that her concentration camp experiences could never serve as an excuse for the messy, chaotic quality of her present-day existence.

And so she continued to write her diaries, not really knowing why, until one day she was overcome by an attack of the-devil-take-it desperation and destroyed them—only to start a new diary in a moment of renewed hope.

She had now gone 'diaryless' for the whole stretch of that short, sunless summer, which had vanished more rapidly than the summer before and the one before that. Blotted from her memory, the past had turned into what she called 'a black hole.'

Today was Friday. Sarah had a dread of Fridays. She had a superstitious anxiety about this day, an apprehensive fear of approaching danger, which she could not shake in spite of all attempts to reason with herself. She had always gotten the worst marks at school on a Friday. The war had broken out on a Friday. Her mother had died in the camp on a Friday. President Kennedy had been shot on a Friday. She had discovered on a Friday that her husband was unfaithful to her. On a Friday she had gone to see the doctor, and on a Friday she was operated on. In addition, she retained the memory of one late Friday afternoon, after a selection in the camp. Those women whose lives had been spared returned to their barrack and climbed up onto their bunks in the dark.

It was then that Crazy Bluma exclaimed, 'Children, have you forgotten? Today is Friday, Sabbath eve! Quick! Let's light the candles and bless them!' And in the dark Bluma went through the motions of lighting the Sabbath candles, while all the other half-mad women in the barrack—those whose lives had so recently been spared—covered their faces with their hands and mumbled the blessing of the lights, whether they knew the words or not.

So every Friday morning Sarah's superstitious self was apprehensive, even though her reasonable, enlightened self looked forward to the coming day with a heart full of hope.

Her morning went as usual. She sent the children off to school, tidied the kitchen, and served breakfast to Moniek, her husband, who discussed the news in the morning paper with her. He spoke to her of the racial problems in South Africa and discussed Poland's stand with regard to the Common Market. She did not wish that he would speak of something more personal, more intimate, that he would murmur a few affectionate words, because this had not happened for a very long time; perhaps it had never happened.

Sarah had always clung to the unrealistic belief that two people who loved each other before the war and had found each other after the war were touched by divine grace, so to speak; that they were bound to one another by an exceptionally powerful bond of devotion, and that such a man and woman were different from other couples by virtue of their love's miraculous salvation. In her mind such a marriage, even when not cemented by religious vows, was sacred. Such a woman and such a man had been appointed by fate to alleviate and soothe each other's pain and distress.

As a matter of fact, Sarah had once worked up the courage to raise this topic with Moniek, albeit in a vague form, presenting her thoughts in a less romantic wrapping. But Moniek's response was to burst out laughing, and he laughed so heartily that she was forced to laugh along with him. Such a fool she had made of herself.

She had no idea how long ago this scene had taken place. Her memory was terrible. All she could remember was that in the past her heart had often filled with longing for an intimate moment during breakfast that would supply her with energy and good cheer for the rest of the day. But the need for such a moment had faded, and she now considered this fading to be a charitable gift from fate. Nevertheless, it was unfortunate that the older a woman grew, the less affection she received, although she needed affection more than ever. But perhaps this was nature's subtle way of preparing her for death, numbing her before she tasted the real thing.

As she sat at the breakfast table opposite Moniek, Sarah kept her eyes fixed on the door. It was too early for the mailman, yet sometimes a nice bundle of letters did slip through the slot in the door just at breakfast time. She did not recall that anything exciting ever arrived in that bundle of letters, which usually consisted of bills, city-hall circulars, bulletins, and business letters for Moniek. Yet the sudden leap of her heart at the sight of the envelopes falling onto the floor gave her pleasure. She could still feel the taste of excitement as she tore her lips from the cup of coffee and rushed to the door to pick up the mail.

She hoped that this pleasurable experience would happen again during today's breakfast. When it did not, she went about her housework, hoping that perhaps something pleasurable would happen later on. It was a new day, a new morning, carrying the secret of unknown hours to come, each one liable to reveal the seed of a new beginning. Her superstitious self remembered that it was Friday, but during the morning hours her optimistic, life-loving self got the upper hand over her dread.

And so she continued to expect the arrival of the mail, without fully admitting to herself that she had not yet given up on it. The slot in the front door was a window of promise. Perhaps it would bring a solution to her loneliness, a solution to her troubles with Moniek and the children; perhaps it would bring her recognition as a valuable human being, perhaps a message of love or praise, something to heighten her sense of dignity, to make her feel like somebody special, like a person to whom people wrote letters and with whom they needed to communicate; perhaps it would make her feel like a person who was fully alive and whose days did not fall into black holes of nothingness.

Sarah's Saturdays and Sundays were the dullest, drabbest days of her week, because there was no mail on Saturday or Sunday. She scolded herself for making a *deus ex machina* out of the mail. But her superstitious belief in the power of the mail was stronger even than her superstitious fear of Fridays. She doubted whether she would ever be rid of both of these weaknesses.

The mailman had probably passed while she was busy at the sewing machine, stitching felt flowers onto the decorative pillow slips on the living-room sofa. With Moniek gone and the children at school, Sarah had the day to herself, and the best part of it was the morning, when she sat at the sewing machine deciding on the designs for the pillow decorations, when all her ideas about color and fabric texture were just right, and everything she did had an air of beauty and excitement about it. Yes, in the morning, when she could still feel the imprint of Moniek's cold peck on her cheek, she gave herself the treat of doing something of value for herself alone. She did not mind the untidy house. There was time enough to be wasted on housecleaning.

Then, when she rose from her seat at the sewing machine to get another cigarette, she glanced at the floor beneath the slot in the door to make sure that there really had not been any mail today. She lit her cigarette and went back to the sewing machine. She worked for a while, executing her original designs, but the work went more slowly. Her head ached; she was sleepy. What a sham art was after all! Once, she had thought art to be the ultimate expression of truth, coming just after love in importance in her life. But nowadays she was confused about love and no longer knew what art was all about. She abhorred the canvasses displayed at the art galleries, the so-called masterpieces of contemporary art. They irritated her. They seemed to mock her with their displays of childish doodles in crazy colors. The same was true for modern music, which drove her out of her mind with its deafening noise, producing visions and sounds aimed at dulling the senses. The musical instruments boomed, the singers shouted, their bodies and faces distorted by passion. Was this ugliness art? Had all the beauty seeped out of life after the war?

The flowers she had stitched onto the pillow case began to hurt her eyes with their clashing colors. They too were lies. They were ugly, nauseatingly so—or was it the cigarette that was ugly? She hardly derived any pleasure from that lazy puffing. However, she continued working and puffing until she grew tired. Then she stood up and turned her attention to the disorderly house. Her nausea increased. She felt like weeping and sleeping.

She started to make the beds. As she straightened her son's bed, so disorderly from his playing on it, her eyes filled with tears. She threw herself on the untidy blanket and spread her arms across the bed as if she were embracing his body. She loved that boy of hers. She imagined him next to her as she caressed his slim figure. He was so busy discovering the world, he had little time for her. She missed him badly. 'What does he really feel for me?' she asked herself, thinking of the boy who was about to leave his childhood behind. Could need be described as love? And what would be left of it when he needed her no more?

She reproached herself for wasting her time, squandering her life, for sleeping so much during the day, for her frequent attacks of weeping. It was her indulgence in self-pity that nauseated her, she thought. She got up from the bed and cleaned the boy's room, collecting the piles of comic books from the floor, putting away his clothes, replacing his guitar and accordion in their usual places.

She moved on to her daughter's room. There was little to do here, thank heaven. The bed was made, and the things lying around were probably meant to be lying around. Of late Sarah had been feeling a little like a stranger in her daughter's room. Here lived a beautiful somebody who had once been part of her—once, she hardly remembered when. Sarah swept the floor, while in her imagination she saw the girl's graceful body, her budding breasts, and the flow of her long, blond hair, which reflected the sun's luster. She saw her smiling, saw the dreamy sparkle of the blue eyes, which could change into panther green when she was in a rebellious rage, calling her mother a liar. And perhaps Sarah was a liar after all, but in a different sense of the word. She just no longer knew what was true. She no longer knew who she was herself, or whether she was at all.

She stepped out of her daughter's room and entered her own bedroom. First she dusted off the night tables and arranged the stacks of books that stood on them. Lately she could read no more than a page or two before falling asleep. Somehow the books, even the best works of fiction, had lost their magic. They had betrayed their promise. Was there something wrong with literature, with art in general? Or was the problem life itself? Or perhaps the books no longer served as a substitute for some other needs within her? Or she had lost the ability of entering another reality besides her own, of being capable of imagining herself into someone else's life, because she was so absorbed with her own?

All she felt was that if everything was a lie, literature was the greatest lie of all. She had been raised on literature. It had fed her dreams and provided her with an education. But now she could not forgive its shortcomings, could not forgive the fact that it had so poorly prepared her for life, although she still loved books, piling them up on her bedside table, collecting them on her library shelves. She was constantly adding new volumes, since she could not pass a bookstore without going in to buy, returning home with a neat package under her arm. Would she ever read all the books that she now owned? Of course not. But if she did read them, what difference would it make?

She turned to face the double bed. How vast that bed sometimes seemed! A white-sheeted desert between body and body. If a bed could listen, or feel, or tell a story—would the story it told be the truth?

Sarah had two scrambled eggs for lunch. While eating, she remembered that she had to run over to the grocery store; there was no milk left in the refrigerator. She wrapped herself in her old worn-out coat, and for a split second her fur coat came to her mind. She seldom wore it anymore. There were hardly any occasions for it. She did not mind this. She felt more at home in her familiar shabby, old coat. It better suited her disposition. In fact, she felt guilty for possessing a fur coat. Even though she was not an ardent animal lover, she nevertheless felt an affinity for animals.

She glanced quickly at herself in the mirror and tidied her hair. She should start going to the beauty parlor again, she thought as she ran out into the street. She hated spending long hours at the beauty parlor, and she hated the stiff, fluffed, teased hair that resulted from her sessions there. She even hated the smell of the hair spray. But taking care of her hair might give her a lift. She might acquire a more youthful look by covering the gray. All women dyed their hair nowadays. There seemed to be no woman around with natural hair color and a natural hairdo and a natural face to go with it, a face bearing witness to the passing of time. So what? The main thing was that women were more beautiful today than they had been in the past, although their beauty was of a superficial kind.

But shouldn't she at least start taking care of her figure? What a shame to be walking around wearing those flat hush puppies! They looked like slippers. She should get used to wearing shoes on raised heels, which made a woman look and feel uplifted and less flat-footed. And why not wear the fur coat after all? The animal whose fur it had been was dead anyway. Wrapped in the fur, she might perhaps better demonstrate her affinity with the living creature whose pelt she now wore.

The fresh breeze and the mild sunshine of an early-fall afternoon caressed Sarah's face. The unbuttoned sides of her old coat flapped like wings around her. She felt dirty and sloppy. It was not an apt comparison, yet a trace of that same self-disgust she had sometimes felt in the concentration camp because of the rags she wore returned to haunt her.

But what did she care? Where was she going and who was going to see her? Except for an occasional 'excursion' to the grocery store, she was alone in the house all day long, and when Moniek was home, he rarely noticed what she was wearing. On those rare occasions when she dressed for the theater or for an acquaintance's family celebration she could only get compliments from Moniek by begging.

'How do I look?' she would ask.

And he would answer obligingly, 'Nice,' or, more generously, 'Very nice,' looking through her rather than at her.

Perhaps she should buy herself a dress in spite of everything. In the past buying a new dress or any other item of clothing—something bought exclusively for herself—would have helped to lift her spirits. But she no longer felt like shopping for clothes; she was unable to work herself into the proper frame of mind to undertake the excursion.

She grinned at herself as she imagined her picture in a quiz magazine and underneath it the caption: 'What is wrong with this woman survivor? Why can't she enjoy the life fate has bestowed on her?'

Then she noticed the mailman standing on the corner of the street, his mailbag utterly, painfully empty. There he stood next to her, his work done, waiting to cross the street on his way home. She nodded at him, but he did not respond. Perhaps he did not recognize her. After all, hers was only one door in a street full of doors.

She ran ahead of him, paying no attention to the lights. Suddenly she heard a harsh squeak, a raw screech of tires against asphalt. She did not turn her head, yet she knew. There had been an accident. The mailman. Her heart began to pound. She ran into the grocery store without turning her head. She asked for a bottle of milk, and while she waited, she thought she saw the dead mailman lying sprawled on the street. Serves him right—for his empty mailbag, for not responding to her greeting. That took care, also, of another unlucky Friday.

Sarah took the bottle of milk in her hand. What a pleasant, cool whiteness it had, how good it was to hold it in her hand. She would have much loved to cool her hot face against the bottle that very minute or open it and take a few sips. But no, she would not do that in public.

She left the store. At the bus stop on the corner the mailman was still standing, waiting for the bus to take him home. She was relieved. There had been no accident. She smiled at him. He glanced at her, and this time he lifted two fingers to the rim of his mailman's hat in a kind of military salute. How lovely that was! She fell in love with him on the spot! Yes, she fell in love, and perhaps that was really the only solution, the only answer to all the questions: that rare moment when one person's loneliness saluted the loneliness of another, that moment was happiness. That was all there was to it.

With her entire being she felt the beauty of this sunny afternoon in the fall. Yes, basically she was madly in love with life and therefore terrified of her particular brand of loneliness, which heralded the approach of death. She was not the suicidal type at all. It would have never occurred to her to willingly stop her own heartbeat. Just the contrary. She could never get her fill of living. Hadn't she once written a story for her children about a fly born in the fall, and how it was better to be alive in that season than not to be alive at all?

She knew what she would do. She would go home, prepare dinner for her husband and children, and then pack; take a valise, throw in a few items of clothing, take the few hundred dollars that she had saved, write a note to the children telling them not to worry about her—and leave; go somewhere in search of the mail that never came, in search of the exciting news that never reached her, in search of friendship, that honest, serious friendship that she had known in the camp. She would take action to make things happen. Take a step toward your goal, and it will take a step toward you. She, Sarah Zonabend, would do it! She would be free again.

The breeze playing with the sides of her coat gave her a delicious feeling of abandonment; it seemed to be lifting her up on wings. Her steps were light, her body ready to soar. She swung the bottle of milk in her hand just as she had her school bag long ago when she had run home full of the joy of life and freedom: 'No homework today! Hurray! Today is Friday! No school tomorrow!'

She entered the house and looked around. Scattered around the sewing machine lay the colorful pillow slips on which she had worked that morning. Slowly she approached them. The work looked definitely unprofessional and shabbily executed. She was a dilettante in everything she did. Everything came out half-baked from under her hands, devoid of any masterful finishing touch. Yet, the sight of her work stirred something within her and brought tears to her eyes. Perhaps all that was needed was to remove the brown patch in the center of the design and replace it with some blue. . . .

She set down the milk on a nearby table and, still wearing her coat, sat down by the machine. Her eyes filled. She knew that these were not the tears that she sometimes shed when admiring a work of beauty. It was rather that so many of her tears seemed to have filled the clumsy flower cups sewn onto the pillow cases; so much of her own self was embodied in that disjointed, amateurish piece of work. Her eyes were so full that she could hardly see the flowers that she wanted to fix. Anyway, it was time to prepare dinner.

She stood up, took off her coat, and picked up the milk. On her way to the kitchen she noticed the telephone. It had not rung even once during the day. Nor had it rung yesterday. Perhaps it was out of order? She smiled a bitter smile and picked up the receiver in order to check for a dial tone. The buzzing sound mocked her. The telephone was functioning all right. There was something else that did not function. Perhaps she should get rid of that obnoxious buzzing by telephoning somebody herself? But whom should she call? Perhaps one of her former camp sisters who after the liberation had turned into ersatz friends, full of meaningless chatter and phoniness. What would she and the woman on the other end of the line talk about? They could not bring up the subject of the camps this Friday afternoon. And how much entertainment would they derive from cheerfully discussing the insignificant details of their daily lives? And even if Sarah went directly for the jugular by starting a heart-to-heart conversation—how sincere could she be on this Friday afternoon, when the person on the other end of the line was as confused as she was and just as preoccupied with her own loneliness and her own dinner preparations?

Sarah entered the kitchen and started to peel some potatoes. She washed the lettuce. Suddenly she dried her hands and reached into the table drawer for a pencil. The next moment she was sitting at the kitchen table, bent over her old notebook, from which half of the pages—those filled with the notes from her former diary—were missing. Next to her lay the shavings of the peeled potatoes, and next to the bowl of the freshly washed salad stood the white milk bottle, which she had forgotten to put into the refrigerator.

'Dear diary,' she wrote, laughing softly to herself like a little girl enthralled by the act of confiding a secret to her diary. 'You are the only trip I am capable of taking, the only phone call that I am capable of making, the only letter I am both writing and receiving. Today is Friday and, thank heaven, nothing has happened.'

Translated by Goldie Morgentaler

Naïm Kattan

Naïm Kattan was born in Baghdad in 1928, where he attended a Hebrew school and learned Arabic, French, and English in preparation for his studies at the law faculty of the University of Baghdad. He left Iraq at the end of the Second World War for Paris to study literature at the Sorbonne before moving to Montreal in 1954. He was head of the literary section of the Canada Council from 1967 to 1990 and in 1994 was appointed to the faculty at the Université du Québec à Montréal. His first book of essays, *Le réel et le théâtral* (1970), won the Prix France-Canada in 1971 and was translated by Alan Brown as *Reality and Theatre* (1972). He has continued to publish several collections of essays, novels, and short stories. His first novel, *Adieu, Babylone* (1975), translated by Sheila Fischman as *Farewell, Babylon* (1976), describes his childhood in Baghdad and forms the first part of a trilogy, with *Paris interlude* (1979) depicting his university years in France and *La fiancée promise* (1983) portraying his settling in Canada. The present short story, translated by Phyllis Aronoff, displays the exotic presence of Iraq's Jewish community in Montreal as it tries to acculturate to the established Canadian community. 'La danseuse' was first published in Kattan's collection *La distraction* (1994).

Naïm Kattan

The Dancer

She would start getting ready for the ceremony as soon as she received the invitation, which generally arrived a month before the wedding. When she first came to Montreal, she was invited to two or three weddings a year. Cousins, or vaguely cousins. Then the weddings became more and more elaborate, the hotels more fashionable, but the invitations fewer. She went from one generation to the next. Now it was the children of cousins, or vague cousins, who were getting married. Tonight the ceremony was taking place at the Ritz-Carlton, whose hall, smaller but more elegant than that of the Queen Elizabeth, she preferred. The weddings she liked the least were those that took place in synagogues, except perhaps the Shaar Hashomayim, where she had gone when the Aghabada boy married a wealthy Canadian girl. But not many Iraqi Jews went to that establishment.

When she learned of Gainser's engagement to the Mukamal girl, she wondered if she would be invited. Then there was the large envelope. Her heart pounded. That evening at the table, casually, she announced, 'We've received an invitation to Gainser's wedding. Did you see?'

'It's about time he got married, that one. He was living with an Italian girl for two years. The brothers were getting threatening. She left him, fortunately.'

'We'll have to buy a gift.'

'You take care of it.'

Above all, she mustn't show her excitement. 'I don't know what to wear.'

'Wear your red dress, the one you wore to the last wedding.'

'Everyone's seen it.'

'You think they'll remember it? You haven't worn it for a year.'

She was about to protest, to say, 'Exactly,' but stopped herself in time so as not to let her excitement show. 'It looks good on me, though, doesn't it?'

'It does look good on you,' he said quietly.

This year marked the thirtieth anniversary of their arrival in Montreal. Lena was called Latifa then, and Solly, Selim. Their children, Jane and Kevin, were six and four.

Solly had been born in Tehran. His Iraqi parents had grown rich there, but they were not among the prominent families. Solly, with his heavy features, his thick lips, his large, flat nose, and his dark complexion, looked like an Iranian or a Bedouin. In other words, he was far from handsome. He had gone back to Baghdad to marry a girl from there. Matchmakers had presented him with a selection of candidates, all afflicted with some defect. One limped slightly, another had a face covered with scars from bites by an insect unknown outside of Iraq. But there were not only physical flaws. There were girls from families that were not very desirable who had inherited chronic diseases or tarnished reputations (an aunt of loose morals, an uncle who was a swindler or a crook). Finally, there were the daughters of impoverished families who were no beauties. . . . Latifa was the second of four daughters. Her elder sister, who had brown eyes and pale skin, had had a procession of suitors. At twenty she was already well set up, married to a doctor. Latifa was twenty-five. With her dark complexion and black eyes, she was considered homely. And there was no dowry to compensate for her ugliness. Selim was far from handsome, and his name was without distinction. But he was rich and young. However, his wife would have to leave her country. All things considered, Selim and Latifa were made for each other. The wedding took place in Baghdad. Contrary to custom, it was Selim who paid for it. Latifa wanted a dancer and a singer at her wedding. Selim, in love with his wife-to-be, yielded to her every wish. It embarrassed him to admit that he found her beautiful, more beautiful than her sisters. One day he would declare his love for her, but she already realized it, she was sure of it.

Selim put off his return to Tehran from month to month. Should he set himself up in Baghdad? The political situation, especially the uncertain future of the Jews, discouraged him from doing so. He promised Latifa he would take her to America. 'We'll spend a year or two in Tehran organizing our departure.' Latifa was not unhappy in Baghdad, although she resented her father, and especially her mother, for treating her like a poor relation, the ugly duckling of the family, and did not appreciate the constant comparisons with her brown-eyed, pale-skinned sisters. Then Jane was born, whose real name was Hanna, after her late grandmother.

'We'll have to wait until she's old enough to travel,' she told her husband, whose business was doing better and better. Then Kevin was born. 'We'll have to wait. . . .'

The family had to leave Baghdad for Tehran. There was an exodus of all the Jews. In Tehran life for the Jews was uneventful. Here and there little groups of troublemakers or little marginal journals exhorted the Muslims to support their brothers in Palestine. But the echoes that reached the Jews were muffled and infrequent and didn't seem threatening. Selim went to the American consulate. Immigration visas were hard to obtain, and there were so many applications that it would take twenty years before his turn came. He became frightened. Where should they go? A cousin of Latifa's had just gone to Montreal. She sang its praises in a letter. The die was cast. Canada was the family's future home.

They arrived in the middle of summer. Latifa had never suffered so much from the heat. Her cousin and the little community of Iraqis talked constantly of the horrors of the cold and snowstorms. There was nothing she hated as much as the heat and humidity.

Secure in his capital, and with a trusted man left in Tehran to take care of the interests he still had there, Selim was in no hurry. He started by looking for a house in the town of Mount Royal, where there were already two Iraqi families. The neighbours, although they were Canadian and not Jewish, were calm and peaceful, the streets wide and clean. Every day Latifa visited one or two houses. Selim finally chose a property on Laird Avenue with a large yard with fruit trees and flowers. They furnished the house with copies of French and English furniture. By the first frost, the family was comfortably ensconced in its new home. The children took up English, and Arabic was now reserved for the parents when they were alone.

Selim looked for a business. He was offered all kinds of stores and shops. He wanted to put his knowledge to use and to keep busy. 'Idleness is fatal for a man,' he said. 'He starts playing cards night and day, drinking, and womanizing.' Cards were a pleasant, harmless pastime. Every Saturday the Iraqis got together at one of their homes to play. In Tehran Selim had been a moderate player. Once a week. At midnight he would put on his jacket and leave. Latifa sometimes played with the ladies, and she would get up as soon as her husband gave her the signal that it was time to leave. In Montreal they found a similar group and went back to their old habit. The same jokes, the same audacities, the same food. The only difference was the absence of domestic servants. 'Good riddance,' said Latifa with a sigh. She had never been able to give them orders or prevent their petty thieving.

One afternoon Selim came home later than usual. 'I tried to telephone, but the line was always busy,' he explained to Latifa, who was dying of anxiety. 'We're not in Baghdad any more. Nothing can happen to me here. Nobody even knows I'm Jewish.'

He gathered the children in the living room. His chest swelled with pride, he solemnly intoned, 'I'd like you to meet Solly.' He drew Latifa toward him. 'And this is Lena.'

'We don't have the same names any more?' exclaimed Jane.

'Your names are fine. As of today, your parents are Canadians.'

'What about our passports?' objected Latifa.

'I've consulted a lawyer. Don't worry. Everything will be in order. We're keeping our family name.'

'Oh . . . ,' murmured Jane, disappointed.

'That's not all,' he added. 'Solly is now the owner of a business—'Solly's Cars.' Get your coats on. We're going there.'

'What about dinner?' asked Lena.

'We'll go out for dinner.'

There was a car at the door. Solly drove them to Décarie Boulevard. They passed huge, brightly coloured, flashing signs one after another: Used Cars, Voitures Usagées.

'A garage!' said Lena, imagining her husband with oily hands and black arms.

'No, Lena. Not a garage. An automobile business. New and used.'

The lot, squeezed between two others, seemed small. Solly indicated its boundaries.

'Is that all?' asked the boy.

Solly, proud of his ambitious son, retorted, 'You want all the lots, do you? Yes, that's all. It's enough for a hundred cars. It's not bad.'

The wind blew, cold and damp.

'And you'll be outside all day?' asked Jane.

'That's a good daughter, worrying about her father. No, I have an office.'

'He led them to a wooden shack and proudly took a key from his pocket. Three chairs, a small desk, a hot plate, a cabinet.

'Everything is there. Telephone, files.' He opened the cabinet. 'Even a coffee maker. Every comfort.'

'And the cars will all be left outside?' asked Lena.

'Yes. There aren't any thieves here. And anyway, I have insurance.'

The months and years passed. The children grew, went to school, spoke English. Solly made a good living. He sold his used-car business and bought a large garage for Ford cars on Saint Denis Street. Saturdays the family played cards at the home of one of the Iraqi families. When her turn came, Lena spent a week preparing the food. Jane had nothing but scorn for this kind of food, and Solly apologized, 'Once in a while. Otherwise the Baghdad cooking will make us sick.'

Lena discovered exercise and dancing—belly dancing—to keep trim. The Canadian woman who taught this dance to a dozen women heavy with age presented it as a health measure. The heady music reminded Lena of her wedding and all the weddings she had attended as a girl in Baghdad. Alone, she circled the living room to the music of bygone days, observing herself in the big mirror. She found it hard to take the scornful jokes of the teacher, to whom this dance was only a type of callisthenics for which the dancers received male homage in the form of bank notes slipped into their bra. The other women sniggered like fools. Lena did not attend the twelve sessions she had paid for in advance.

All alone in front of the mirror she rediscovered movements and gestures she knew. She had only to let go, to obey her body, and the movements came of themselves, reviving an ancient knowledge. The dance lifted her up, made her light and undulating; her body asserted itself irresistibly. She stopped in front of the mirror to catch her breath. She was beautiful, more beautiful than the cabaret dancer at her wedding.

She inspected her arms, her thighs, her mouth, her nose. She was more beautiful than all the blondes in the world. A dancer. Unlike any ever found in a cabaret in Baghdad. And what if Solly suddenly burst in? He'd fall on his knees, he'd love her as no man ever loved a woman. And all the men, all the other men . . . she imagined them there, very close, behind a screen of lights, of huge candelabra sparkling with a thousand flames, dazzled by her dance, her splendor.

One day Jane came home from school early. Lena was still wearing her dancer's costume.

'What are you doing, Mother?' she asked in astonishment and burst into laughter.

'Go to your room. Can't you see I'm exercising?'

'But you dropped out of the class.'

'Leave me alone, Jane,' she pleaded, exasperated. 'Go to your room.'

She felt alone. Her daughter would always be a stranger. She would not understand.

One evening, when the children were in bed and Solly was at a meeting of dealers, she put on her dancer's costume—a gold brassiere and skirt of silvery strips. She put on some music and moved away from the mirror. She was not going to look at herself. She saw herself, dark and beautiful, the gaze of all the men hanging on her every movement.

She heard Solly come in but did not stop dancing. She knew he was there, a drifting shadow, watching avidly, his mouth slightly open. He wanted her, completely naked, but the dance made her invulnerable. It was she who chose, and no man could approach her or put his hand on her skin without her consent, and that included Solly. Had he known that she was a dancer, that his wife was a dancer? He turned on the living-room light. She froze.

'Don't stop, Lena. I want to see you.'

She continued her dance, but it was no longer the exercise from her Canadian class.

'Do you know I've never seen a cabaret dancer better than you? You have a gift. An artist. You could have gone to Egypt and been in the movies. Tahia Carioca would have been afraid of the competition.'

She rushed to her room, changed her clothes, and threw herself on the bed. She wanted to cry. She hated Solly, who didn't understand, couldn't understand.

He came and joined her and held her lightly against him.

'Luckily I married you in time. You could have ended up in a cabaret.'

She despised him, the fool, for reducing her to a prostitute, for being so crass. Yet, he was her husband and he loved her, she knew, dark though she was, *because* she was dark. But he considered himself her savior. Poor fool. He would never understand what she felt, this body that was beginning to live apart from him, from any man, and yet all the men were there in a circle, and they were shouting their admiration and applauding like mad.

For many months Lena did not dance anymore. She slipped on her costume a few times and played the Arabic record, but she found herself ridiculous—'a real cabaret dancer.' Sometimes she would wonder if that adored and scorned dancer was so contemptible. The idea of being the mistress of some tribal chief, minister, or commanding officer, the kept woman of some businessman, the one-night conquest of a senior official who would give up everything for her filled her with terror. She wouldn't dare. She could never. Even with Solly, she could hardly . . . And he was her husband. How could a dancer, a real dancer, spend the night with a tribal chief or a Bedouin? She imagined herself a prisoner, degraded—and every night, on the cabaret stage, she would regain the integrity of her body and would feel powerful, beautiful, and so happy!

And then the day of the great event arrived. Lev's wedding, the reception at the Queen Elizabeth. He was a cousin of Solly's, who in Baghdad had been called Fuad. He had been found in a kibbutz near Haifa by the dark, heavy daughter of the wealthy Rubin, who had lost hope of finding a taker in Montreal. Lena wore a dress of red chiffon with paillettes. She no longer tried to hide her dark skin under dreary, dull-colored dresses. She was no longer in Baghdad. Ugly, blond, blue-eyed girls were a dime a dozen. She smiled at everyone and punctuated her pleasure with cries and hugs. And she drank and she ate. The wealthy Rubin had spared no expense—two bands, one Western and the other Arabic-Israeli. After the *hora*, the band played the music of her forgotten everyday dance. Women and men swung their hips without style, coarsely miming the movements of the dance. Without thinking, she found herself at the center of the floor. Oblivious to the crowd, the noise, the room, she began to twirl. The band followed her and accentuated the rhythm, bending to her will. Her body had become the music, and the band guessed every movement of her desire, obeying the rhythm that she dictated, that she imposed. She heard the shouts and applause in an indefinable fog. She was all alone on the floor. They had given her room. They encircled her, vibrating to the movements of her thighs, her breasts, her belly. Her raised arms moved freely, imperiously. Everyone breathed in time with her. There was no more wedding, no hotel hall. Baghdad and Montreal had disappeared in the shadow of this dance floor where she, the lone dancer, silenced the crowd and made it shout. The band stopped playing.

She was on the floor, dripping with sweat, panting, seeing nothing but a confused mass of faces. Men and women clasped her in their arms, embraced her. Rubin brought her over to his table. 'I haven't seen anything like this since Tahia Carioca.' Their words jumbled together. 'Too bad that here it's associated with prostitutes.' 'If only Canadians could appreciate it.' 'You're a true artist.'

Driving home, Solly was on his guard, somber, silent.

'I'm a bit tired,' she murmured, her head leaning against the seat.

'You must be.'

The children were asleep. In their bedroom Lena undressed and threw herself on the bed. Half asleep, she thought she heard Solly say, 'My wife is a dancer. I'm married to an artist.'

He never talked to her about the dancing. They both knew that at every wedding, for fifteen or twenty minutes, Lena would be the dancer, the Tahia Carioca of the Iraqis in Montreal, the queen of the evening. And Lena lived in anticipation of the next wedding.

Translated by Phyllis Aronoff

Monique Bosco

Born in Vienna in 1927, Monique Bosco received her early education in France; in 1948 she came to Montreal, where she earned her Ph.D. in 1953 at the Université de Montréal. In 1963 she became a professor in the university's French department. She has published several novels and collections of short stories and poetry. *Un amour maladroit* (1961) won an American first-novel award. Her third novel, *La femme de Loth* (1970), won a Governor General's Award and was translated as *Lot's Wife* (1975). In 1996 she received the Prix Athanase-David in recognition of her life's work. Recurrent themes of bitterness, anger, and the solitude of rejected love pervade her work with its strong feminist perspective. The following excerpt from her novel *Sara Sage* (1986), translated by Phyllis Aronoff, depicts a sister's exclusion from the male-dominated Jewish world at the moment of her brother's circumcision. Set in France during the Second World War, this feminist novel revises the patriarchal biblical story of Sarah.

Monique Bosco

EXCERPT FROM *Sara Sage*

I had always heard Edna declare that there was nothing more wonderfully fulfilling than those days of the birth of a new creature born of one's flesh. So like, so unlike, perfect from head to toe, fierce and greedy, seeking the breast with incomparable trust and passion.

'So good. Sleeps all night. Gurgles all day.'

And now a frenzy of panic and dread surrounded that baby. With veiled words, Raguel intimated that between me and the new arrival there had been many disappointments. He refused to tell me more.

'Ask your mother.'

The same old story.

Men do not seem to have words or explanations for anything important.

So many hours in the main square, debating gravely.

And what do they do in the synagogue, in front of the Torah finally unveiled, those who can read, the learned, the scholars, interpreters of the law?

From Edna alone I sometimes had the impression of receiving a little light and clarity. And now Edna was reduced to this: nothing but a howling, suffering beast we heard crying and sighing for days.

Why did women have to suffer so to give birth, while our cats have always performed the ritual of birth with stunning ease?

In vain they tried to make me leave the basket where she went and dropped her young, one by one.

Four, sometimes five. And it happened with a sureness and speed that filled me with admiration. I never ceased being fascinated by the ordinary basket where the little cats rubbed against each other, their eyes still sealed.

'What about us? How many will we have?'

The cradle they had prepared seemed marvelous to me. Very

large, decorated with lace and ribbon. With a little pillow embroidered with fruits and flowers. Just one little pillow. Who would lay their head there? Taking turns, no doubt. Sometimes the little cats were all similar, and no one could tell right away if it was a male or female kitten that had arrived.

I persisted: 'Do you think there'll be a lot of them? Blond and dark boys, or girls with lots of curls?'

Finally I understood that at most there would be one nice, big, lively boy in the wicker cradle prepared with so much love and care. Raguel, harried, finally told me there had been many little angels—as he called them—who had died right after coming out of Edna's belly. For her, who had prayed, then cried out so, these children hadn't even had the strength to utter a feeble greeting. Others, born before term, were just big enough for Edna and Raguel to know that another little boy had been refused them.

'The Lord has given. The Lord has taken away.'

Raguel refused to count his losses. God, in his wisdom, had apparently decided thus. So he took up a shovel and spade and went to bury this forbidden fruit far and deep in the blackest earth of the orchard.

'All sons.'

He allowed himself neither comments nor curses, but the garden, where he had once worked from dawn to dusk, had become overgrown with brambles. No more fruit or flowers. Even the huge, century-old fig tree had been sterile for several summers.

But this time Edna had a beautiful belly. Her nine months had gone perfectly. Sometimes she would take my hand and place it on that round ball, which was growing from day to day.

'Do you feel it? Do you feel how it moves and tosses and turns and rolls within?'

And I felt this long awaited baby move and stir and almost heard it cry. And I, too, was impatient for it to break open its shell and emerge from its wrapping like a ready chick, a ball of fuzzy down.

'We'll both take care of it.'

I was fidgeting with impatience.

'When the moon is perfectly full and round, it will be time.'

And every night I watched for it as it was shining like a big, luminous disk in the dark sky.

I clapped my hands. 'That's it.'

But they told me that, contrary to all appearances, no, the moon was not completely round. And fear, a strange fear, seized me. And I saw Edna become nervous and lose some of her good humor and confidence.

Far from growing, it seemed to me that the moon had begun to wane. And I insisted on going to bed very early, I closed my eyelids with rage, feigning sleep.

And I awoke with a start to Edna's cries. I rushed into her bedroom and was immediately chased out.

Once again confusion reigned, and Edna's cries were more desperate and hoarse than before.

How fragile and vulnerable seemed my world, yesterday so deliciously calm and serene. Incomprehensible. Apparently, daughters came out of their mother's bellies practically by themselves, with no effort. Only sons clung to her womb, refusing to leave the warm, shady grotto, the sweetly damp cavern where they had nestled so long. Finally, there was a long cry. Every trace of agitation disappeared. Silence. Then a weak, hoarse cry. The newborn. I knew that at last a son had been born. Raguel burst out sobbing while Edna proudly held out that thing that was round yet thin, with a few scant hairs stuck to its skull, its frail limbs trembling convulsively.

I felt relieved and unhappy, uneasy and sad, delighted and jealous all at the same time. The event had finally happened.

'Let us all praise his coming.' With what extravagant care we prepared to rear this son, this savior of the threatened race. Nothing was beautiful, fresh, or sterile enough for this child-king. Father and mother vied in attendance at his bedside. Jealously guarded, night and day. As in the tales and legends they sometimes read to me, they seemed to fear that a wicked fairy would spring up near his cradle and cast an evil spell on him. They would hardly let me near him.

Me, Sarah, who had prayed so for the birth of this baby. This baby now took up all the space despite his small weight. He changed Edna's voice, and she no longer spoke softly and long to me as she had always done, but seemed constantly preoccupied with him, him alone. Even when I coughed to break your heart—and I sometimes had painful coughing fits—Edna's only concern was to keep me away so as not to contaminate the new wonder. And if I fell and scraped my knees till they bled, she had the maid wash my sores—she called them, scornfully it seemed to me, 'booboos'—denying them even the help of iodine or mercurochrome.

'It will heal by itself, in the air.'

Once I would have been given the most delicate gauze and constant attention.

What was I to make of all that?

Edna pronounced: 'You're big now. My big girl. My good, sensible girl.'

I did not feel myself destined, already, for goodness.

Sometimes I was stirred by great waves of rage and revolt, as if to confirm that I had not really become sensible—at least according to Edna's new criteria for me. What she had formerly found delightful and funny about me—and enjoyed recounting to all her friends—now aroused in her only a kind of irritation tinged with contempt.

No longer was there any question of equality between us or of sharing the everyday tasks in raising this child-miracle. Whenever I was about to pick him up, Edna intervened.

'He's still so small, so delicate. The slightest shock could be fatal to him.'

I did not want to contradict her, but it seemed to me that this was not the right way to raise a boy who was called on to play someday such a great role. Why did she shelter him and bundle him up like this, fearing every ray of sunshine or gust of wind?

This future leader of armies, this fearless, resolute general—who would teach him to sit tall in the saddle and advance against the enemy at dawn and even at nightfall?

'You'll make an invalid of him.'

I immediately regretted my words and did not add what had been causing me to burn with curiosity for weeks. In the circle of women, generally so quick to celebrate every birth with unrestrained emotion, I sensed a strange reticence. Raguel had gone back to his work in the orchard and vegetable garden. But no one said anything about celebrating the ceremony of circumcision with pomp and opulence. Wouldn't God be angry at this delay in obeying his commandment? How could they dare to exempt this child of destiny from the first law of the covenant?

I heard whispering. 'How pale this child is, livid, greenish mauve, ivory, pale blue, you'd say, yes, blue.'

What strange breed had belatedly sprouted in Edna's hothouse?

Sometimes I heard Edna murmuring almost inaudibly. As if she was counting the baby's heartbeats. Like a metronome, regularly. Which, just as regularly, became irregular. And each time Edna sighed and clutched to her bosom, her heart, this infant who usually refused to nurse at the breast that was always offered.

Ridiculous baby that could allow itself the luxury of disdaining this warm, sweet milk it was begged, cajoled, and badgered to deign to drink.

'This child is not gaining enough weight. He needs the strength to resist.'

To resist what? I wondered. These words of the midwife alarmed Edna even more. They shocked me, who was always thirsty and hungry and no longer received any praise for cleaning my plate, even of spinach or turnips.

'Poor little sweetheart, my dove, my pigeon, my wonder,' cooed Edna to him. And the cradle was still in their bedroom, and Edna never left the bedroom, not caring what might happen elsewhere in the house. And she forced herself to drink stein after stein of beer so that her milk would flow more abundantly, creamy and light, so that her son would not have to make the slightest effort when suckling; but he turned his head away as if in fear and loathing when she urged him a little more vigorously.

A strange struggle, which I watched in painful fascination. Because sometimes, despite my jealousy, I felt a sympathy for this baby who was so extraordinary. Because all around me, among the women and the busybodies in the neighborhood, I had noticed that children always demanded the breast, grasping it firmly in their little hands for fear that it would be gone too soon. Only this long awaited brother seemed to expect nothing of this abundant breast, this exquisite manna that I myself still dreamed of as a paradise lost.

Maybe these were signs that marked children predestined for a fabulous fate. They did not need, as others do, that maternal ritual, that nourishment in which everything was fastidiously cooked, counted, and measured.

Ceremonies of the bath. They practically threw me out whenever the little boy was to be immersed in the warmed water. Sometimes I managed to stay. Then I sensed the tension of Edna and her maid when with endless precautions they finally put him into his little white bath. The baby—and I was surprised that he had not been formally named—seemed as terrified as they. Quickly they sprinkled a little water on him and wrapped him up again in dry cloths heated to the right temperature.

'But he's changed color again.'

Edna stated it. The servant tried to reassure her.

I had indeed seen the skin, so delicate, change from azure to mauve pink, like the barometer I had been given that forecast bad weather. It was one of the first gifts I ever got, and I considered it a very precious, magical thing. I followed the instructions extremely rigorously, consulting it only for major occasions. And now this innocent baby possessed the power to change color at the slightest fluctuation in temperature.

I dared not question Edna further, and I tried to forge my own convictions, to understand the order of things—or, rather, the disorder—with its oddities that were so numerous that I sometimes despaired of ever understanding anything. Finally they named my little brother Emmanuel. And the circumcision was to take place the following Sabbath. Raguel had decided this after discussing it at length with the rabbi. And I heard my parents in the bedroom talking long and late into the night, even until dawn. And that night, for the first time, my little brother started to cry in the night, too, as if he suspected the butchery they were planning for him. In the morning Edna's eyes were red. She saw me looking at her with a mixture of pity and terror. My all-powerful mother, defeated. How horrible. Edna took me in her arms as she used to, holding me very tight, covering me with kisses in which I thought I detected the bitter taste of tears, punctuating her caresses with disjointed words in which I could hear that I was very lucky to be a girl, preserved and protected from the murderous madness of men, maniacs for law and order, who only knew to obey the strongest one and never questioned anything—sheep turned into tigers, ferocious tigers, devouring each other, preying on the innocent. And she, always so respectful of her 'spouse,' as she usually liked to call him, seemed ready to denounce him along with the rest, so great was her fury.

'Don't you go and get married. You no longer have freedom or the right to speak.' I couldn't believe my ears. Later, when Edna demanded that I make up my mind and marry, I recalled her indignant tone that day, which I have never been able to forget, to excise from my memory.

'So is this circumcision really horrible?'

I had got the impression that this ritual offering of every male on God's altar was required for the honor of belonging to the privileged group.

And that 'bird' Edna spoke of, that tiny spigot I had glimpsed between my fragile little brother's legs—the only tangible difference between us—a slice of it had to be offered to a God as demanding and stupid as the one in my books of history and legends in the chapters on primitive civilizations. A barbarous God who exacted bloody human sacrifices from his faithful. And this brother who was so fragile that at the mere contact with water he seemed ready to faint with weakness and terror—now the tools of butchers were going to attack his most secret, tender flesh. I took my mother aside.

'Do you want me to take him away, far away, and hide him?'

Edna sobbed even harder. 'Poor dear. You don't realize. Emmanuel is very ill. He's not like other children. I will always be fearful for him. Not only this Saturday.'

And she went into long, complicated medical explanations, from which I understood only that my little brother had a hole in his heart. A heart that wasn't closed properly. A heart open and vulnerable. Therefore, we must at all costs avoid shocks and irritations. He could succumb to the most innocuous illness, the slightest fever.

'You understand why I've been neglecting you somewhat.'

I again was filled with love for my poor parents, whose long unfulfilled desires and aspirations were thwarted.

With their wish finally granted after so many disappointments and bereavements, they found themselves more miserable than ever. But Raguel's puritanical view of the world prevented him from pouring out curses and abuse or trying to avert the punishment he sensed coming. He again took on the furtive, guilty, ashamed manner I had seen in him for so many years. He stopped working, although he couldn't afford not to work. He appealed to his faraway relatives, who until then had been carefully kept out of the drama because their distance made secrecy possible. So, forsaking all pride, Raguel appealed to his rich cousin Tobit, soliciting a large sum of money to provide for 'whatever might happen.' Tobit exacted a promise from him: I understood that with this ignominious request Raguel, my father, had made a pledge of the only property 'at his disposal,' his only daughter, the youngest member of the clan, healthy in body and mind and destined to become a woman with many good qualities, because 'her mother brought her up strictly, according to the sound principles and the most stringent rules of the tribe.' My heart skipped a beat. I must have turned blue myself, or purple. I had a pain in my heart, which was beating wildly. I felt burning hot and freezing cold at the same time, rigid with horror and shame and fear for the future. But there would be no future. Everything was settled, decided in advance. Here was this father I had thought so virtuous, so detached from mercenary concerns, selling me, delivering me up in exchange for a little gold like some piece of merchandise, without consulting me, speaking of me in terms that were insulting and sordid. I had thought myself free and strong, proud and good. I had been praised only for reasons that were false and vulgar. Nothing was mine any more. I had become a thing, deprived of freedom, personal desire, freedom of choice, and free will. A mere animal that could be sacrificed with impunity on the altar of the ancestors. Emmanuel had had to suffer only a minimal bodily loss. I would be delivered whole, against my will, to a master, I, the pledge of this new covenant among the men of the clan.

Edna and I spent the Saturday of Emmanuel's circumcision huddled together. I did not have a moment of diversion or lightness. With all my energies straining, I implored fate not to harm this baby who was so frail and innocent. And indeed, he appeared not to have suffered when he was finally returned to us safe and sound. I had made so many promises through that long day to ward off bad luck. I would even, I had promised myself, give up young women's pleasures so that this little brother who was so threatened might be saved. Yes, I would be sterile and shameful like the women stricken with this disgrace, but I would voluntarily forswear commitment for life. So there would be no man in my bedroom to murmur my stories to through the nights and no child to carry, 'fruit of my womb.' And my breasts would remain small, and no one would drink from them.

Translated by Phyllis Aronoff

Régine Robin

Régine Robin was born in 1939 in Paris to Polish-Jewish parents. She received her Ph.D. in history from the Université de Paris before emigrating to Montreal in 1977, where she teaches at the Université du Québec à Montréal. She is a member of the Royal Society of Canada, recipient of the Governor General's Award, and winner of the prestigious Prix Jacques Rousseau (1994). Her interdisciplinary, postmodern prose explores the interfaces of history and fiction as she examines multicultural identities in shifting from Canada to the United States to Europe. Among her publications are *L'amour du Yiddish* (Paris, 1984), *Le réalisme socialiste* (Paris, 1986), which won the Governor General's Award, and a biography of Kafka (Paris, 1989). The present selections are from her novel *La Québécoite* (1983), translated by Phyllis Aronoff as *The Wanderer*. The translated title captures the multiple punning of the French title and suggests nomadic meaning and identity in Robin's writing. A fascination with signs and languages in Montreal, Paris, and eastern Europe runs through the novel.

Régine Robin

EXCERPT FROM *The Wanderer*

No order. No chronology, no logic, no lodging. Nothing but a desire for writing and this proliferation of existence. To fix this porousness of the probable, this micro-memory of strangeness. To spread out all the signs of difference: bubbles of memories, pieces of vague reminiscences coming all together without texture, a bit grey. Without order, they were loose series, colours without contours, lights without brightness, lines without objects. Fleeting. The black night of exile. History in pieces. To fix this strangeness before it became familiar, before the wind suddenly changed, freeing rushes of obvious images. The longings could be experienced but they couldn't be tamed. You couldn't analyze them. They would suddenly impose themselves. No representation of exile. Unrepresentable. With no present, no past. Just blurry faraways, bits, traces, fragments, gazes all along these urban travellings. To fix the strangeness right away because the longing would break through the surface of the days by surprise. It was language, language taking its pleasure all alone, body without subject. Nothing but language. It was snatches at first, of conversations heard in cafés, along the streets, in lines waiting, in the métro. It's a settlement. You're not trying to understand. It has nothing to do with a contract. Look, I'll tell you something. I'm selling the building on Rue Censier to the common property. I don't know. The contributions aren't equal, ninny. Separate as to property? You don't think about it. It's true, listen, it's logical. With the inheritance from my parents, I buy another building—incidentally, you know, it's proportional to our contributions, but no, you have to make a big thing out of it. You're beautiful, beautiful, don't ever use makeup again. You understand, it couldn't go on. I told him. Snatches whispered in the dark at the movies. It's a building on Avenue Foch. If I get kicked out, what will you do? That slut Nicole. And what if I had nothing, if

I didn't have anything. If you find someone better than me, you leave, and all I have is myself. That's the problem. You're an idiot. Half-whispered snatches, confusion. Confessions. Misunderstandings. That's not what I meant. What I mean is. You said it. You didn't say it, say it, tell me, repeat, don't say that. A building on Avenue Foch, did you say? He owed money. Let's go, let's leave. It's not very nice out, not warm. Already summer, but we won't have any summer this year. It upsets me, I'm already all jittery. Let the sky fall on my head. Horn, brakes, squeal of brakes in the rain, spraying, splashing. They're in no hurry to serve us. She'll make an omelette. We'll see. A Ricard and a Casanis, please. Sounds of pinball machines, of cassettes playing low or spewing noise. But still, there aren't fifty million morons. I'll remember later. He had a problem yesterday, work bothered him—I don't know anything about it. Of course not. What does that mean? We don't know anything about it. What do you feel like eating? Green and red stripes from the traffic lights at the corner, greenish reflections of the crosses of pharmacies, dazzling, headlights flashing. The voices move away, move closer. Their inflections are unpredictable. Every year he says he'll retire. If only he didn't bother people with it. The Pernod is sweet—it tastes different. What a nut! Cheap bracelets at Félix Potin. A decaf please. Sounds of buses, of the cash register. Hoarse voices, warm voices, mingling of voices. I touch them, I finger them, I hug them to me. Bits of dreary everyday, snatches of radio broadcasts, television theme songs. Zitrone. Giquel. El Kabbach. Hit parade, ads, news, TV newsmagazine. Scraps of routes along the métro lines. Line 10. Austerlitz without sun, without victory. We were leaving for the Landes. The smell of urine and vomit always dominated the station. Sadness, dirt, the station crossed, the endless wait for a taxi on the return, the arrival early in the morning, the first *café crème* after vacation. You had arranged to meet your husband in Rouyn-Noranda, at the local bistrot on a little square—but there was no square and no local bistrot in Noranda-Rouyn. The meeting with a city. You often got lost, coming back to the same place a thousand times, recognizing the signs, the shops, the quality of the air hanging over the intersections. A month later, familiar routes had replaced the hesitant, awkward wanderings of the early days. Cities take on colour in the early morning. There are also colourless cities tinted with water, snow. Fog and siren cities, factory smokestack cities, park cities, flower cities. You loved all cities. The hallucinatory breathing of American cities seen from a plane at night, like an instrument panel, an electronic screen of criss-crossed lines of light, webs of light in the night.

Downtown,
old ring,
new ring,
outer boulevards,
beltways,
boulevards periphériques,
ramps,
highways,
freeways,
turnpikes,
parkways,
thruways,
Stadmitte,
Zentrum,
midtown,
downtown,
centreville.

This desire for writing. Yet it was so simple to start at the beginning, to follow a plot, to resolve it, to speak of an off-place, a nonplace, an absence of place. To try to fix a few signs, hold onto them, wrest them from the void. Nothing but a mark, a tiny little mark. You had to fix all the signs of difference: the difference of the smells, of the colour of the sky, the difference of the landscape. You had to make an inventory, a catalogue, a nomenclature. To record everything in order to give more body to this existence. Your slightest doings, your encounters, your appointments, your movements—the curious names of the big stores:

SIMPSON
EATON
THE BAY
OGILVY
HOLT RENFREW

MARKS & SPENCER
WOOLWORTH
KRESGE
DOMINION
STEINBERG

All this would surely end up having the density of a life, an everyday life. Would it be possible to find a position in language, a purchase, a fixed point of reference, a stable point, something that would anchor the words when there was only a tremulous trace of text, a mute voice, twisted words? To take the right to speak. What words? To keep quiet? Humiliation again? To wear the star again? Broken text. To root out fear, shame, solitude. To speak for—for nothing perhaps. To speak because. The noise—nothing but noise, babble, rubble.

I don't know how to speak, exclaims Moses
perhaps to keep quiet—
but a voice, a little tinkling voice
to cross the violent sheets of silence—
just speech—words to the letter
it's the unfinished that's important—
death
is but a shadow
There will be no beginning
no story
No order—no chronology
no logic
no lodging—
omega will never come. Because nothing starts at
alpha—the first letter of the Bible is bet, *the second*
letter; the last letter is tav, *index of the future*
open–
to keep quiet perhaps–
perhaps—
To write—with the six million letters of the Jewish
alphabet

You had loved this country, you had breathed in the blue mist, the autumnal smells of fresh-baked bread and dead leaves, the currents of cool air on the milky mountain. JUSSIEU. The polonia trees in the square, the newspaper kiosque and the student cafés across from the university. CARDINAL LEMOINE. Going up the street to get to the Mouffe. King Henry at the corner of Rue des Boulangers, where we bought Glenfiddich and Pilsener beer. Continuing on Rue Monge to the square—bistrots, market twice a week, the shade of chestnut trees, evening on Place Monge. MAUBERT-MUTUALITÉ. How many meetings at La Mutualité, the hall empty or full? Everyone to La Mutu! We aren't going to La Mutu! On October 27, 1960, we didn't go to La Mutu—who remembers? How many Algerian wars, strikes, frustrations, celebrations, rages, commemorations at La Mutu? MABILLON. The student restaurant before the Mazet opened. We went to the Mab, it was better than the Inter. SÈVRES-BABYLONE. The Bon Marché store and the Lutétia café. It was before they built the Maison des Sciences de l'Homme. Already the nice neighbourhoods. VANNEAU. Chez Germaine, on Rue Pierre-Leroux. A greasy spoon where everyone knew each other, where the owner went around with a tea towel. When you wanted to wipe your hands, you'd yell, 'Germaine, the towel!' Germaine's Basque chicken and cherry clafoutis. Café Vanneau right near the métro, where you could read on the walls about the bird the place was named for:

> *The lapwing is found in Kamchatka and Europe, where its habits and migrations are similar. It has very strong wings and uses them a great deal. It flies for long periods at a time, rising very high. On the ground, it darts, jumps, and moves in short flights. This bird is very cheery and is always in sprightly movement, frolicking in the air. It holds itself for several seconds in all kinds of positions, even with its breast upward or on its side with its wings perpendicular, and no bird gambols and flutters about more nimbly.*
>
> [*signed*] BUFFON

Conversations barely intercepted. I'll call you. I'll give you a ring. Don't go. Give me a ring. Call me. I love you. I don't love you. Tell me you love me. Of course I love you. I love you with cream, I don't love you with chocolate. Regret for words already spoken, crystallized, stored up, itemized. DUROC. Café François-Coppée and Boulevard du Montparnasse. The imagination of a distant city. False returns. Her name is despair. As usual, right. I don't know why I have this tune in my head—la la la la. Don't be mad at me, my little Loulou, if the cops are on my tail. The imagination clings to puddles, gutters, sidewalks. It was a pale grey menu, a bistrot menu. They tumbled out in purple memory layers. All the cafés with their different names. There were the Bougnats

Bougnat des Folies
Bougnat de Lagny
the Chopes
Chope de Choisy
Chope de Montreuil
Chope lorraine
Chope des martyrs
Chope des sports
Chope normande
just La Chope
on the Place de la
CONTRESCARPE
There were the CANONS
CANON *de* TOLBIAC
and
the BOUQUETS
BOUQUET DE VERSAILLES
BOUQUET DE L'OPÉRA
BOUQUET DU NORD
BOUQUET DE BELLEVILLE
BOUQUET D'ALÉSIA
There were the CARREFOURS
THE TERMINUSES
THE BARS DE LA POSTE
DE LA PAIX
DES SPORTS
THE CLAIRONS
THE MARRONIERS
THE TROUBADOURS
THE SAUVIGNONS
not counting THE DUPONTS
NO JEWS OR DOGS ALLOWED
DURING THE WAR

Like the failure of exile itself. It's all one or all the other. How much did you say? They're going to pay you? Before the end of the year? A good strong espresso. Good. I'm getting out. I'm shoving off. I'm taking off. I'm hitting the road. I'm off. I'm weighing anchor. I'm setting sail. Sailing. 'After sailing for three months, they arrived. It was a dangerous crossing. The ship pitched and rolled, even in good weather. The round-keeled sailboats were unstable. "You will pay 6,000 pounds," states the royal order of March 12, 1534, "to the navigator Jacques Cartier, who is going to the New Founde Landes to discover certain islands and countries where large amounts of gold are said to be found." '

Hello, asthmatic breathing of the city. You're feeling good. The pink neighbourhoods, the lilac neighbourhoods, the blue neighbourhoods, the grey neighbourhoods. Wanderings. Strolls. Listening to the sounds, the smells—cinnamon cities, curry cities, onion cities.

Stops at storefronts
crossings in covered passageways
return to the large squares
descents into train stations.

To feel the wind, the fine rain, the murky reflections in the puddles. What anguish some evenings with the sidewalks eternally wet. To fix the difference of all these banks scattered through the city like flies:

Canadian National Bank
Canadian Imperial Bank of Commerce
Bank of Montreal
Bank of Nova Scotia
Savings Bank
Bank of Canada
Federal Development Bank
Mercantile Bank of Canada
Provincial Bank of Canada
Toronto Dominion Bank

bank—bank—the land of banks—the big bank country—the big bank power *in God we bank.*

She would live in Snowdon, west of the mountain and the Notre-Dame-des-Neiges cemetery, on one of the shady streets around Victoria, parallel or perpendicular to Queen Mary. A neighbourhood of immigrants with awkward English, where the accents of central Europe still survive, where you hear Yiddish spoken and it's easy to find pickles, braided challah, matzoh meal.

They would live in the ramshackle house of an old aunt who had come here just before the war, by chance probably, like Mordecai Richler's grandparents. The grandfather had sailed to Canada third class, leaving a *shtetl* in Galicia in 1904 right after the start of the Russo-Japanese War and the horrible pogrom at Kishinev. He originally had a railway ticket to Chicago. On the boat, he met another Jew from the same sect who had family in Chicago and a ticket for Montreal. The grandfather knew someone who had a cousin in Toronto, which he discovered was in Canada. One morning on the deck, the two men exchanged their tickets.

But no. That's not how Mime Yente would have come. She would have left her native Volhynia in March 1919, when the soldiers of Petlyura, having beaten the Red Army, took Zhitomir. Her father, the baker in the market square, would have been killed by the Whites—found strangled amid his round loaves, with his eyes wide open. In London, Mime Yente would have married Moishe. They would have settled in the East End, in Whitechapel, finding work in a clothing factory, a sweatshop. More than once in those terrible years, they would have been seen at the soup kitchen on Brune Street, as poor as Job. Moishe would have worked tirelessly in the Jewish trade union movement, in the radical scene that was then seething with activity. They would have been through the general strike of 1926, which lasted nine days. The aunt would still remember speaking to the troops that occupied the neighbourhood. Then, with the money they had saved by working like slaves, with incredible determination, they would have bought a bakery, a *bakerai*, on Fashion Street in the heart of the old ghetto. A miserable storefront, but no matter! They would have become real celebrities, suppliers to Bloom's, the famous restaurant where all the Jews from central Europe went. Yente would still be able to tell stories about Jack the Ripper and Martha Turner, Polly Nichols, Annie Chapman, Elizabeth Stride, Catherine Eddowes, and Mary Jane Kelly, his victims. The aunt would have travelled to Paris during the trial of Samuel Schwartzbard, who had killed Petlyura. Schwartzbard was a poet who had taken part in the events of 1905 and organized the Jewish self-defence during the terrible pogroms. He had escaped his pursuers and lived underground in Paris as a watchmaker. Back in Russia in 1917, he had rejoined the Red Army. Then, in 1920, much of his family had been slaughtered by Petlyura's troops. After that, his one goal had been to find Petlyura and kill him—which he did in May 1926. The aunt would have been a witness at his trial.

'The man was a liberator. He avenged us. He gave us back our dignity,' she would have said in court, this shy little bit of a woman. Back in London, hearing of Schwartzbard's acquittal, she would have given out round loaves and challah to everyone in Whitechapel and Stepney. And then, on October 4, 1936, the aunt would have taken part in the battle of Cable Street, which pitted trade unionists, Communists, and workers against Mosley's fascists. Mosley had announced that he was organizing a march through the East End. This was immediately understood by the people in the shops as a provocation. Three thousand Blackshirts mobilized on Cable Street. At the intersection of Cable and Leman Streets, they came up against barricades erected by the crowd. More than a hundred thousand workers had massed to block their way. They shall not pass. *No pasarán*. When a truck was overturned, the police charged. Stones and bricks rained down on the cops. All the dockers from Wapping and St. George's were there. The Commissioner of Police, after arresting several workers—one must do what one must do—ordered Mosley and his troops to turn around and go back along the Embankment, where they dispersed. That night there was dancing in the East End all night long. And among the dancers was Mime Yente, with her rolls.

They would have left London just before the war, a little tired. Like so many others, Moishe and Yente would have crossed the ocean and ended up here in Snowdon. They'd have bought that ramshackle house and the tiny bakery on Décarie just north of Isabella. Almost all the customers would have been Yiddish-speaking. What a pleasure to make challah, wheat bread, balls of rye bread, and black bread with kimmel, sesame, or sunflower seeds, and bagels, little cheesecakes, strudel, and hamantashen. People would have come from all over.

Moishe would have died a long time ago. The aunt would have sold the bakery to some Hungarian Jews from Budapest. She would have retired to her house—that's where she would have greeted her—I'm not sure when. That rickety house that was sinking into ruin would be her place, her real country. A large maple tree on the street side would almost completely hide the dark, cracked brick. They would have had the lower floor of the duplex with separate entrances, while old Yente reigned imperiously over the upper. It would have been very easy for them to furnish their four rooms and basement. They would have put some old pine chests in the living room that looked out directly onto the street, with an old sofa in earth tones under the window where in the summer the leafy shadows of the maple tree played. There would be old-fashioned lace curtains from Chez Quentin and pots of plants hanging in front of the window. An oak table bought at a secondhand store on St-Denis or Duluth would go in the dining room. The two other rooms would consist of a rather monastic bedroom and a messy book-filled office with simple bricks-and-boards shelves and rough trestle tables covered with old reels of tape, multi-coloured file folders, books, pencils, ashtrays, unused chequebooks, and cleared Visa and Bell bills. The basement, down a steep flight of stairs, would contain a large kitchen, the bathroom, the furnace, and a laundry room Yente would also have access to. The kitchen would be brightened by small windows that let in the daylight, at least in summer—in winter the windows would be blocked by the heavy snow. Although the kitchen was large, they wouldn't have enough money to furnish it properly. She would have dreamed of tiles on the floor and rustic pine furniture, with ivy trailing down from the top of the cupboards. They would have had to make do with a formica table—a house-warming gift from the aunt, who meant well—chairs found at a garage sale, and a stove and fridge bought on credit at The Bay, but she would have insisted on having the old-fashioned curtains here too, and a sophisticated art nouveau light fixture. The effect would be pleasant but nothing more. The bedroom, on the ground floor, would open directly onto a garden that was quite big for the neighbourhood, where Mime Yente would long ago have planted rose bushes. In summer, they'd take out the kitchen table and some deck chairs and at sunset they'd sit out in their oasis daydreaming. The guardian of the hearth would be Bilou, a lazy, music-loving marmalade cat a bit past his prime. He'd spend most of his time on the ledge in front of the middle window between the lace and the glass, taking in the view of the maple tree and the houses across the street, calmly waiting for them to come home, wondering where they could be—at the university, the library, the movies, with friends, at the store—gazing into the distance, happy to do nothing. A real cat's life. Near the front door would be the piano brought from Paris.[. . .]

Stop. Don't know anything, got to tell them everything. Solomon, that's okay. Some tribes, I'll say, ten in all, got lost in the desert on the other side of the Sambatyon River, which is impossible to cross. These tribes were supposed to be found again at the coming of the Messiah. Then there would be three days of darkness over Constantinople, but light in the dwelling places of the children of Israel. Recount the legend in a solemn voice. The Messiah would come back from the land of the exiled tribes on the other side of the Sambatyon. He would be mounted on a heavenly lion with a seven-headed serpent for a bridle, and he would be breathing fire. At that signal, all kings and all nations would bow down before him. He would arrive in Jerusalem at the western wall, which was believed never to have been deserted by the divine presence. On that day, all Jews who had died in Palestine would come back to life; those who had died in the Diaspora would come back to life forty years later. Show them that reality and legend are intermingled, and that the Jews believed this. A beautiful story. One class. Twelve classes to go, on the false Messiahs of the sixteenth century. My death of a cold! With my health! Natasha, you're so far away, so far! They met. Diego Pines, the Portuguese, wanted to become a Jew. He changed his name to Molcho Melech, meaning 'king,' and wanted to have himself circumcised. The other one, Reubeni, talked him out of it. It seems he circumcised himself. Uproar in the class, better skip this episode. He set out travelling and began to believe he was entrusted with a divine mission. He studied the Talmud, preached, gathered disciples, fired up crowds. The other one, meanwhile, told of his fabulous voyages, how he had been captured and sold into slavery to Arabs and taken to Alexandria, and then bought back by some Jews. He too started messianic propagandizing. Claimed to be the emissary of the king of the lost tribes of Israel on the other side of the Sambatyon. One class on his travels, the fantastic stories. Eleven classes to go. Nice and warm. Sunday morning at my desk with a good hot coffee, slices of bread with Philadelphia cream cheese and smoked salmon or whitefish, nice and warm at the window looking out on the highest branches of the maple tree. Natasha, help me. A two-room apartment, I think. Mama is spreading goose fat on kimmel bread. I leave for *cheder*. It's dark. I have to light my way with a lantern with a flickering flame. I'm afraid. What if the angel of death with a thousand eyes came after me! He said that to hasten the day of redemption, a certain stone in the western wall had to be moved, and that he was the only one that could do it. Went to Damascus, returned to Alexandria, left for Venice, and arrived in Rome in 1524 on a white horse and was received by Pope Clement VII. Said he was the commander in chief of the army of his brother, the leader of the ten lost tribes on the other side of the Sambatyon. Proposed a treaty of alliance with the pope against the Muslims in exchange for giving Charles V and Francis I letters for the kingdom of Prester John. Wealthy Jewish leaders raised money for him and gave him a silk banner embroidered with the ten commandments. So they were able to con rulers and popes, to play on their contradictions and penetrate the slightest cracks in their defences, and play on the legend and the belief in the coming of the Messiah. Morton sky-colour is getting bogged down. Don't know anything. Got to tell them everything. That the mysterious kingdom of Prester John was Ethiopia, and that Clement VII wasn't just anybody, but a Medici, the nephew of Lorenzo the Magnificent. Nothing to do with Saint Lawrence Street, I'll say. A real pope, who excommunicated Henry VIII of England. A real power, the pope, not just anybody. A leader of war as well. A head of state. Written test. You have two hours. Charles V abdicates. He's had it. He leaves everything to his brother Ferdinand and his son. He's had enough. In ten pages, explain why; you're not allowed to use your notes. You'll have to remember the important dates, the History, the dates—and silence please. One class for the written test. And our two saviours? Patience. The Jews have been waiting a long time for the Messiah, they can wait a little longer.

Translated by Phyllis Aronoff

Robert Majzels

Robert Majzels is a novelist, playwright, and translator, who was born in Montreal in 1950 to survivors of the Shoah. He is the author of three novels: *Hellman's Scrapbook* (1992), *City of Forgetting* (1998), and *Apikoros Sleuth* (forthcoming). *City of Forgetting* was short-listed for the 1998 QSPELL Fiction Award and translated into French as *Montréal barbare* (2000). His full-length play, *This Night the Kapo*, won the 1992 Dorothy Silver Playwrights' Award in Cleveland and first prize in the 1994 Canadian-Jewish Playwrights' Competition. His recent translations include two novels: *The Waiting Room* (1999) by Anne Dandurand and *Just Fine* (1999) by France Daigle, for which he won the Governor General's Award in translation. From 1986 to 2000 he taught creative writing at Concordia University in Montreal. He is presently living and writing in Beijing. In this excerpt from his first novel, the protagonist writes letters home from the asylum and recalls events of his childhood in Montreal with flashbacks to his father's experiences in a concentration camp. The page from his forthcoming novel, *Apikoros Sleuth*, outlines the multiple Talmudic discourses in a postmodern spy fiction.

Robert Majzels

EXCERPT FROM *Hellman's Scrapbook*

Room 303
Hochelaga Memorial Institute
Montreal, Quebec

Monday, March 10, 1980
1:10 A.M.

For Papa. Because you were first. Do you remember? The old Rabbi, withered white skin, hoarse Yiddish whisper; Avram, his stooping gait, his long slender hands, serious hands; Steiner, squat, tough, with broad cheekbones and bright black eyes. And you, Papa, crouching on the rough wood floor by the three-tiered bunk in the dark. You can barely make out the others huddled around the light of a candle stub, the light playing on the smooth round surface of Steiner's shaven head. You are gathered around the Rabbi, who is seated on the bunk, ancient and weary and leaning on Avram's arm. His voice is hollow, incorporeal, the words are lost. Do you remember, Papa? Because I do, every bit of it.

I was six years old on a spring Saturday morning and, for some reason, you had decided to take me to the synagogue. Neither you nor Mama was a believer, but you'd had some sort of relapse, or maybe you felt it was something you ought to do for your only son, if only just once, or then again maybe I was just a prop, an excuse for you to go back and test the waters.

Mama was against it. She kept up a steady argument even as she fiddled with my tie and made quick, nervous jabs at the lint on my jacket. She said if you wanted to go, you should go, but you didn't have to take the boy with you, it meant nothing to the boy. You kept insisting that you didn't want to go. It was for the boy you were going. He doesn't want to go, she said, fussing at my hair and stabbing my ear with a red-lacquered fingernail. Let him decide that, you said. He's only a child, she said. How can he decide? You argued I would decide later: by taking me to the synagogue you were giving me the option. If later be doesn't want to go, he'll stop going, you said. But she shook her head and pressed her lips together: if he decides later, she said, he can start going later. He should at least know what it is, you said, pulling on my arm. She licked her thumb and rubbed at a smudge she imagined on my forehead until I felt my skin burn: what it is, what it was, he'll never know, he can't know.

In the end, you took me by the hand and we went out, Mama shouting after us from the doorway so that several people in full Sabbath suits and starched dresses heard her: You want to show him something? Take him to the circus. The circus is better than the synagogue.

The synagogue was down on Mackenzie Street, on the northern edge of the Snowdon district. This was before the Caribbean and Asian immigrants began moving in, before the city stopped cleaning the streets and the landlords let the houses run down, before the Jews had scrambled their way up and out to the suburbs. The congregation was poor, but there were a few who were already rising and these would have stopped to chat and be seen on the steps of the temple. I have a memory of some men joking and poking at each others' paunches. One of them called out to you as we started up the steps. We walked over and I stood among black shoes and sharp creased trousers, listening to the tail end of an anecdote.

So what do you think the shmuck does? He shaves three feet off one of the bales. You believe that? The bastard is cutting three feet off every shipment. Just to spite me. You think he's making any money like this? Not a fucking cent! He's doing it for spite. Just to spite me.

I don't know why I still remember those words, except that every time he said the word 'spite' a fine spray came down on my face. I tend to recall scraps of conversations like that, more for some particular physical effect than because of their meaning.

You pulled me up the steps and I could feel the dampness in the palm of your hand. From the top of the steps I saw *yarmulkas* bobbing and swaying. There were snatches of talmudic debate: So he says, a bird in your hand is worth a hand in the bush. And loud bursts of laughter. This was your first time in a North American synagogue. I started to feel a queasiness somehow transferring from your warm wet palm to my dry little hand. The feeling worked down into my intestines, which began to churn in anger. The Rabbi came out to greet us—young, with plump, clean shaven cheeks, a tapered suit and a silk *yarmulka*. You had my skull cap in your left hand, I guess you'd been putting off my actually wearing it—but when the Rabbi extended his greeting, rather than let go of my hand, you jammed the beanie on my head and gave him an awkward left.

The Rabbi said he was glad you had decided to come. He was smiling very broadly and he held your hand in both of his. You nodded, looked around at the congregation. He let go of your hand and swung an arm around your shoulder. Believe me, he said, he'll thank you some day, and he bent down and cupped my face in his hands. I felt your grip tighten on my fingers. One day, the Rabbi repeated, he'll thank you. Then he pulled his hands away from my face in a broad gesture, as though he were releasing a homing pigeon. He waved at his congregation. A man needs his roots, he said so they could hear him. We watched him move among his flock and that queasy feeling flowing from your hand into my guts got worse. I was afraid. I glanced up at your face. You were staring down at the crowd, daydreaming, drifting in memory. I felt my small boy's soul slip free from its tight little Sabbath suit.

The wooden steps lead down into the cellar of the barracks. The cement walls sweat a foul green slime and your bladder is bursting. Speaking is not permitted—in any case, you are too tired, too heavy with the mud of the quarry. In the cellar the smell of men's bodies mingles with the stink of urine and human faeces. You're kept a long time at the head of the stairs, and then, all at once, the line moves forward, bringing you to the foot of the stairs. Along the wall of the basement: ten toilet bowls, without seats, without partitions, without paper. Ten men leave the line and lower their trousers to squat over the urns. You try not to stare but the scene will not release your gaze: ten men, a minion, crouching on the toilets with their pants down around their ankles and their bone-white knees shining under the naked bulbs overhead. Your turn soon. It is not the fear of the guards, of death, that prevents you from breaking ranks and clawing your way up out of the cellar, but rather the urine stretching your bladder. You may also need to shit. You can think of nothing else: your mind is tied, inexorably bound to your bowels. You must make a decision before your turn comes: to risk forcing a weak trickle of shit or just urinate quickly and get away. The Kapo blows his whistle.

He is standing in the corner, at the end of the row of toilets. This Kapo is unlike any other prisoner: a giant, big with bulging rolling flesh, not just over his belly and arms, but up to his neck and face, pressing round two tiny dead eyes. Perhaps this explains why the guards have adopted him: a clear case of the Jew-freak, the human aberration. They've put him in charge of the toilets, given him a whistle and taught him to count ten times ten before signalling the next batch of men onto the bowls. They have also given him a whip, a short leather whip with a knot in the end.

Now the Kapo shifts his weight forward, turns the whip loosely between his thick fingers and blows his whistle again. The knotted tip of the whip trails in a puddle of urine on the floor. The men on the bowls fumble with their trousers and move away. One prisoner is too slow. You can see him hanging back, one hand on his pants, halfway up off the toilet, straining to cut off his business at the Kapo's command. He is too slow. The Kapo shouts, curls the whip under the low ceiling and across the room. A line of blood appears on the left cheek of the prisoner, just below his eye. He cries out, just a short yelp, more in surprise than in pain. Now he struggles quickly away from the toilet, his pants still tangled around his shins. The whip fills the room again and another red line forms, across the man's bare thigh. The guards watch quietly.

Again and again the whip lashes out, slashing at the prisoner's shirt, slicing the pale skin of his upraised arms, his back, his neck. At first the man screams with each lash, but after a while he crumbles to the ground, hugging his knees. The Kapo keeps on whipping. And whipping. And whipping. He is sweating and breathing hard with the effort but he does not stop. At some point the prisoner dies, but you can't tell exactly when. There is no last cry, no final jerk of movement to mark his passing; only his indifference to the whip tells you he is gone. When the Kapo finally stops, there is nothing to distinguish between torn flesh and blood and shreds of shirt. For a moment the Kapo stands there panting, sweating, staring dully, like a bull in a post-coital daze. Only now, one of the guards orders two prisoners to gather up the body and carry it out of the cellar. The Kapo slumps down on a small wooden stool in the corner and stares at the wall.

You hurry forward with the others and squat on the bowl. An idea comes to you like an unwanted child that will not be denied: you are lucky to be in this group, he's not likely to kill again for a while. Still you piss quickly, and you watch the Kapo the whole time.

We were sitting by then in the middle of a bench near the rear of the synagogue. You had let go of my hand for a moment, and I felt dizzy. The Rabbi was making an announcement—Mr. Goldstein had made an important donation. Everyone began to applaud. I could feel something like a long snake uncoiling in my stomach. As Mr. Goldstein rose to acknowledge the congregation's applause, I doubled over and heaved my sunnyside eggs and toast down onto my shiny black shoes. You bent over me, gripping my shoulders and pulling out your fresh laundered handkerchief to wipe my mouth. I was only vaguely aware of the commotion all around us.

You tried to reassure everyone: Everything is all right. Please, don't worry. He does this when he's nervous, it's nothing, really.

You weren't lying, not entirely. I was a nervous kid. At the time, I had this habit of starting the day off every morning by throwing up. I don't even know what it was at school I was anticipating with such dread. I wasn't a bad student, and I managed, by working very hard at it, to avoid the teacher's attention. Still, I guess the dangers were always present: a teacher can turn on you anytime. And there's always the other children. Whatever the reason, the vomiting happened so regularly that everyone in the house just took it in stride. In fact, it had become part of the family routine:

6:30—Papa's alarm;
6:35—Mama prepares breakfast while Papa showers and shaves;
6:45—Mama wakes David;
6:50—David's turn to wash and dress;
7:00—everyone at the table for breakfast;
7:30—David throws up (Hurry up, David, or you'll be late);
7:35—Papa leaves for work;
7:45—David off to school.

You and Mama had decided it was only nerves, it would wear off as I grew older. The truth is, these things never go away, they simply take on different forms. As I grew older, and all my childish fears turned out to be completely justified, I threw up more sparingly and expressed myself in other ways. In any case, neither of us was particularly alarmed at my performance in the temple; we had both grown accustomed to it.

The Rabbi, on the other hand, did not take it well. His service had been interrupted, people were twisting in their seats to get a better look and murmuring: Whose boy is that? What's the matter with him? Where's his mother? Everyone loves to see a father bring his son to synagogue, but when the child begins to throw up, it is generally agreed his mother ought to be there.

Please, Mr. Hellman, the Rabbi pleaded.

Everyone turned to see Mr. Hellman drag his son into the aisle, the faithful parting as the puky boy tottered blindly past, pausing at the back of the hall to empty the rest of his breakfast. Mr. Hellman had to abandon his overworked handkerchief: he shoved the boy's soft white *yarmulka* over the boy's mouth and swept him out the temple's massive doors.

I remember the feel of the sun on my face. You took my hand and we crossed the empty street to the park. The sky was freshly washed, pale blue. The trees were full-blown maples, their broad leaves green kites whistling softly overhead. We strolled off the path and onto the grass, not speaking. The park was empty and quiet, except for the distant, high-pitched sounds of children playing.

A warm and not unpleasant weariness had settled over me; I was content to sit by your side on the wooden bench, to pick at the flaking green paint and dangle my bespattered shoes. I guess I was ashamed, and frightened. But mostly, I felt tired. And lightheaded. And something else: a jittery sensation in my fingers and toes, and a dry sponginess in my mouth. Of course, that little boy sitting on a sun-parched bench in the park beside his father was too young to recognize the symptoms; the dangers of addiction meant nothing to him. So they sat in silence together for a short time—perhaps a very long time—just resting and listening to the trees sing. Something compelled the little boy to slide his hand over the splintered seat, close to his father's warm, woollen thigh. He hesitated, half afraid, while the father, lost in his dream, shifted his weight and unconsciously covered the little boy's hand with his own. He was gazing off into the maples; the boy slowly turned his hand over and pressed their palms together.

Steiner is waiting for you upstairs. We'll have to move the Rabbi into the lower bunk, he says.

He won't be able to breathe down there, you object.

He can't get up any more. Every night he's pissing all over me.

They'll take him. Soon they'll come for him.

No, they won't, Steiner replies harshly. This is our Rabbi. We must take care of him. Help me move him down.

You follow Steiner to the bunk. You haven't the strength to resist. These barracks, they've turned out to be a nightmare. They should have been better than the old wooden shacks—the brick walls keep the wind out, the toilets are a luxury—but now . . . now there's the Kapo down there. And the Rabbi is dying. So you follow Steiner. Since the Rabbi has become too sick to move from his bunk, too sick to work, someone else must take the lead. Avram is too deeply entangled in the Talmud, not practical; the others lack the necessary education; and you, you lack Steiner's certainty. Steiner is a practical man, a Warsaw veteran. His idea of paradise is clear and solid: Palestine, to be won at the head of an army, Jacob driving his enemies into the sea. Your dream is vague: a distant feeling of stillness, trees, grass, sun. So, follow Steiner.

The Rabbi is lying in the top bunk. He is mumbling in something which resembles prayer but is more likely fever. Steiner grasps the old man's arms and slides him over to the edge of the cot. He is waiting for you to help. Come on, Hellman, he says, you can have the top bunk, you're healthy still.

You step up on the edge of the lower bunk and take hold of the Rabbi's ankles, your fingers recoiling for an instant at the touch of brittle bone. Take the bunk, you tell him, I don't want it.

Together you swing the body down, like kindling, to the bottom tier. Steiner lays his hand on the old man's forehead, as though to keep him from floating up off the bunk.

Simon steps up behind you. Why don't I take the top bunk? I'm healthier than any of you. I wouldn't piss all over you, Steiner. At least not by accident.

Shut up, goy, Steiner says. I wouldn't desecrate the Rabbi's bunk.

Simon laughs and points to the Rabbi. Your god isn't much good. Why is he killing the Rabbi instead of me, the unbeliever, the Goy-Jew?

Steiner, the traces of a stocky body, the still strong, thick hands, moves toward the younger man. Wait, your turn will come.

You step between them. He's only a child. . . .

He's an animal, Steiner hisses, moving forward.

Simon shifts the weight of his wiry body onto the balls of his feet and grins. Yes, an animal, he whispers. Only this animal knows where he can find some potatoes.

Ghosts begin to rise from their bunks and gather.

Where? Steiner asks.

I'll show you, if you're not afraid. He turns for the door and pauses, watching while each man makes his secret calculations: what is the ratio of desperate hunger to the sum of dogs plus guards plus bullets waiting outside?

Striped shadows drift silently back to their cots. But you and Avram and Steiner remain. You follow Simon out into the cold, shit-brown evening, he darting expertly in the bunkhouse shadows between white death circles of light, and you stumbling breathlessly behind. Already your head is spinning, your digestive acids are churning, your stomach is like a gaping mouth. The hunger beast is calling: Potato, potato, potato.

Simon's silhouette glides across the open ground toward the ditches. You follow in a running crouch, stopping to huddle together on the edge of the pit, shivering and panting white bursts of pain into the cold air. Up in the tower against the moon, you can see the high-collared coat of the guard, his breath a gentle plume above the shining barrel of the automatic rifle.

Simon glances up at the tower briefly and scrambles over the side of the ditch. It's he who is leading now: even Steiner knows that Simon, working as a fireman, pulling the heavy cart loaded down with hoses—and sometimes bodies—has explored every inch of the camp. In spite of his age he has been here since the beginning; he knows the risks, the little things that give you an edge, the places to hide. But on the other hand, you think, he is reckless, far too reckless.

He makes his way down the length of the trench to a spot beside a small mound, and motions for you to follow. The mound is a jute sack, stretched tight and lumpy, like a bag full of fists. One corner has already been broken or gnawed open. Simon reaches in, produces a potato. A whole, brown, perfect potato. Each of you is passed one like it. You cradle yours in your hands for a moment. It's almost round, with a fold like a mouth on one end, and several small spongy eyes. You raise it to your lips. It's hard, cold, and odourless, like a dream. You push it between the edges of your teeth, stretch the muscles of your jaw and bite. But the potato is frozen solid. You gnaw desperately at the surface, your tongue shoving its way recklessly in among your teeth, groping for a loose bit of skin, a single juicy eye, anything. Is it possible you have forgotten how to eat solid food? Do we forget such things: chewing, swallowing? You spin crazily around for help. Steiner is squatting on his hind legs, gripping his potato in both hands. Tears are streaming down Avram's cheeks. A small animal cry escapes from the back of your throat.

Steiner, brandishing his potato like a stone, rises and grabs hold of Simon. You idiot, they're frozen.

Simon shakes his head. Why don't you ask your god to warm them up for you? He climbs up the side of the ditch and whispers down: Come on.

You make your way back up out of the pit, into the black snout night, through crazy crisscrossing searchlights and across to another trench. This one is not empty. Your eyes sting from the quicklime freshly poured over the corpses.

Are you mad? Avram hisses.

Warm steam pours off the quicklime like breath. Simon crawls down the side of the ditch and gently rolls his potato into the lime.

What are you doing? you ask in a shrieking whisper.

Simon touches a finger to his lips and points up at the tower. Then he bends over his potato and continues to roll it carefully back and forth in the quicklime.

After a long time, at last, the scent of potato cooking. Just a hint at first, mingling with the bitter lime, then thickening. You fill your lungs greedily, barely allowing yourself the time to exhale between deep breaths. You ignore your burning eyes, your running nose.

Avram whispers: It's sacrilege, a desecration. But he speaks softly and no one moves.

Simon crouches, watches the potato, occasionally gathering a bit of his sleeve in his hand and adjusting the potato's position. He ignores you now, ignores your protests, your doubts; he lets the potato speak. Some time passes—a long time, a short time, you don't know—and Simon nudges the potato out of the chalk, wipes it on his shirt, rises. Standing before you now, Moses with his magic staff before the Egyptians, he bites deep into the flesh of his miracle and begins to masticate slowly, luxuriously. And all the time watching you, watching you with dark round eyes. Not gloating, not teasing, just watching, watching you watching him.

Saliva fills your mouth faster than you can swallow. You turn away and wipe your chin on your sleeve; the saliva keeps coming, pouring through your lips, down your chin, your neck. . . . Maybe you are not the first to break ranks, but soon you too have fallen to your knees, shoving the others for a spot at the edge of the pit. You burn your fingers jabbing barehanded at the potato to turn it, to speed its cooking. Simon stands behind, eating quietly and studying his new converts.

You wait just long enough for the pulp to soften before digging out your potato, and, still on your knees, you bite and swallow without bothering to chew. Your hunger leaps up into your throat to seize the food.

Simon nudges Steiner with the toe of his muddy shoe. Well, do I get the upper bunk?

You stop eating for one brief moment to look up at Simon. His face is calm, expressionless. We have to eat, he says. You break off a bit of the potato and put it in your pocket, to bring back to the Rabbi. But when you get back to the barracks the Rabbi is too sick to chew or swallow solid food. He lies, tossing and muttering in his cot. You bend close to his ear. The taste of potato lingering on your breath, you whisper your name. But the Rabbi no longer recognizes you.

March 11, 1980

Dear Father,

Hello.

Hi.

Hello, how are you? Just a note to let you know I am . . . I hope you are well. . . . I'm much better. . . . I'm fine.

Dear Papa,

Dear Father,

Papa

Hi, Papa,

Dear Papa,

Sorry for not writing sooner; time passes so quickly. . . .

I've been so busy. . . . I'm just getting settled in

Dear Papa,

Dear Papa and Mama,

I miss you very much

I miss you and Mother Mama very much

I am looking forward to seeing you and Mama very soon

Robert Majzels

EXCERPT FROM *Apikoros Sleuth*

Before we were narrative, we were boots and vertigo. We leapt across a canyon of traffic. We flung ourselves into the net of language. A horse was an inch of music. Dogs danced, wings gathered rock. Now we are the small brown pigtail of a mystery trailing behind its solution. We pour murder out of a tenement and lay the limp and soggy rag of story in the street.* The police have parked the realistic code (always straddling a sidewalk) beneath their lights flashing. They are an empty vehicle crackling speech in a canyon of traffic. He crawled past it. That tale is a parade marching on someone's borrowed crutches. All the more difficult to cross the highway. A passerby will pause and look from a bristling

upon his head. He turned his toes the way he had come. To look across at the twenty-second floor. The native is on the ground and the stranger is in the sky.[α] What droned in the chapel of his stomach? Must we churn this? From where he had come, a war of charm had underestimated black murder. Now, any act was great. He gazed back across from where he had gazed across at the cross for so many years. Into the cracked mirror of a canyon of traffic. He saw uniforms (two) bending and unbending in a room and a half of stooping and unstooping. What were these detectives of deadly sin retrieving?[Ω] Now that we have come to this. We sit upon a volume of argumentation and clutch a curtain of souls. Shall we say

אב בת גש דר הק וצ זפ חע טס ינ כמ
אג בת דש הר וק זצ חפ טע יס כנ למ
אד בג דת הש ור זק חצ טפ יע כס לנ
אה בד הת וש זר חק טצ יפ כע לס מנ
או בה גד ות זש חר טק יצ כפ לע מס
אז בו גה זת חש טר יק כצ לפ מע נס
אח בז גו דה חת טש יר כק לצ מפ נע
אט בח גז דו טת יש כר לק מצ נפ סע
אי בט גח דז הו ית כש לר מק נצ ספ
אכ בי גט דח הז כת לש מר נק סצ עפ
אל בכ גי דט הח וז לת מש נר סק עצ
אמ בל גכ די הט וח מת נש סר עק פצ
אנ במ גל דכ הי וט זח נת סש ער פק
אס בנ גמ דל הכ וי זט סת עש פר צק
אע בס גנ דמ הל וכ זי חט עת פש צר

*On reading Charles Dickens: I can't understand it and can't believe it. I live only here and there in a small word in whose vowel I lose my useless head for a moment. The first and last letters are the beginning and end of my fishlike emotion.
Franz Kafka, *Diaries*

[α] One who sees his past always thinks: because of; or but this is not so; or just as, so too; or the event that happened, happened that way; or act, deed, event, precedent.

[Ω] When is a tenement house not a home? When you can no longer return there.

way pregnant with disaster and to a shifty eyed mule under a load of curtained text. I struggled for a visible expression. I tried to read the nervous lip beneath his bushy moustache and above a shouting shirt. If there is a difficulty, this is the difficulty. To practice exegesis in the street comes to identify a criminal. How should we act?+ Someone else is always an anticipation. Wondering if we can continue in this way. We can crawl past it. We can edge into Cratylus' river of traffic,° but can we cross it? Panic snaps the mind; to walk repairs it. The street was a long poem; he went down to the end of the verse. He thought how assiduously a murder obeys the rules of the road. On the other side the mountain poured greenish weeds into the city. He was inclined to go up. A ways. He flexed his ankles, his knees blazed on ahead. Someone's sweat, perhaps even his, gathered in the small of his back. He earned it. Until he paused on the slope to extinguish his lungs. A chestnut tree leaned hard against him. It might have been raining. Instead, the sun piled warmly globules of irony

+If the relationship with the other involves more than relationships with mystery, it is because one has accosted the other in everyday life where the solitude and fundamental alterity of the other are already veiled by decency.
Levinas, *Time and the Other*

°Cratylus' version of the river, in which one cannot bathe even once; where the very fixity of unity, the form of every existent, cannot be constituted; the river wherein the last element of fixity, in relation to which becoming is understood, disappears.
Levinas, *Time and the Other*

אצ בפ גע דס הנ ום זל חכ טי צת קש

He was not prepared to be driven into that countryside. He counted his options on the fingers of his nose. There were none. The landscape paused. The hearse of failure pulled up behind the flashing blood of the law. More time gathered among the weeds. He muttered to himself in the language of sleep. Something[δ] was calling him back to the scene(s) of the crime. Having already come this far, the journey demanded repetition. Shall we descend that bitter slope of disappointment? At the corner light, he paused to recognize a Ukrainian janitor's head momentarily fill the open door. Still he crawled back along the way he had fled.

At times like this we often think of our mothers. And mine too, for that matter. Performing rites, such as eating, washing, drinking, sacrificing.

[δ]Perhaps a horsey habit, perhaps the lure of disaster, perhaps the refusal to believe he had not been dreaming or merely the familiar comfort of a damp cot.

He pulled that outer door in time to hold it open for a backward stretcher-bearer followed by the stretcher and the other bookend. Whereas his heart took him by the throat and flung him back along the sidewalk, his knees would not flee. They drew him toward that stretcher. When death disappears into the hole in the rear of an ambulance it draws a crowd. The living jostle with each other's anonymous odours in anticipation of an inevitable momentary glimpse when the sheet slips away from the Other's face. He jostled with the best of them. He peered and saw. What? A face, bloodless, but still recognizable. His own. Gazing skyward::

Robyn Sarah

Robyn Sarah, born in New York City in 1949 to Canadian parents, has lived for most of her life in Montreal, where she graduated from McGill University and Quebec's Conservatoire de Musique et d'Art Dramatique. She is the author of two short-story collections, *A Nice Gazebo* (1992) and *Promise of Shelter* (1997), as well as collections of poetry, which have been gathered in *The Touchstone: Poems New and Selected* (1992). *Questions about the Stars* (1998) is her most recent collection of poems. Her writing has appeared in the *Threepenny Review*, the *New England Review*, the *Antioch Review*, the *North American Review*, the *Malahat Review*, and the *New Quarterly*. 'Looking for My Keys' (1997) shows her dedication to domestic details and the congruities and incongruities of Montreal past and present, with its Chasidic traditions surviving in contemporary society. This short story shares qualities of Kafka's and Agnon's writing.

Robyn Sarah

Looking for My Keys

It was on a Friday afternoon that I lost my keys, somewhere between home and the regular round of streets where I do my errands. That is to say, I had my keys with me when I left my house, on foot, to do my errands, and I did not have them when I returned.

It is important, I think, to understand that we are not talking here about a person who loses keys. I do not lose keys. My children lose keys, I yell at them about it, recently they've gotten a little better—I think I only had to make two replacements this year. As to myself, I lose hats sometimes, I lose gloves; umbrellas I lose almost religiously, and I have even been known to lose single shoes, if such a thing can be imagined; but I do not lose keys. If by chance I misplace them, they are quick to turn up; if I happen to leave them somewhere—very unusual—I remember where, almost as soon as I miss them; and when I go back for them—there they are.

The closest I ever came to losing my keys before this was one day about five years ago, coming home from Berman Paint where I'd gone to buy a half-gallon of peach-coloured furniture enamel to paint my kitchen table. I had meant to paint the kitchen table, which was a horrible tomato-soup colour, for years—not only because it needed a paint job (having been bought second-hand and a little banged up), but because it clashed with the masonite countertop in the kitchen of my rented flat. The countertop was a pebbled shade of more or less salmon pink, a difficult shade to match, and I had often had the thought that if I could only find paint that colour, both the table and the counter would be happier and the kitchen would take on a positively rosy glow.

But I could not very well take the kitchen counter with me to Mrs Berman's store, and painting the table was not enough of a priority for me to remember, in passing the paint store (which I did frequently), to go in and ask for a book of colour samples to bring home. So years went by. In fact, I had almost stopped noticing that the table clashed with the counter and that it needed painting, when someone gave me a gift: a peach-coloured coffee mug. This, when placed on the counter, appeared to exactly match it.

I was depressed at the time, let's not go into why, and when I am depressed, I like to do a little something to fix up my immediate surroundings—say, get rid of a constant low-grade irritant like a leaky faucet or a sticking door, put up a shelf where a shelf has long been needed, wash windows, buy a cheap lamp for a dingy corner. So, now that I had something portable that matched the elusive pink of the countertop, it seemed like a good time to paint the kitchen table. I saw at once that I could take the coffee mug to Mrs Berman's.

Let me explain that the particular habit I have developed of carrying my keys accounts both for the fact that I so seldom lose them, and also for how I happened to lose them this time. I carry my keys in my purse if I am away from the house for an extended period; but if I am just out briefly, on a neighbourhood errand, I don't like to have to bother, on my return, to fish around in my purse (which is large and full of all kinds of things) on the front stoop. So I carry my keys in my hand. No, I carry them on my hand. I slip the keyring, which is a perfectly plain ring, no doodads, over my index finger, where it fits comfortably and not too loosely; and I grasp the keys lightly in my palm. I find the feel of them comforting, like worry-beads. Also, I read somewhere in a magazine that if a woman walking alone at night carries her keyring in her palm, keys slipped between her fingers can make a spiked fist with which to surprise and fend off an attacker, if need be. Actually, I have tried this—making the spiked fist, I mean; fortunately the occasion has not arisen for me to test it—and I find it a little awkward. Besides, could I ever bring myself to ram this fistful of metal into human flesh? But, in theory, it is one more reason to carry my keys the way I do.

If it happens that I need my hands, I slip the keys into my purse. Thus, if my keys are not on my finger, where I can easily see and feel them, then I know that they must be in my purse; I make it a point never to put them down anywhere else, if I am not at home. That way it is not easy for me to lose my keys.

Once not long ago, on the way home from the pharmacy, I realized that my keys were not in my hand, and as I turned up my block, I began feeling around for them in my purse and did not find them. I turned around straight away and retraced my steps: the pharmacy; before that, the post office; before that, the bank. My keys were not in any of those places. I was surprised and alarmed. It occurred to me that while I was in the post office, I had had to submit a claim card for a parcel, and then I had had to sign for the parcel; and that both the card and the parcel had my address on them, and that behind me there had been a line-up of people. There is usually a line-up of people in the post office, especially since they closed the branch at the photocopy centre and everybody has to go to the one in the stationery store.

Perhaps I had put down my keys on the counter while I signed for the parcel. It was unlikely, but I am sometimes absent-minded. Then someone standing behind me could have quietly pocketed my keys, having made a mental note of my address by glancing at the parcel. People are desperate these days; you see them everywhere, going through waste bins for bottles to return for cash, scavenging for useable items. My friend told me that sometimes at night, when he goes to drop off paper or bottles at the recycling bins, he will see a person fishing papers out of the paper bin (that's when the bin is full enough for a person's hand to reach paper, but it usually is, because they are so slow to empty the bins in this backward metropolis)—he will see a person systematically sifting through papers and checking out the addresses on certain envelopes. It's easy to recognize a government envelope, and in this way a person can tell who receives government cheques by mail, and where in the neighbourhood they live, and what day of the month the cheques get mailed on. Even if I had such information, I would not know to what practical use it could be put, but some persons can apparently use such information. And obviously a person who knew my address could make use of my keys, whereas one who did not, could not.

It happened, though, that on that particular occasion, I returned home to find that I had not had my keys with me to begin with: they were sitting on my desk, in plain view. And then I remembered that I had left the house in a hurry, in company of my friend, and that he had locked the door behind us with his key, and I had not bothered to check to make sure I had mine with me; I had simply assumed my keys were in my purse.

I was greatly relieved. I don't like to feel mistrustful of people, ordinary people who live in my quarter and stand behind me in the post office line. It hurts me to feel I can't trust people. During the years when I lived alone—I say 'alone' but I always had my children with me of course—I was not careful about the door, I didn't have the habit of locking it when I was at home, even after dark—at least not until I was ready to go to sleep, which in those days was often not until very late. It was my friend who, in the months when we began seeing each other, used to telephone me in the evenings to ask me sternly whether my front door was locked—this, once he had come to know my habits. At first it irritated me; I used to tell him shortly that I had lived in this neighbourhood all of my adult life and had never kept my door locked when I was at home and awake, and that it was for me to decide when to lock my door in the evenings. This was not, I argued, an American city; not like the cities he was used to. But I knew that he had a point, that the city was changing. And something in his protectiveness won me over. I began locking my door obediently when he told me to, and then I began locking it routinely on arriving home; and I felt, not that the locked door protected me, but that in obeying the voice of my friend in my head, telling me to lock it, I was entering a safe harbour of a kind, and accepting a great blessing that had descended, unasked-for, upon my life.

Now that I live with my friend, I can be more casual. I feel safe with him, and anyway, if I forget to lock the door, I can be pretty sure that he will do it.

The day I went to Berman Paint, you may have figured this out for yourself, what threw me was the coffee mug. Not on the way there, though. On the way there, I carried the mug in my purse—it just fit, and the purse still closed. I smiled to myself when I thought of opening my bag, taking out the coffee mug, putting it down on the counter in front of Mrs Berman, and asking for furniture paint to match it. Would she imagine that I was painting my table to match my coffee cup? Would she find that eccentric? Mrs Berman didn't turn a hair, she only smiled very faintly. She is an older lady and since Mr Berman passed away several years ago, she runs the store by herself. She is a person of few words, and nothing ever seems to surprise her.

I thought of explaining that I had brought the cup because it matched the counter and that I really wanted to paint the table to match the counter, but it seemed too complicated. People don't want to know the 'why' of what you do; it tires them. Mrs Berman reached behind her and took a sample book down from the shelf and opened it to a page of rose, orange, and pink squares. She moved the coffee mug slowly down the page and stopped at Dewy Peach, then moved it across the page to Coral Dust, then back again.

'Which do you think?'

'It looks a little light,' I said of Dewy Peach.

'They always dry darker.'

'They're both pretty close,' I said. If I had had the sample book at home, I could have decided, but since I was in the store, I looked to Mrs Berman to be the expert.

Mrs Berman pursed her lips briefly and said, 'The other one might dry too dark.' She went in back, to mix my colour. Then, since I was paying by credit card anyway, in addition to my paint I decided to buy a few other things: sandpaper, a gallon can of solvent, a couple of new brushes, a can of Varathane I had various uses for, some sealer for around the kitchen sink. Mrs Berman put it all in two plastic shopping bags. 'Can you manage?'

I carried a bag in each hand and my purse slung over my shoulder. 'Don't forget your cup,' said Mrs Berman. Since my purse was already zipped up, I slipped the handle of my coffee mug over my finger.

The door to my house wasn't locked when I returned, because my children were out on the front steps, talking to their friends. So it wasn't until later in the day that I missed my keys. I cast through my mind, the only place I'd been all day was Mrs Berman's, so I telephoned the paint store, confident that I must have left my keys on the counter while signing the credit card slip. But Mrs Berman said no, she hadn't found any keys. She put me on hold while she checked again—the counter, the floor around the counter. No, she told me again, no keys.

Then I did what I always tell my children to do when they misplace a thing: I went over in my mind every detail I could remember of my trip to the paint store and back. And I realized almost at once that the coffee mug—the fact that I had left the store with it hung over my finger—would be a clue. Wouldn't I have been carrying my keys over the same finger? Yes, I remembered them jingling against the cup. Then I remembered that the shopping bags had been heavy and awkward, and that about a block from the store, the strap of my purse slipped off my shoulder and I had had to stop. I remembered putting my bags down on the hood of a parked car while I shifted the purse over my head to the other shoulder, school-satchel style, so it couldn't slip off. Then I picked everything up and resumed my way, only, perhaps I had not picked *everything* up? In addition to the shopping bags, I must have put my keys and my coffee mug down on the hood of the car, and perhaps, having slipped the coffee mug back onto my finger, I was deluded into thinking I had my keys—satisfied that I had slipped something over my finger. Then, I would have left my keys on the hood of that parked car on Fairmount Street.

It seemed too much to expect that the car would still be there, but I walked back over to where I remembered stopping. The car was gone, but even from half a block away I could see something lying on the curb, gleaming in the sun, right where the car had been. I came closer and there were my keys, waiting for me, winking. It's funny how vividly I remember this moment, the immense satisfaction of picking up my keys from the pavement. The squareness and rightness of my keys being *right there*, exactly where I'd figured I must have parted with them. A little feat of memory, a successful exercise of self-knowledge, proof that I could always recover what was important, even if I temporarily lost sight of it.

The children were happy with the newly painted table, and even happier when—having painted it—I was inspired to go out and buy four old Windsor-style chairs in a used furniture store, and to paint them the same colour. Our old chairs, a scruffy and mismatched assortment of leftovers, went out on the back porch. 'It's so nice in here now, Mummy,' said my son, 'like a *real* person's kitchen, like my friends' houses.' And I was a little shocked at this glimpse of how I'd been living, not noticing the shabbiness, unaware that my children noticed, calculated, compared.

Much has changed since then. My keys are not even the same keys, since I and my children now live in my friend's house, a few blocks away. My peach-coloured coffee mug broke, long before I moved. Since my friend had a perfectly good kitchen table set, a solid oak one that had belonged to his grandparents, there was no need for me to keep my pink table when we decided to live together; but I didn't want to part with it altogether, so it is now at my friend's chalet in the country. Sometimes when we go there I look at it and think about how painting it was the beginning of my being good to myself, after a long time of living numbly from day to day, in the wreckage of my failed marriage. The colour of it warms me, it is the colour I remember waking myself up with.

On Friday, too, when I discovered my keys were missing, I began going over my day step by step. I knew that this time I had not left my keys at home, because no one else had been home when I left the house, and I remembered locking up. I made sure the keys were not in my purse by turning it out onto my lap on the front steps, emptying everything; and by feeling along the seams of the lining for holes. Once or twice, I have thought my keys lost, only to find they had slipped through a hole in the lining, into the space between the purse leather and the liner. This time they had not.

Then I made a mental list of my errands: to the bank to deposit cheques, to the travel agency to pick up a train ticket, the grocery store for fresh fruit, the kosher bakery for braided challah loaves, back to the bank because I'd run out of cash, the corner store for milk. Theoretically, my keys could have been left in any of these places. It was also possible I had dropped them on the street. Dimly I thought I remembered walking along jingling my keys, calculating how many errands I had to do, and thinking it made more sense to put my keys away—slipping them into my purse as I walked. I did not quite see how, but my keys could have caught on the zipper somehow and fallen outside the bag, instead of falling into it. But wouldn't you think I'd have heard them fall? No, not necessarily. The traffic is loud along Park Avenue, and in addition, it being spring, pavement cutters were at work on several corners—I remembered wincing at the racket each time I passed them. There was nothing to do but retrace my whole route.

My keys were not at the bank. I remembered which tellers I had dealt with, Nelie and Brigitte, and I asked each of them directly. I checked the counter where I had filled out my deposit slips, and to make absolutely certain I asked the assistant manager as well. Nobody had turned in keys.

So I headed on to the travel agency. The name of it is Mazel, which means 'luck' in Hebrew—I think a nice name for a travel agency, we all hope for luck when we travel. It is run by a neighbourhood family of Hasidic Jews. Usually I book my train tickets at the station itself, but this time I had decided to try the travel agency because it is closer and more convenient. Now that I make short trips more and more frequently in connection with my work, it is sensible to have somewhere close by where I can make all the arrangements.

A very young, pretty Hasidic woman had undertaken to book my tickets earlier in the week, and I had picked them up from her that afternoon. I could tell that she was a married woman by her wig, which for some reason made her look even younger. She had smiled handing me my ticket, and had asked a little shyly what was the purpose of my trip; when I told her I was scheduled to give a talk, for my work, she wanted to know what was the subject of my talk and for whom was I working? I knew that for her, such inquiries constituted ordinary courtesy and were in no way intended to give offence. Had I told her I was Jewish, she would have wanted to know if I came from here, and who my parents were and where they came from, and whom I had married and how many children I had and so on. She would have asked me these things casually, with a lively familial interest, as if I were related.

As I walked back in that same direction in search of my keys, I passed many Hasidic families in the street, and I knew that the stir of activity, the speed and purpose with which they were moving, was because it was Friday and the Sabbath was approaching. I myself am Jewish, but I grew up in a home that was not religious, and I have never been observant in the strict tradition. Passing them I reflected briefly, as I often do walking these streets, on the differences between their lives and mine.

Remind me some day to describe to you the beauty of these families—the serenity and innocence of the young women's faces, the attractiveness of the children, dressed always so prettily; the quiet affection family members show towards one another, the gentle protectiveness with which very small children guide and oversee even smaller children. I do not know how people can speak ill of them, unless it is out of envy: they are so clearly happy and secure in their ways. My friend thinks that I romanticize them, but I see what I see. Yet I know that I myself could not live as they do, a life so circumscribed.

My friend is also Jewish; he grew up in a much more traditional home than mine, yet he, like my former husband, has let go of most of it, apparently without conflict. His last girlfriend, with whom he lived several years, was not Jewish. When we decided to live together, I asked him whether he wanted me to keep a kosher kitchen, but he only laughed and said gently, 'Why would you want to get into all that?' Nevertheless he is respectful of religious people, he does not need to justify himself by deriding them, as some do. Sometimes I see in his eyes a serenity that reminds me of theirs, an at-homeness in the world, and I think it is this above all that I love in him.

The travel agency is on the second floor, above a bank. Climbing the stairs I heard something that made my heart beat faster—I heard a jingling, as of keys. I thought, Someone right now has picked up my keys from that young woman's desk and is looking around to see who might have left them. But when I turned the corner below the landing, I saw a very large, tall Hasidic man closing and locking the doors of the office. He startled me a little, standing there at the top of the stairs in his black clothing, partly blocking the sunlight that filtered in through a dusty window.

I saw that the keys that he had in his hand were his own keys; they were not mine.

'Are you looking for somebody?' he asked me formally.

I said, 'I was here earlier today to pick up a train ticket. I lost my keys and I thought I might have left them here. Do you know if anybody found a set of keys?'

He shook his head. 'I don't think so,' he said. 'Who made you the ticket?'

I mentioned the woman by name.

'I think she would have told me, if she found something. She left half an hour ago,' he said. 'We close early on Friday. You can check again with her maybe next week?'

'All right,' I said, although I was sure that my keys were not there. I thought of wishing him a good Sabbath, but I did not want to complicate things for either of us by revealing that I was Jewish, so I only thanked him. As I started downstairs, he called after me, in a voice still formal but not unfriendly, 'I hope that you find them.'

My keys were not at the grocery store, the kosher bakery, or the corner store. They were not on the sidewalk; I kept my eyes peeled for them coming and going. Sometimes I had to stop and think: did I cross the street at this corner, or the next one? If my keys had fallen on the ground, it was important that I retrace my path exactly. But this time my good memory, my thoroughness, did not bear fruit. I did not find my keys. My keys were gone. Maybe they had fallen into a hole left by the pavement cutters. Maybe a child playing had found them lying on the pavement, and had carried them off somewhere—to a parent's safekeeping, or to be used in a childish game, or stored away with a child's treasures.

My keys were gone, and without reason I felt, for a moment, bereft and naked in the world.

I returned home hot and tired and a little upset with myself. My daughter was on the front steps, waiting for me. 'Mummy, where were you for so long? I was just going out to try to find you.'

'I lost my keys, and I had to go back and look for them,' I told her.

'And did you find them?'

'No,' I admitted.

'There, Mummy, you see,' she said. 'You tell us that you never lose your keys, but you do. So you shouldn't get so angry at us when we lose ours.'

Then she let me in with her keys, took the bag of challah loaves from me, and ran to set the Sabbath table, for even though I am not religious, I light candles on Friday evenings, I serve a Sabbath meal.

'I lost my keys,' I told my friend when he arrived home a few minutes later, and I waited for him to scold me for my carelessness; but he only came next to me and lightly kissed my forehead and tilted my chin upward so he could look into my face.

'Are you so upset about it, then?' he asked, affectionately, stroking the hair back from my forehead with gentle fingers.

'Only because I can't understand how it happened,' I replied, and then I was quiet, thinking about how easily one could have a new set of keys made, and how strange it was that one could feel such a keen disappointment, not to have found the old ones.

Judith Kalman

Judith Kalman was born in Budapest in 1954 and grew up in Montreal. She received her B.A. from Concordia University and her M.A. in creative writing from the University of Windsor, Ontario, where she studied with Joyce Carol Oates and Alistair Macleod. She now lives with her two sons in Toronto. *The County of Birches* (1998) won the Danuta Gleed Literary Award; in addition, Kalman has been the recipient of National Magazine Award (1996) and the Tilden Canadian Literary Award (1995). 'Personal Effects,' one of the interconnected stories of *The County of Birches*, shows the transition between Old World and New World as the post-Holocaust family prepares for departure from Hungary to Montreal.

Judith Kalman

Personal Effects

The Budapest flat was long and sprawling. For a little one, it was endless. Along the floorboards worn so smooth I had only to watch out for the rugs with rough naps. If I slipped and slid on them, I'd get something red and sore. Some of the rugs were soft, though, and thin with age. They'd turn up and bunch and trip me if I wasn't careful. The rugs were islands with their own landmarks, like the raised bristly whorls at the centre of the one by the kitchen. I liked to sit on it in my warm felt pants and pat the horsehair surface gingerly. See how I could tame it? Along that brown river of a hallway, there were archipelagoes of throw-about worlds. I saw my mother take them and shake them and sometimes hang them out the window. She would try to rearrange them, but I made sure they found their right spots at last, the thick woolly tassels combed neat and flat. The brown river parted for doorways, some always closed to me. 'Karcsi's room. Stay out,' said my mother, then to my sister: 'Close Karcsi's door, before the baby finds his fiddle.' And doors I wouldn't want to open, ever. The one with the great roaring thing that shook and rattled while it regurgitated water with a terrible rushing force.

On weekends Apu came home. His tread on the landing was our mother's cue to pull off her apron and tug her sweater smooth. There would be sweets if I foraged deep enough into the big coat's pockets. And the coarse rub of thick arms around me. Skin loose and tender as he held my face to his. I thought I smelled the animals on his coat. He talked about cattle, pigs, but it was just the soft musky fur of the coat's lining, sweetened by the smell of him. Karcsi would come out of his room to shake hands and would be asked to join us for dinner, although he ate with us most nights as part of his lodging, and his place was always set on the dining-room table.

We celebrated Christmas because everyone else did, and so we wouldn't seem too different being Jews. The big flat was surprisingly close with warm aromas and flickering lights. Evening lamps glowed. Up on the deep ledge above the dining-room door frame three small fir trees glistened with pink marzipan bells. I was allowed to finger them lightly when someone held me up. If it was a visitor, we were given a taste. The rough sugar coating grazed before it melted on my tongue. Pink, soundless bells, though their sugar, hard like crystal, made me imagine a little tinkling. I would gaze up from the floor, feeling sated.

The clapping made me startle. Who was this? Who was coming? The grown-up voices knowing and festive. Mikulás. Look. Look. Like a big brown bear. His great coat turned inside out to show the furry lining, and a white pillowcase over his shoulder. What? Who is it? Mikulás. Your Apuka. Look, silly, what is there in his sack?

My first memory was heat. I saw it. Waves of heat dancing. Later I imagined a small room with a black stove. I put red flames into the picture, flickering behind a grill. But I knew the image first through my pores. A pulsing reddish glow I ingested with each breath and sigh of my tiny, gorging body. The long rambling flat was difficult to heat during the coal shortage in 1954. Karcsi the boarder had a separate stove in his room, so that was the room my mother took for the new baby. Karcsi moved out onto the divan. At dawn he met the coal cars pulling into the freightyard and paid the black market prices my father had left him the money for, his fine musician's fingers gripping a sack of coal that by breakfast he let slide against the nursery furnace.

My sister came in to warm up. She stood first by the stove, and looked into the cradle at me. When my mother lay down to nurse me on the bed, my sister nestled her brief length along the curve of our mother's spine and took strands of our mother's long hair, twisting them around her finger. I felt heat, indistinguishable from the dance of gold shadows.

Out in the country on the state farms, my father trudged over crusty fields to inspect livestock. Wide hands thrust into the deep pockets of his heavy fur-lined coat, he spun dreams of spring crops and fall yields. Trusting implicitly that his family was safe and warm and unbeholden. How did he do that? Assume decency. My father anticipated decency in others before he would suspect anything else. Decency in others, even though he had had to leave his first wife and their child for a final labour service in 1944, and they disappeared with every other member of his family, in smoke. When I was born, Karcsi the lodger gave up his bed, and my father entrusted him with all that he had.

The shattering of glass behind us was a sound like day, clear and explosive. In the halls, apartment doors swung open, and from all of them people ran, spilling into the stairwell. My heart thrilled hopefully. Such excitement. With trembling fingers my mother buttoned up my little blue double-breasted coat, then I was swept up by Apu and tucked like a loaf under his arm. But I could walk as well as Lili, I protested, squirming. No time. My sister's able legs were a flick of white ankle socks in leather lace-ups as they flew away below me. I was bounced down the stairs urgently. My mother wore her warmest coat although we were inside. It flapped open as she hurried, suitcases in both hands. Sun poured down with us right to the basement.

Inside the basement was a camp. All the families from our apartment house were together. This was new and interesting. Bundles. Families spread on blankets. Food unwrapped, passed from hand to hand. From outside a deep rumble and vibration, distant and stirring. 'Boom-boom!' I clapped gleefully. But my sister's hands covered her ears, and her face froze yellow as she hissed, 'Shut up, idiot.'

I learned a name for the camp-out in the basement. It was the Revolution. I tried the word in my head as my parents reassured Lili. Rev-o-lu-tion. There was fighting, but a revolution wasn't war, they explained. This revolution wasn't about Jews. War, Lili told me while our parents exchanged courtesies with the adults on the neighbouring mat, was when Jews were pulled from their homes and burned in ovens. This was only a revolution. Everyone in the tenement—Catholics, Jews, regular Hungarians called Communists—all of us there were equally at risk.

I took in the dim, densely bodied basement, learning and absorbing it like any new situation. It became part of me, the hours stretching into a predictable pattern of rhythms that I turned into the rituals of daytime and nighttime. The walk with my sister to the improvised bathroom. Threading our way past, and sometimes through, the personal effects of strangers. Habitual distrust in the glances cast at us, before they noticed we were children. Faces swerving at each unexpected noise, apprehension their common feature. I learned not to thrill so gladly to the drone of guns.

In the midmorning hush of a city that for days had been punctuated by bursts of shellfire and shattering glass, my father slipped away from us, out through a slice of light admitted by the basement entrance. They went out that day for the first time, men mostly, escaping tentatively through the fragment of light to forage a few facts that might let us know what was going on. No one was certain of the enemy. Hungarian troops were familiar but—Apu lowered his voice thinking Lili and I weren't listening—the Hungarians had in their ranks some of the old Arrow Cross members who had murdered Jews in the war. And the Russians were so touchy they might mistake anyone for an insurgent. Russians were generally feared, it seemed. But that day it was quiet, and the basement residents seemed to tacitly agree that it might be safe enough to go out to investigate. One after another, the men broke from their family groups.

It felt strange, the grown-up men gone. Almost like before, when the men used to go to work. We were left as of old, the children with the women, but my mother didn't appear her customary certain self. She had held Apu back for a moment before he left, as though changing her mind about letting him go. After he was gone, she tried to pull herself together. 'Come, Lili. Let's make up the sleeping mats, then we will have a hand or two of rummy if you still want to play cards.' Lili dropped her book in surprise at our mother's unusual proposal, for, even here in the packed basement, our mother found countless chores to do.

When the door flung inwards throwing in the harsh daylight, when the light burst in on us, it was as much an assault, that brilliant flare, as the bereted silhouette that followed. He had booted in the door, brandishing his rifle. The severe light seemed to radiate from his khaki-clad figure. He waved his gun at us as though we meant to hurt him. A sudden stillness seized all of us in that basement. Lili's hand was a small sculpture with cards fanned around it. We were still, as though not to alarm him. Don't move. Careful. Don't scare the strange doggy. See his sharp teeth.

'*Minden rendben van?*' Hungarian. Someone dared to answer, so perhaps a Hungarian soldier was not so bad. 'Yes,' a woman close to the door whispered, 'yes, all right. Everything here is fine.' He tipped his beret, a peacetime courtesy, and, relieved to withdraw without incident, backed out the door, his pointing rifle our last glimpse of him as it had been our first. My mother's voice didn't lose its shrill fear, not even months later when she drew on this incident during my parents' arguments and endless speculations. 'When that soldier burst in and we didn't know who or what he was, which would be better, Hungarian or Russian, all we were aware of was the weapon he carried, and our own pitiful dread.' She wasn't going to cringe like that again. Enough! 'I saw Auschwitz, now this!' She wasn't going to raise her children in fear. 'I've had enough cringing and hiding and hoping against the worst that always happens. I want something better to hope for. Milk the children can swallow without gagging.' Voice rising: 'I'm already thirty-seven years old! . . .'

When we finally emerged from the basement it was like blinking at a miracle. In my father's arms, ascending the stairs lowly, squinting into the light with every footfall. I entered our flat with the two men, my father and our tenant violinist. The windows splayed open. Before leaving the men had released the latches to minimize the impact of explosions. My father held me to keep me away from shards of broken glass. Wind gusted through the open windows. It seemed to me that the wind was sweeping in the very sky, there was so much cold light. It brought an emptiness into the unlived rooms. A purity. As if all had been wiped clean, sterilized by the light and blue air. Rooms that had lived something we had been spared—or denied; a life of their own. No longer the same rooms we had lived in. The men's voices boomed. The flat felt so empty. There were our things, the horsehair recamier and sturdy credenza, the framed photographs and fringed lampshades, even the throw rugs Apu stepped over as he hurried eagerly down the hall, checking everything. But they seemed insubstantial, almost transparent to me in that windy light. They had lost their solidity. Everything was light and airy as though even the thick oak table could be blown away in a breath of wind. The men's shoes resounded on the hardwood that skirted the carpets. It was as if we'd never lived there. As though in our absence someone had cleared out our personal claim to these belongings. Now there was only the idea of a sofa, the shadow of an armchair. All had filled with a light that was blue, clear, and so jagged it might slice you if you dared move. I flinched when my father laughed and our violinist put his head outside and waved. Human gestures seemed out of place to me, and risky, in that rare ether.

We were in a little car, hurtling past windbreaks on a highway. I was sandwiched between my sister and my father, conveyed into the countryside away from everything familiar. The sensation of being propelled against my will was as strange to me and as wild as I would find the ride, in years to come, in a Canadian amusement park, blasting around and around so fast my teeth were ground together. My mother's food packets were tucked inside my father's pockets. My mother had stood in her apron on the street, waving good-bye.

Apu liked to tell Lili stories about his life before the war on his family's country estate. Sometimes I caught references to the tobacco plantation and the horse-drawn carriages. When I heard him mention crop rotation, I imagined the fields spinning like the arms of the windmill in one of my picture books—one year up, one year down. Lili and I grew to imagine all that was good and beautiful to have risen out of his family's turf. The metre-long braided loaves of *challah* from my grandmother's kitchen, and tables set for twelve, sometimes twenty. Apu said his family had grown as rich and bountifully as the yields that fed and clothed them. They had lived on the land and nurtured it as lovingly as their offspring for three generations. These stories were part of the climate of our Budapest flat. Lili and I were accustomed to them. They had filtered into us like rain soaks a plant, and we understood that just as the seasons bloom and fade, so had my father's rural past.

Now he was taking us to the country. My father's fabled world was lost, but he was taking us nonetheless to see something he said was very special. Spring. Animal babies. Whizzing along in the little car, far from my mother and from Budapest, I wasn't sure what to expect.

Spring, ushered in by the rankness of wet winter rot, assailed us on arrival. The ground was mushy under our feet as though it would suck us in. The sodden fetid air we could only marvel at when our father said with relish, 'Smell it? That is the earth blowing out its winter breath.' Our offended urban nostrils flared in distaste. Feeling chilly in the damp air, we tramped along the muddy furrows. I looked to my sister for some cue, something to help me interpret the unpleasant sensations made more confusing by my father's obviously happy stride. Her boots seemed to sink into the furrows. Each step, as she pulled it up stickily, was laborious. She was ahead of me by six years. She was my measure, my yardstick. Hers the first impression.

'There was a calf born just this week,' my father told us. 'Isn't that lucky?' His voice sounded full with the pleasure of giving. But we weren't prepared for the dense stench of the barn and the rows of enormous beasts with their hot vaporous breaths. Lili had to be urged forward as Apu went down the row, patting the sides of the animals and pulling up their eyelids. I scrambled like a puppy beneath his feet. I was afraid to take a step away from him. I clung to his trousers until he had to pick me up. When he did, when I was up, oh, it was too late to look away. Something I wanted to hide from, but too riveting. One after the other he had pried open their eyes, checking for health. He had seen nothing to suggest disease. Not anything like what accosted us as a beast swung around presenting a back end that was red, so rawly red, every possible shade of red and plum unfolding like the layered petals of a giant bloom, all blood and flesh and tissue. A festering bovine backside from whose centre a black vermin seeped and crawled. I couldn't scream, lest putrid gore fill my mouth. Apu sucked back his breath in disbelief and turned, too late, to divert my gaze. My sister was already retching, a loud, raspy choke and surge.

As Apu held us in his arms outside the barn, trying to comfort us, he whispered into our hair and wept. He held us close, then wiped my sister's streaming nose with his monogrammed handkerchief. He stroked our soft hair, cradled our delicate bones, and whispered over our heads what sounded like a prayer, but was just the name of his other little daughter, the first one, our half-sister—lost in an

Auschwitz oven. 'Clarika,' he kept reminding us. He remembered her in each caress he ever gave us; in each kiss on our foreheads and flip of a storybook page, she was always beside us, loved just the same. We were everything to him, I felt, but also we were never enough. As my father prayed over our heads his lost daughter's name, I imagined he saw the gulf between them stretch wider and wider.

Going home in the car, we didn't talk about the newborn calf we'd seen, or the baby chicks and new lambs. I played back the red gore of disease, and saw it mirrored in my poor father's dismay. He who had grown from the earth, who loved the smell of horseshit and fodder. I believed he could have grown a forest in a bed of salt, and in our Canadian garden he would grow a veritable arbour of fruit trees and flowering shrubs and beds that never wilted. How it broke him to see his children repelled so virulently by the living earth, and severed from the generations who had cultivated this land, loved it and nourished it and built from it a dynasty.

My family left Hungary in 1957. My mother retold the scene so often over the years, it acquired the quality of something tangible, like a family icon. My mother's hands had locked over those of her daughters, me on one side and Lili on the other. Her head turned to look over her shoulder at our father, who stood framed against the tenement. 'With or without you,' she said, putting argument and persuasion behind her. She led us down the front walk of the building, and said with finality, 'We're going.' My father stood rooted at the entrance. He was a man of European height, to become small only by North American proportions. His arms hung by his sides, and his face was carved in loss over loss. As he watched us, his face began to break down along these creases until it was the face I recognized later in galleries of modern art: the face of our century, its features skewed and misaligned. When he left the portal of that building his figure diminished with each step. By the time he reached us his shoulders had rounded, his chest sunk into his belly. He turned into the father of my childhood, the one I really knew. The man who never again trudged through fields of corn or patted the flanks of horses, who from that moment was always close by our sides, our Apu. A man for whom borders opened, but whose world shrank around the shoulders of his family.

Norman Levine

Norman Levine was born in Ottawa's French Lower Town in 1923 to parents who had emigrated from Poland. He joined the Royal Canadian Air Force in 1942 and after the war graduated from McGill University in Montreal (B.A. 1948; M.A. 1949). He attended King's College in London with a fellowship from 1949 to 1950, but gave up academia for a career as a writer. After living in St. Ives, Cornwall, he went to Toronto in 1980 and now lives in the north of England. Levine's first two books were poetry collections: *Myssium* (1948) and *The Tight-Rope Walker* (1950). His war novel, *The Angled Road*, appeared in 1952. In 1958 his best-known work, the autobiographical *Canada Made Me* was published in both English and American editions, although the first Canadian edition of this work did not appear until 1979. Levine's other works include: *One Way Ticket: Stories* (1961); *From a Seaside Town* (1970); *I Don't Want to Know Anyone Too Well, and Other Stories* (1971); *Selected Stories* (1975); *I Walk by the Harbor* (1976); *The Lower Town* (1977); *Thin Ice* (1979); *Why Do You Live So Far Away* (1984); *Champagne Barn* (1984); and *Something Happened Here* (1991). He was also the editor of *Canadian Winter's Tales* (1968). Levine's stories have appeared in both popular and small-circulation magazines in England and Canada; many of them have been broadcast by CBC and BBC; and his collections have been widely translated in Holland, Switzerland, Germany, and France. Influenced by Orwell, Hemingway, Graham Greene, and Chekhov, Levine's short stories have become his strongest genre. They are marked by a spare style that complements the struggles of a poor artist in exile from both Canada and England. His fiction has been translated into German by Heinrich Böll and has found a significant audience in Germany. The present story is taken from *Champagne Barn* (1984) and depicts the isolated life of a Jewish writer, who visits the only Jew in small-town northern Ontario.

Norman Levine

By a Frozen River

In the winter of 1965 I decided to go for a few months to a small town in northern Ontario. It didn't have a railway station—just one of those brown railway sidings, on the outskirts, with a small wooden building to send telegrams, buy tickets, and to get on and get off. A taxi was there meeting the train. I asked the driver to take me to a hotel. There was only one he would recommend, The Adanac. I must have looked puzzled. For he said,

'It's Canada spelled backwards.'

He drove slowly through snow-covered streets. The snow-banks by the sidewalk were so high that you couldn't see anyone walking. Just the trees. He drove alongside a frozen river with a green bridge across it. Then we were out for a while in the country. The snow here had drifted so that the tops of the telegraph poles were protruding like fence posts. Then we came to the town—a wide main street with other streets going off it.

The Adanac was a three-storey wooden hotel on the corner of King and Queen. It had seen better times. Its grey-painted wooden verandah, with icicles on the edges, looked old and fragile. But the woodwork had hand-carved designs, and the white windows had rounded tops. Beside it was a new beer parlour.

Fifty years ago it was the height of fashion to stay at the hotel. It was then called the George. The resident manager told me this, in his office, after I paid a month's rent in advance. His name was Savage. A short, overweight man in his sixties, with a slow speaking voice, as if he was thinking what he was going to say. He sat, neatly dressed, behind a desk, his grey hair crew-cut, and looked out of the large window at the snow-covered street. The sun was shining.

'Well,' he said slowly. 'It's an elegant day.'

His wife was a thin, tall woman with delicate features. She also hardly spoke. But would come into the office and sit, very upright, in a rocking chair near Mr Savage and look out of the window. The office connected with their three-room flat. It was filled with their possessions. A small, bronze crucifix was on the wall. Over the piano a large picture of the Pope. There were a few coloured photographs: a boy in uniform, children, and a sunset over a lake.

I rented the flat above. I had a room to sleep in, a room to write and read, and a kitchen with an electric stove and fridge. To get to them I would go up worn steps, along a wide, badly lit corridor—large tin pipes carried heat along the ceiling. But inside the rooms it was warm. They had radiators and double windows.

I unpacked. Then went to the supermarket, by the frozen river, and came back with various tins, fruit, and cheap cigars that said they were dipped in wine. I made myself some coffee, lit one of the thin cigars, and relaxed.

I saw a wooden radio on the side-table in the sitting-room. A battered thing. I had to put twenty-five cents in the back. That, according to a metal sign, gave me two hours' playing time. But that was only a formality. For the back was all exposed, and the twenty-five cents kept falling out for me to put through again.

Listening to the radio—I could only get the local station—the town sounded a noisy, busy place, full of people buying and selling and with things going on. But when I walked out, the first thing I noticed was the silence. The frozen, shabby side-streets. Hardly anything moving. It wasn't like what the radio made out at all. There was a feeling of apathy. The place seemed stunned by the snow piled everywhere.

I quickly established a routine. After breakfast I went out and walked. And came back, made some coffee, and wrote down whatever things I happened to notice.

This morning it was the way trees creak in the cold. I had walked by a large elm when I heard it. I thought it was the crunching sound my shoes made on the hard-packed snow. So I stopped. There was no wind, the branches were not moving, yet the tree was creaking.

In the late afternoon, I made another expedition outside. Just before it got dark, I found a small square. It began to snow. The few trees on the perimeter were black. The few bundled-up people walking slowly through the snow were black. And from behind curtained windows a bit of light, a bit of orange. There was no sound. Just the snow falling. I expected horses and sleighs to appear, and felt the isolation.

That evening I had company. A mouse. I saw it just before it saw me. I tried to hit it with a newspaper, but I missed. And as it ran it slipped and slithered on the linoleum. I was laughing. It ran behind the radiator, I looked and saw it between the radiator grooves where the dust had gathered. It had made a nest out of bits of fluff. I left food out for it. And in the evenings it would come out and run around the perimeter of the sitting-room, then go back behind the radiator.

Birds woke me in the morning. It seemed odd to see so much snow and ice and hear birds singing. I opened the wooden slot in the outside window and threw out some bread. Though I could hear the birds, I couldn't see them. Then they came—sparrows. They seemed to fly into their shadows as they landed on the snow. Then three pigeons. I went and got some more bread.

On the fourth day I met my neighbour across the hall. He rented the two rooms opposite. He wore a red lumberjack shirt and black lumberjack boots with the laces going high up. He was medium height, in his forties, with pleasant features. And he had short, red hair.

'Hi,' he said. And asked me what I was doing.

'Writing a book,' I said.

'Are you really writing a book?'

'Yes.'

'That must be very nice,' he said.

And invited me into his flat. It was the same as mine, except he didn't have a sitting-room. The same second-hand furniture, the used electric stove, the large fridge, the wooden radio.

I asked him what he did.

'I work in a small factory. Just my brother and me. We make canoes. Do you like cheese?'

'Yes,' I said.

He opened his fridge. It was filled with large hunks of an orange cheese.

'I get it sent from Toronto. Here, have some.'

I met the new occupants of the three rooms behind me next morning. I was going to the toilet. (There was one toilet, with bath, for all of us on the first floor. It was in the hall at the top of the stairs.) I opened the door and saw a woman sitting on the toilet, smoking a cigarette. She wasn't young. Her legs were close together. She said, 'Oh.' I said sorry and closed the door quickly. 'I'm sorry,' I said again, this time louder, as I walked away.

A couple of days later she knocked on my door and said she was Mrs Labelle and she was Jewish. She heard from Savage that I had a Jewish name. Was I Jewish? I said I was. She invited me back to meet her husband.

The people who rented these rooms usually didn't stay very long. So there was no pride in trying to do anything to change them. But Mrs Labelle had her room spotless. She had put up bright yellow curtains to hide the shabby window blinds. She had plastic flowers in a bowl on the table. And everything looked neat, and washed, even though the furniture was the same as I had.

Her husband, Hubert, was much younger. He looked very dapper. Tall, dark hair brushed back, neatly dressed in a dark suit and tie and a clean white shirt. He had a tripod in his hand and said he was going out to work.

'Savage told us you were a writer. I have started to write my life story—What the photographer saw—I tell all. You wouldn't believe the things that have happened to me.'

His wife said that the mayor was trying to get them out of town. 'He told the police that we need a licence. It's because he owns the only photograph store here. He's afraid of the competition. We're not doing anything illegal. I knock on people's doors and ask them if they want their picture taken at home. He's very good,' she said, 'especially with children.'

After that Mrs Labelle came to the door every day. She knew all the other occupants. And would tell me little things about them. 'He's a very hard worker,' she said about the man who made canoes. 'He doesn't drink at all.' Then she told me about the cleaning woman, Mabel. 'She only gets fifteen dollars a week. Her husband's an alcoholic. She's got a sixteen-year-old daughter—she's pregnant. I'm going to see her this afternoon and see if I can help. Be careful of Savage. He looks quiet, but I saw him using a blackjack on a drunk from the beer parlour who tried to get into the hotel at night. He threw him out in the snow. Dragged him by the feet. And

Mrs Savage helped.' She complained of the noise at night. 'There's three young waitresses. Just above me. They have boys at all hours. I don't blame them. But I can't sleep. I can't wash my face. It's nerves,' she said.

Then I began to hear Mr Labelle shouting at her. 'God damn you. Leave me alone. Just leave me alone.' It went on past midnight.

Next day, at noon, she knocked on the door. She was smiling.

'I found a place where you can get Jewish food.'

'Where?'

'Morris Bischofswerder. He's a furrier. Up on the main street.'

I went to the furrier. He had some skins hanging on the walls. And others were piled in a heap on the floor.

'Do you sell food?' I said.

'What kind of food?'

'Jewish food.'

He looked me over.

He was below middle height, stocky, with a protruding belly. A dark moustache, almost bald, but dark hair on the sides. He was neatly dressed in a brown suit with a gold watch chain in his vest pocket. He was quite a handsome man, full lips and dark eyes. And from those eyes I had a feeling that he had a sense of fun.

'Where are you from?' he asked. 'The West?'

'No, from England.'

'All right, come.'

He led me through a doorway into the back and there into his kitchen. And immediately there was a familiar food smell, something that belonged to my childhood. A lot of dried mushrooms, on a string, like a necklace, hung on several nails. He showed me two whole salamis and some loose hot dogs.

'I can let you have a couple pounds of salami and some hot dogs until the next delivery. I have it flown in once a month from Montreal.' He smiled. 'I also like this food. Where are you staying?'

'At the Adanac.'

His wife came in. She was the same size as Mr Bischofswerder but thinner, with grey hair, a longish thin nose, deep-set very dark eyes, the hollows were in permanent shadow, and prominent top teeth.

'He's from England,' he told her.

'I come from Canada,' I said quickly. 'But I live in England. The place I live in England doesn't have snow in winter. So I've come back for a while.'

'You came all the way from England for the snow?'

'Yes.'

They both looked puzzled.

'I like winters with snow,' I said.

'What have you got in England?'

'Where I live—rain.'

'Have you got a family?' Mr Bischofswerder said, changing the subject. 'Is your mother and father alive?'

'My mother and father lived in Ottawa, but they moved to California eight years ago.'

'I bet they don't miss Canadian winters,' Mrs Bischofswerder said.

'We have a married daughter in Montreal and five grandchildren,' he said proudly, 'four boys and one girl.'

'Sit down,' Mrs Bischofswerder said. 'I was just going to make some tea.'

And she brought in a chocolate cake, some pastry that had poppy seeds on top, and some light egg cookies.

'It's very good, isn't it?' she said.

'I haven't had food like this since I was a boy,' I said.

'Why are you so thin?' she said. '*Eat, Eat.*' And pushed more cookies in my direction.

'I wonder if you would come to *shul* next Friday,' Mr Bischofswerder said.

My immediate reaction was to say no. For I haven't been in a synagogue for over twenty years. But sitting in this warm kitchen with the snow outside. Eating the food. Mrs Bischofswerder making a fuss. It brought back memories of my childhood. And people I once knew.

'I'll come,' I said.

'Fine,' he said. 'If you come here around four o'clock, we'll go together. It gets dark quickly.'

That night the Labelles quarrelled until after two. Next day, at noon, Mrs Labelle knocked on the door. 'He didn't turn up. This woman was holding her children all dressed up. I told her to send them to school.'

'Is this the first time?'

'No. It's only got bad now. He's an alcoholic.'

She began to weep. I asked her inside. She was neatly dressed in dark slacks and a small fur jacket. 'My sisters won't have me. They say I've sown my wild oats.'

'Would you like some coffee?'

'Thanks. We had a house in Toronto. I have in storage lots of furniture—a fur coat—real shoes—not shoes like this. And where would you see a woman of my age going around knocking on doors? I'm sure I'm going to be killed. He calls me a witch. I found a piece of paper with a phone number. And a name—Hattie. I called up and said to leave my husband alone. I found another piece of paper. It said Shirley. They're all over him. He's a good-looking guy. And when he's working—these women are alone with him. You know—'

That afternoon, while I was writing, the phone went. It was Mrs Labelle.

'I'm in someone's house waiting for him to come and take the picture. Can you see if he's in. He hasn't turned up.'

I knocked on their door. Mr Labelle was sitting on the settee with a middle-aged man in a tartan shirt, and they were both drinking beer out of small bottles.

I said she was on the phone.

'Say you haven't seen me,' he said.

'Yes,' the other man said. 'Say you haven't seen him.'

But Labelle came after me and stood by the open door. 'Why don't you just say hello?' I said.

He went in and I could hear him saying, 'I'm not drunk. I'm coming over.' He hung up and closed the door.

'I'll tell you,' he said. 'Man to man. I'll be forty-one next month. And she's fifty-eight. We've been married fifteen years. I didn't know how old she was when we married. Then she was seven months in a mental home. I used to see her ever day. At two. I had to get my job all changed around. But I'll tell you what. I knocked up a woman two years ago. And she heard about it. The child died. She can't have children. She won't give me some rein. I've had her for fifteen years. Don't worry,' he said. 'I won't leave her. You may hear us at night. I shout. I'm French Canadian. But I'll look after her.'

He went back and got his camera and tripod. And he and the other man went down the stairs.

Ten minutes later she rang up again.

'Is he gone?'

'Yes,' I said.

That evening around nine, there was a gentle knock at the door. It was Mrs Labelle, in a red dressing-gown. 'He's asleep,' she said. 'Thank you very much. He hasn't eaten anything. I make special things. But he won't eat.'

It was quiet until eleven that night. I could hear them talking. Then he began to raise his voice. 'Shut up. God damn it. Leave me alone. You should have married a Jewish businessman. You would have been happy.'

On Friday afternoon I put on a clean white shirt and tie and a suit. And went to call on Mr Bischofswerder. He was dressed, neatly, in a dark winter coat and a fur hat. We walked about four blocks. Then he led me into what I thought was a private house but turned out to be the synagogue. It was very small. Around twenty-four feet square and twenty feet high. But though it was small, it was exact in the way the synagogues were that I remembered. There was a wooden ark between a pair of tall windows in the east wall. A few steps, with wooden rails, led to the ark. The Ten Commandments, in Hebrew, were above it. A low gallery extended around the two sides. In the centre of the ceiling hung a candelabra with lights over the reading desk. There were wooden bench seats. Mr Bischofswerder raised one, took out a prayer book, and gave the prayer book to me.

'Shall we start?' he said.

'Aren't we going to wait for the others?'

'There are no others,' he said.

And he began to say the prayers to himself. Now and then he would run the words out aloud so I could hear, in a kind of sing-song that I remembered my father doing. I followed with my eyes the words. And now and then I would say something so he would hear.

I had long forgotten the service, the order of the service. So I followed him. I got up when he did. I took the three steps backwards when he did. But most of the time we were both silent. Just reading the prayers.

Then it was over. And he said.

'Good Shabbus.'

'Good Shabbus,' I said.

On the way back, through the snow-covered streets, it was freezing. Mr Bischofswerder was full of enthusiasm.

'Do you realize,' he said, 'this is the first time I've had someone in the *shul* with me at Friday night for over three years.'

For the next seven Friday nights and Saturday mornings I went with Mr Bischofswerder to the synagogue. We said our prayers in silence.

Then I went back with him to his warm house. And to the enormous Sabbath meal that Mrs Bischofswerder had cooked. Of gefilte fish with chrane, chicken soup with mandlen, chicken with tzimmes, compote, tea with cookies. And we talked. They wanted to know about England. I told them about the English climate, about English money, English society, about London, Fleet Street, the parks, the pubs. How I lived by the sea and a beautiful bay but hardly any trees.

And he told me how the trappers brought him skins that he sent on to Montreal. That he was getting a bit old for it now. 'Thank God I can still make a living.' He told me of the small Jewish community that was once here. 'In 1920 when we came there were ten families. By the end of the last war it was down to three. No new recruits came to take the place of those who died or moved away. When we go,' said Mr Bischofswerder, 'all that will be left will be a small cemetery.'

'Have some more cookies,' his wife said, pushing a plateful towards me. 'You have hardly touched them. You won't get fat. They're light. They're called nothings.'

Mrs Labelle knocked on my door. She looked excited. 'I'm selling tickets,' she said. 'The town's running a sweepstake when will the frozen river start to move? Everyone's talking about it. I've already sold three books. Will you have one? You can win five hundred dollars.'

'How much are they?'

'Fifty cents.'

'I'll have one,' I said.

'Next time you go to the supermarket,' she said, 'you'll see a clock in the window. There's a wire from the clock to the ice in the river. As soon as the ice starts to move—the clock stops. And the nearest ticket wins.'

She gave me my ticket.

'Good luck,' she said. And kissed me lightly on a cheek.

She looked, I thought, the happiest I had seen her. My ticket said: March 26th, 08:16:03.

That night I noticed the mouse had gone. No sign of it anywhere. It was raining. The streets were slushy and slippery. But later that night the water froze. And next morning when the sun came out it was slush again. The snow had started to shrink on the roofs; underneath the edges I could see water moving. I walked down to the river. It was still frozen, but I saw patches of blue where before it was all white. Crows were flapping over the ice with bits of straw in their beaks. The top crust of the river had buckled in places. And large pieces creaked as they rubbed against each other. Things were beginning to break up. It did feel like something was coming to an end here.

Next day, just before noon, Mrs Labelle came to the door. She looked worried. 'Savage told us we have to leave. I went to see him with our week's rent in advance. But he said he didn't want it. He said we were making too much noise at night. The waitresses make noise, but he doesn't mind them. I don't know where we'll go. We've been in Sudbury, in Timmins, in North Bay—'

'It's OK,' Mr Labelle said, coming to the door. 'We'll be all right,' he said to her gently. And started to walk her back toward their door. Then he called out to me. 'If we don't see you, fellah, good luck.'

'Same to you,' I said.

'But where will we go Hubert?' Mrs Labelle said, looking up to his face.

'There's lots of places,' he answered. 'Now we got some packing to do.'

After the Labelles had gone, it was very quiet. I had got the reminders I wanted of a Canadian winter. I had filled up three notebooks. It was time that I left. I went down to the office and told this to Mr Savage. He suggested that I stay until the ice started to move.

But I left before it did.

I took a light plane, from the snow-covered field with a short runway. From the air, for a while, I could see the small town. But soon it was lost in a wilderness of snow, trees, and frozen lakes.

Matt Cohen

Born in Kingston, Ontario, in 1942, Matt Cohen grew up in Ottawa, where he lived until 1960. He obtained his M.A. from the University of Toronto in 1965 and taught religious studies at McMaster University from 1967 to 1968. In 1970 he moved to a farm north of Kingston, where he wrote most of his fiction. In 1975/1976 he was writer-in-residence at the University of Alberta; in 1979/1980 he served as visiting professor of creative writing at the University of Victoria; and in 1981/1982 he was writer-in-residence at the University of Western Ontario. His first novel, *Korsoniloff* (1969), deals with a schizoid philosopher, who narrates his life and Korsoniloff's passionate and amoral life. Cohen then wrote a series of regional novels around the fictional town of Salem in southern Ontario: *The Disinherited* (1974), *The Colours of War* (1977), *The Sweet Second Summer of Kitty Malone* (1979), and *Flowers of Darkness* (1981). In a few of his short stories Cohen turned to Jewish subjects, but not until *The Spanish Doctor* (1984) did he develop a full-length novel about Jewish history around the time of the Spanish Inquisition. The Santangel, Halevi, and Benares families form his exploration into Sephardic Jewry, and the present story, taken from *Café Le Dog* (1985), focuses on the longevity of the Benares lineage now located in Toronto. He has also translated from the French and published *Freud: The Paris Notebook* (1991). Shortly before his death in 1999 Cohen won the Governor General's Award for his last novel, *Elizabeth and After*.

Matt Cohen

The Sins of Tomas Benares

A narrow, three storey house near College Street had been the home of the Benares family since they arrived in Toronto in 1936. Beside the front door, bolted to the brick, was a brass name-plate that was kept polished and bright: DR. TOMAS BENARES.

Benares had brought the name-plate—and little else—with him when he and his wife fled Spain just before the Civil War. For twenty years it had resided on the brick beside the doorway. And then, after various happinesses and tragedies—the tragedies being unfortunately more numerous—it had been replaced triumphantly by a new name-plate: DR. ABRAHAM BENARES. This son, Abraham, was the only child to have survived those twenty years.

Abraham had lost not only his siblings, but also his mother. The day his name-plate was proudly mounted Tomas could at last say to himself that perhaps his string of bad fortune had finally been cut, for despite everything he now had a son who was a doctor, like himself, and who was married with two children.

By 1960, the Benares household was wealthy in many ways. True, the family had not moved to the north of the city like many other immigrants who had made money, but during the era of the DR. ABRAHAM BENARES name-plate the adjoining house was purchased to give space for an expanded office and to provide an investment for Abraham Benares' swelling income as a famous internist. The back yards of both houses were combined into one elegant lawn that was tended twice a week by a professional gardener, an old Russian Jew who Tomas Benares had met first in his office, then at the synagogue. He spent most of his time drinking tea and muttering about the injustices that had been brought upon his people, while Tomas himself, by this time retired, toothless, and bent of back, crawled through the flower beds on his knees, wearing the discarded rubber dishwashing gloves of his son's extraordinarily beautiful wife.

Bella was her name. On anyone else, such a name would have been a joke; but Bella's full figure and dark, Mediterranean face glowed with such animal heat that from the first day he met her Tomas felt like an old man in her presence. Of this Bella seemed entirely unaware. After moving into the house she cooked for Tomas, pressed her scorching lips to his on family occasions, even hovered over him during meals, her fruity breath like a hot caress against his neck. After her children were born she began to refer to Tomas as grandfather, and sometimes while the infants played on the living room floor she would stand beside Tomas with the full weight of her fleshy hand sinking into his arm. 'Look at us,' she said to Tomas once, 'three generations.'

A few years after the birth of his daughter, Abraham Benares was walking with her down to College Street, as he did every Saturday, to buy a newspaper and a bag of apples, when a black Ford car left the street and continued its uncontrolled progress along the sidewalk where Abraham was walking. Instinctively, Abraham scooped Margaret into his arms, but the car was upon him before he could move. Abraham Benares, forty-one years old and the former holder of the city intercollegiate record for the one hundred yard dash, had time only to throw his daughter onto the adjacent lawn while the car mowed him down.

The next year, 1961, the name-plate on the door changed again: DR. TOMAS BENARES reappeared. There had been no insurance policy and the old man, now seventy-four years of age but still a licensed physician, recommenced the practice of medicine. He got the complaining gardener to redivide the yard with a new fence, sold the house next door to pay his son's debts, and took over the task of providing for his daughter-in-law and his two grandchildren.

Before reopening his practice, Tomas Benares got new false teeth and two new suits. He spent six months reading his old medical textbooks and walked several miles every morning to sweep the cobwebs out of his brain. He also, while walking, made it a point of honour never to look over his shoulder.

On the eve of his ninety-fourth birthday Tomas Benares was sixty-two inches tall and weighed one hundred and twelve pounds. These facts he noted carefully in a small diary. Each year, sitting in his third floor bedroom-study, Tomas Benares entered his height and weight into the pages of this diary. He also summarized any medical problems he had experienced during the year past, and made his prognosis for the year to come. There had once been an essay-like annual entry in which he confessed his outstanding sins and moral omissions from the previous year and outlined how he could correct or at least repent them in the year to follow. These essays had begun when Tomas was a medical student, and had continued well past the year in which his wife died. But when he had retired the first time from practising medicine and had the time to read over the fifty years of entries, he had noticed that his sins grew progressively more boring with age. And so, after that, he simply recorded the number of times he had enjoyed sexual intercourse that year.

Now, almost ninety-four, Tomas Benares couldn't help seeing that even this simple statistic had been absent for almost a decade. His diary was getting shorter while his life was getting longer. His last statistic had been when he was eighty-six—one time; the year before—none at all. But in his eighty-fourth year there had been a dozen transgressions. Transgressions! They should have been marked as victories. Tomas brushed back at the wisps of white hair that still adorned his skull. He couldn't remember feeling guilty or triumphant, couldn't remember any detail at all of the supposed events. Perhaps he had been lying. According to the entry, his height during that erotic year had been sixty-four inches, and his weight exactly twice that—one hundred and twenty-eight pounds. In 1956, when he had begun compiling the statistics, there had been only one admission of intercourse, but his height had been sixty-five inches and his weight one hundred and forty.

Suddenly, Tomas had a vision of himself as an old-fashioned movie. In each frame he was a different size, lived a different life. Only accelerating the reel could make the crowd into one person.

He was sitting in an old blue armchair that had been in the living room when Marguerita was still alive. There he used to read aloud in English to her, trying to get his accent right, while in the adjacent kitchen she washed up the dinner dishes and called out his mistakes. Now he imagined pulling himself out of the armchair, walking to the window to see if his grandson Joseph's car was parked on the street below. He hooked his fingers, permanently curved, into the arms of his chair. And then he pulled. But the chair was a vacuum sucking him down with the gravity of age. Beside him was a glass of raspberry wine. He brought it to his lips, wet the tip of his tongue. He was on that daily two-hour voyage between the departure of his day nurse and the arrival of Joseph. Eventually, perhaps soon, before his weight and height had entirely shrunk away and there were no statistics at all to enter into his diary, he would die. He wanted to die with the house empty. That was the last wish of Tomas Benares.

But even while his ninety-fourth birthday approached, Tomas Benares was not worrying about dying. To be sure he had become smaller with each year, and the prospect of worthwhile sin had almost disappeared; but despite the day nurse and the iron gravity of his chair, Tomas Benares was no invalid. Every morning this whole summer—save the week he had the flu—his nurse, whose name was Elizabeth Rankin, had helped him down the stairs and into the yard where, on his knees, he tended his gardens. While the front of the house had been let go by his careless grandson, Joseph, the back was preserved in the splendour it had known for almost fifty years. Bordering the carefully painted picket fence that surrounded the small yard were banks of flowers, the old strawberry patch, and in one corner a small stand of raspberry canes that were covered by netting to keep away the plague of thieving sparrows.

This morning, too, the morning of his birthday, Elizabeth Rankin helped him down the stairs. Elizabeth Rankin had strong arms, but although he could hardly walk down the three flights of stairs by himself—let alone climb back up—he could think of his own father, who had lived to be one hundred and twenty-three and of his grandfather Benares, who had lived to the same age. There was, in fact, no doubt that this enormous number was fate's stamp on the brow of the Benares men, though even fate could not *always* cope with automobiles.

But, as his own father had told Tomas, the Benares were to consider themselves blessed because fate seemed to pick them out more frequently than other people. For example, Tomas' father, who was born in 1820, had waited through two wives to have children, and when one was finally born, a boy, he had died of an unknown disease that winter brought to the Jewish quarter of Kiev. So frightened had he been by this show of God's spite that Tomas' father had sold the family lumbering business and rushed his wife back to Spain, the cradle of his ancestors, where she bore Tomas in 1884. Tomas' grandfather had, of course, been hale and hearty at the time: one hundred and four years old, he had lived on the top floor of the house just as Tomas now lived on the top floor of his own grandson's house.

That old man, Tomas' grandfather, had been a round, brown apple baked dry by the sun and surrounded by a creamy white fringe of beard. He had been born in 1780 and Tomas, bemoaning the emptiness of his diary on the occasion of his oncoming ninety-fourth, realized suddenly that he was holding two hundred years in his mind. His father had warned him: men were long-lived relics whose minds sent arrows back into the swamp of the past, so deep into the swamp that the lives they recalled were clamped together in a formless gasping mass, waiting to be shaped by those who remembered. The women were more peripheral: stately and beautiful they were easily extinguished; perhaps they were bored to death by the small, round-headed stubborn men who made up the Benares tribe.

'We were always Spaniards,' the old man told Tomas, stubborn as donkeys.' *Stubborn as a donkey*, the child Tomas had whispered. Had his mother not already screamed this at him? And he imagined ancient Spain: a vast, sandy expanse where the Jews had been persecuted and in revenge had hidden their religion under prayer shawls and been stubborn as donkeys.

And they hadn't changed, Tomas thought gleefully, they hadn't changed at all; filled with sudden enthusiasm and the image of himself as a white-haired, virile donkey, he pulled himself easily out of his chair and crossed the room to the window where he looked down for Joseph's car. The room was huge: the whole third floor of the house save for an alcove walled off as a bathroom. Yet even in the afternoon the room was dark as a cave, shadowed by its clutter of objects that included everything from his marriage bed to the stand-up scale with the weights and sliding rule that he used to assess himself for his yearly entry.

From the window he saw that his grandson's car had yet to arrive. On the sidewalk instead were children travelling back and forth on tricycles, shouting to each other in a fractured mixture of Portuguese and English. As always, when he saw children on the sidewalk, he had to resist opening the window and warning them to watch out for cars. It had been Margaret, only four years old, who had run back to the house to say that 'Papa is sick,' then had insisted on returning down the street with Tomas.

Two hundred years: would Margaret live long enough to sit frozen in a chair and feel her mind groping from one century to the next? Last year, on his birthday, she had given him the bottle of raspberry wine he was now drinking. 'Every raspberry is a blessing,' she had said. She had a flowery tongue, like her brother, and when she played music Tomas could sense her passion whirling like a dark ghost through the room. What would she remember? Her mother who had run away; her grandmother whom she had never known; her father, covered by a sheet by the time she and Tomas had arrived, blood from his crushed skull seeping into the white linen.

They had come a long way, the Benares: from the new Jerusalem in Toledo to two centuries in Kiev, only to be frightened back to Spain before fleeing again, this time to a prosperous city in the New World. But nothing had changed, Tomas thought, even the bitterness over his son's death still knifed through him exactly as it had when he saw Margaret's eyes at the door, when Joseph, at the funeral, broke into a long, keening howl.

Stubborn as a donkey. Tomas straightened his back and walked easily from the window towards his chair. He would soon be ninety-four years old, and if fate was to be trusted, which it wasn't, there were to be thirty more years of anniversaries. During the next year, he thought, he had better put some effort into improving his statistics.

He picked up his diary again, flipped the pages backward, fell into a doze before he could start reading.

On his ninety-fourth birthday Tomas slept in. This meant not waking until after eight o'clock; and then lying in bed and thinking about his dreams. In the extra hours of sleep Tomas dreamed that he was a young man again, that he was married, living in Madrid, and that at noon the bright sun was warm as he walked the streets from his office to the *café* where he took lunch with his cronies. But in this dream he was not a doctor but a philosopher; for some strange reason it had been given to him to spend his entire life thinking about oak trees, and while strolling the broad, leafy streets it was precisely this subject that held his mind. He had also the duty, of course, of supervising various graduate students, all of whom were writing learned dissertations on the wonders of the oak; and it often, in this dream, pleased him to spend the afternoon with these bright and beautiful young people, drinking wine and saying what needed to be said.

In the bathroom, Tomas shaved himself with the electric razor that had been a gift from Joseph. Even on his own birthday he no longer trusted his hand with the straight razor that still hung, with its leather strop, from a nail in the wall. This, he suddenly thought, was the kind of detail that should also be noted in his annual diary—the texture of his shrinking world. Soon everything would be forbidden to him, and he would be left with only the space his own huddled skeleton could occupy. After shaving, Tomas washed his face, noting the exertion that was necessary just to open and close the cold water tap, and then he went back to the main room where he began slowly to dress.

It was true, he was willing to admit, that these days he often thought about his own death; but such thoughts did not disturb him. In fact, during those hours when he felt weak and sat in his chair breathing slowly, as if each weak breath might be his last, he often felt Death sitting with him. A quiet friend, Death; one who was frightening at first, but now was a familiar companion, an invisible brother waiting for him to come home.

But home, for Tomas Benares, was still the world of the living. When Elizabeth Rankin came to check on him, she found Tomas dressed and brushed. And a few minutes later he was sitting in his own garden, drinking espresso coffee and listening to the birds fuss in the flowering hedges that surrounded his patio. There Tomas, at peace, let the hot sun soak into his face. Death was with him in the garden, in the seductive buzz of insects, the comforting sound of water running in the nearby kitchen. The unaccustomed long sleep only gave Tomas the taste for more. He could feel himself drifting off, noted with interest that he had no desire to resist, felt Death pull his chair closer, his breath disguised as raspberries and mimosa.

At seventy-four years of age, also on his birthday, Tomas Benares had gone out to his front steps, unscrewed his son's name-plate and reaffixed his own. In the previous weeks he had restored the house to the arrangement it had known before his original retirement.

The front hall was the waiting room. On either side were long wooden benches, the varnished oak polished by a generation of patients. This front hall opened into a small parlour that looked onto the street. In that room was a desk, more chairs for waiting, and the doctor's files. At first his wife ran that parlour; after her death, Tomas had hired a nurse.

Behind the parlour was the smallest room of all. It had space for an examination table, a glass cabinet with a few books and several drawers of instruments, and a single uncomfortable chair. On the ceiling was a fluorescent light, and the window was protected by venetian blinds made of heavy plastic.

After Abraham's death his widow, Bella, and the children had stayed on in the Benares household, and so on the morning of the reopening Tomas had gone into the kitchen to find Bella making coffee and feeding breakfast to Joseph and Margaret. He sat down wordlessly at the kitchen table while Bella brought him coffee and toast, and he was still reading the front section of the morning paper when the doorbell rang. Joseph leapt from the table and ran down the hall. Tomas was examining the advertisement he had placed to announce the recommencement of his practice.

'Finish your coffee,' said Bella. 'Let her wait. She's the one who needs the job.'

But Tomas was already on his feet. Slowly he walked down the hall to the front parlour. He could hear Joseph chatting with the woman, and was conscious of trying to keep his back straight. He was wearing, for his new practice, a suit newly tailored. His old tailor had died, but his son had measured Tomas with the cloth tape, letting his glasses slide down to rest on the tip of his nose exactly like his father had. Now in his new blue suit, a matching tie, and one of the white linen shirts that Marguerita had made for him, Tomas stood in his front parlour.

'Doctor Benares, I am Elizabeth Rankin; I answered your advertisement for a nurse.'

'I am pleased to meet you, Mrs. Rankin.'

'Miss Rankin.' Elizabeth Rankin was then a young woman entering middle age. She had brown hair parted in the middle and then pulled back in a bun behind her neck, eyes of a darker brown in which Tomas saw a mixture of fear and sympathy. She was wearing a skirt and a jacket, but had with her a small suitcase in case it was necessary for her to start work right away.

'Would you like to see my papers, Doctor Benares?'

'Yes, if you like. Please sit down.'

Joseph was still in the room and Tomas let him watch as Elizabeth Rankin pulled out a diploma stating that she had graduated from McGill University in the biological sciences, and another diploma showing that she had received her RN from the same university.

'I have letters of reference, Doctor Benares.'

'Joseph, please get a cup of coffee for Miss Rankin. Do you—'

'Just black, Joseph.'

They sat in silence until Joseph arrived with the coffee, and then Tomas asked him to leave and closed the door behind him.

'I'm sorry,' Elizabeth Rankin said. 'I saw the advertisement and . . .'

She trailed off. It was six months since Tomas had seen her, but he recognized her right away; she was the woman who had been driving the car that had killed his son. At the scene of the accident she had shivered in shock until the ambulance arrived. Tomas had even offered her some sleeping pills. Then she had reappeared to hover on the edge of the mourners at Abraham's funeral.

'You're a very brave woman, Miss Rankin.'

'No, I . . .' Her eyes clouded over. Tomas, behind the desk, watched her struggle. When he had seen her in the hall, his first reaction had been anger.

'I thought I should do something,' she said. 'I don't need a salary, of course, and I *am* a qualified nurse.'

'I see that,' Tomas said dryly.

'You must hate me,' Elizabeth Rankin said.

Tomas shrugged. Joseph came back into the room and stood beside Elizabeth Rankin. She put her hand on his shoulder and the boy leaned against her.

'You mustn't bother Miss Rankin,' Tomas said, but even as he spoke he could see Elizabeth's hand tightening on the boy's shoulder.

'Call Margaret,' Tomas said to Joseph, and then asked himself why, indeed, he should forgive this woman. No reason came to mind, and while Joseph ran through the house, searching for his sister, Tomas sat in his reception room and looked carefully at the face of Elizabeth Rankin. The skin below her eyes was dark, perhaps she had trouble sleeping; and though her expression was maternal she had a tightly drawn quality that was just below the surface, as though the softness were a costume.

He remembered a friend, who had been beaten by a gang of Franco's men, saying he felt sorry for them. When Tomas' turn came, he had felt no pity for his assailants. And although what Elizabeth Rankin had done was an accident, not a malicious act, she was still the guilty party. Tomas wondered if she knew what he was thinking, wondered how she could not. She was sitting with one leg crossed over the other, her eyes on the door through which the sounds of the children's feet now came. And when Margaret, shy, sidled into the room, Tomas made a formal introduction. He was thinking, as he watched Margaret's face, how strange it was that the victims must always console their oppressors.

Margaret, four years old, curtsied and then held out her hand. There was no horrified scream, no flicker of recognition.

'Miss Rankin will be coming every morning,' Tomas announced. 'She will help me in my office.'

'You are very kind, Doctor Benares.'

'We will see,' Tomas said. It was then that he had an extraordinary thought, or at least a thought that was extraordinary for him. It occurred to him that Elizabeth Rankin didn't simply want to atone, or to be consoled. She wanted to be taken advantage of.

Tomas waited until the children had left the room, then closed the door. He stood in front of Elizabeth Rankin until she, too, got to her feet.

'Pig,' Tomas Benares hissed; and he spat at her face. The saliva missed its target and landed, instead, on the skin covering her right collarbone. There it glistened, surrounded by tiny beads, before gliding down the open V of her blouse.

The eyes of Elizabeth Rankin contracted briefly. Then their expression returned to a flat calm. Tomas, enraged, turned on his heel and walked quickly out of the room. When he came back fifteen minutes later, Elizabeth Rankin had changed into her white uniform and was sorting through the files of his son.

Bella said it wasn't right.

'That you should have *her* in the house,' she said. 'It's disgusting.'

'She has a diploma,' Tomas said.

'And how are you going to pay her? You don't have any patients.'

This discussion took place in the second floor sitting room after the children were asleep. It was the room where Bella and Abraham used to go to have their privacy.

'At first I thought maybe you didn't recognize her,' Bella started again, 'and so I said to myself, what sort of a joke is this? Maybe she didn't get enough the first time, maybe she has to come back for more.'

'It was an accident,' Tomas said.

'So you forgive her?' Bella challenged. She had a strong, bell-like voice which, when she and Abraham were first married, had been a family joke, one even she would laugh at; but since his death the tone had grown rusty and sepulchral.

Tomas shrugged.

'I don't forgive her,' Bella said.

'It was an accident,' Tomas said. 'She has to work it out of her system.'

'What about me? How am I going to work it out of my system?'

At thirty, Bella was even more beautiful than when she had been married. The children had made her heavy, but grief had carved away the excess flesh. She had jet-black hair and olive skin that her children had both inherited. Now she began to cry and Tomas, as always during these nightly outbursts of tears, went to stand by the window.

'Well?' Bella insisted. 'What do you expect me to do?'

When she had asked this question before, Tomas advised her to go to sleep with the aid of a pill. But now he hesitated. For how many months, for how many years could he tell her to obliterate her evenings in sleeping pills.

'You're the saint,' Bella said. 'You never wanted anyone after Marguerita.'

'I was lucky,' Tomas said. 'I had a family.'

'I have a family.'

'I was older,' Tomas said.

'So,' Bella repeated dully, 'you never did want anyone else.'

Tomas was silent. When Abraham brought her home he had asked Tomas what he thought of her. 'She's very beautiful,' Tomas had said. Abraham had happily agreed. Now she was more beautiful but, Tomas thought, also more stupid.

'It is very hard,' Tomas said, 'for a man my age to fall in love.'

'Your wife died many years ago. . . .'

Tomas shrugged. 'I always felt old,' he said, 'ever since we came to Canada.' All this time he had been standing at the window, and now he made sure his back was turned so that she wouldn't see his tears. The day Abraham had been killed he had cried with her. Since then, even at the funeral, he had refused to let her see his tears. Why? He didn't know. The sight of her, even the smell of her walking into a room, seemed to freeze his heart.

'If there was—' Bella started. She stopped. Tomas knew that he should help her, that she shouldn't have to fight Abraham's ghost *and* his father, but he couldn't bring himself to reach out. It was like watching an ant trying to struggle its way out of a pot of honey.

'If there was someone else,' Bella said. 'Even a job.'

'What can you do?' Tomas asked, but the question was rhetorical; Bella had married Abraham the year after she had finished high school. She couldn't even type.

'I could be your receptionist, instead of that—'

'Nurse,' Tomas interrupted. 'I need a nurse, Bella.'

'I can put a thermometer in someone's mouth,' Bella said. 'Are people going to die while you're next door in the office?'

'A doctor needs a nurse,' Tomas said. 'I didn't invent the rules.'

'There's a rule?'

'It's a custom, Bella.'

He turned from the window.

'And anyway,' Bella said, 'who's going to take care of the children?'

'That's right, the children need a mother.'

'We need Bella in the kitchen making three meals a day so at night she can cry herself to sleep—while the murderer is working off her guilt so at night she can go out and play with the boys, her conscience clean.'

'You don't know what she does at night—'

'You're such a saint,' Bella said suddenly. 'You are such a saint the whole world admires you, do you know that?'

'Bella—'

'The holy Doctor Benares. At seventy-four years of age he ends his retirement and begins work again to provide for his widowed daughter and his two orphaned grandchildren. Has the world ever seen such a man? At the *shul* they're talking about adding a sixth book to the Torah.' She looked at Tomas, and Tomas, seeing her go out of control, could only stand and watch. She was like an ant, he was thinking. Now the ant was at the lip of the pot. It might fall back into the honey, in which case it would drown; or it might escape after all.

'You're such a saint,' Bella said in her knife-edge voice, 'you're such a saint that you think poor Bella just wants to go out and get laid.'

She was teetering on the edge now, Tomas thought.

'You should see your face now,' Bella said. '*Adultery*, you're thinking. *Whore*.'

'It's perfectly normal for a healthy—'

'Oh, healthy *shit!*' Bella screamed. 'I just want to go out. Out, out, *out!*'

She was standing in the doorway, her face beet-red, panting with her fury. Tomas, staying perfectly still, could feel his own answering blush searing the backs of his ears, surrounding his neck like a hot rope.

'Even the saint goes for a walk,' Bella's voice had dropped again. 'Even the saint can spend the afternoon over at Herman Levine's apartment, playing cards and drinking beer.'

Tomas could feel his whole body burning and chafing inside his suit. *The saint*, she was calling him. And what had he done to her?

Offered her and her family a home when they needed it.' Did I make Abraham stay here?' Tomas asked. And then realized, to his shame, that he had said the words aloud.

He saw Bella in the doorway open her mouth until it looked like the muzzle of a cannon. Her lips struggled and convulsed. The room filled with unspoken obscenities.

Tomas reached a hand to touch the veins in his neck. They were so engorged with blood he was choking. He tore at his tie, forced his collar open.

'Oh, God,' Bella moaned.

Tomas was coughing, trying to free his throat and chest. Bella was in the corner of his hazed vision, staring at him in the same detached way he had watched her only a few moments before.

The saint, Tomas was thinking, *she calls me the saint*. An old compartment of his mind suddenly opened, and he began to curse at her in Spanish. Then he turned his back and walked upstairs to his third floor bedroom.

In the small hours of the morning, Tomas Benares was lying in the centre of his marriage bed, looking up at the ceiling of the bedroom and tracing the shadows with his tired eyes. These shadows: cast by the streetlights they were as much a part of his furniture as was the big oak bed, or the matching dressers that presided on either side—still waiting, it seemed, for the miraculous return of Marguerita.

As always he was wearing pyjamas—sewing had been another of Marguerita's talents—and like the rest of his clothes they had been cleaned and ironed by the same Bella who had stood in the doorway of the second floor living room and bellowed and panted at him like an animal gone mad. The windows were open and while he argued with himself Tomas could feel the July night trying to cool his skin, soothe him. But he didn't want to be soothed, and every half hour or so he raised himself on one elbow and reached for a cigarette, flaring the light in the darkness and feeling for a second the distant twin of the young man who had lived in Madrid forty years ago, the young man who had taken lovers (all of them beautiful in retrospect), whispered romantic promises (all of them ridiculous), and then had the good fortune to fall in love and marry a woman so beautiful and devoted that even his dreams could never have imagined her. And yet it was true, as he had told Bella, that when he came to Canada his life had ended. Even lying with Marguerita in this bed he had often been unable to sleep, had often, with this very gesture, lit up a small space in the night in order to feel close to the young man who had been deserted in Spain.

Return? Yes, it had occurred to him after the war was finished. Of course, Franco was still in power then, but it was his country and there were others who had returned. And yet, what would have been the life of an exile returned? The life of a man keeping his lips perpetually sealed, his thoughts to himself; the life of a man who had sold his heart in order to have the sights and smells that were familiar.

Now, Tomas told himself wryly, he was an old man who had lost his heart for nothing at all. Somehow, over the years, it had simply disappeared; like a beam of wood being eaten from the inside, it had dropped away without him knowing it.

Tomas Benares, on his seventy-fourth birthday, had just put out a cigarette and lain back with his head on the white linen pillow to resume his study of the shadows, when he heard the footsteps on the stairs up to his attic. Then there was the creak of the door opening and Bella, in her nightgown and carrying a candle, tiptoed into the room.

Tomas closed his eyes.

The footsteps came closer, he felt the bed sag with her weight. He could hear her breathing in the night, it was soft and slow; and then, as he realized he was holding his own breath, he felt Bella's hand come to rest on his forehead.

He opened his eyes. In the light of the candle her face was like stone, etched and lined with grief.

'I'm sorry,' Tomas said.

'I'm the sorry one. And imagine, on your birthday.'

'That's all right. We've been too closed-in here, since—' Here he hesitated, because for some reason the actual event was never spoken.' Since Abraham died.'

Bella now took her hand away, and Tomas was aware of how cool and soft it had been. Sometimes, decades ago, Marguerita had comforted him in this same way when he couldn't sleep. Her hand on his forehead, fingers stroking his cheeks, his eyes, soothing murmurs until finally he drifted away, a log face-down in the cool water.

'There are still lives to be lived,' Bella was saying. 'The children.'

'The children,' Tomas repeated. Not since Marguerita had there been a woman in this room at night. For many years he used to lock the door when he went to bed, and even now he would still lock it on the rare times he was sick in case someone—who?—should dare to come on a mission of mercy.

'I get tired,' Bella said. Her head drooped and Tomas could see, beyond the outline of her nightdress, the curve of her breasts, the fissure between. A beautiful woman, he had thought before. . . . He was not as saintly as Bella imagined. On certain of the afternoons Bella thought he was at Herman Levine's, Tomas had been visiting a different apartment, that of a widow who was once his patient. She, too, knew what it was like to look at the shadows on the ceiling for one year after another, for one decade after another.

Now Tomas reached out for Bella's hand. Her skin was young and supple, not like the skin of the widow, or his own. There came a time in every person's life, Tomas thought, when the inner soul took a look at the body and said: Enough, you've lost what little beauty you had and now you're just an embarrassment—I'll keep carrying you around, but I refuse to take you seriously. Tomas, aside from some stray moments of vanity, had reached that point long ago; but Bella, he knew, was still in love with her body, still wore her own bones and skin and flesh as a proud inheritance and not an aging inconvenience.

'Happy birthday,' Bella said. She lifted Tomas' hand and pressed it to her mouth. At first, what he felt was the wetness of her mouth. And then it was her tears that flowed in tiny, warm streams around his fingers.

She blew out the candle at the same time that Tomas reached for her shoulder; and then he drew her down so she was lying beside him—her on top of the covers and him beneath, her thick, jet hair folded into his neck and face, her perfume and the scent of her mourning skin wrapped around him like a garden. Chastely he cuddled her to him, her warm breath as soothing as Marguerita's had once been. He felt himself drifting into sleep, and he turned towards the perfume, the garden, turned towards Bella to hold her in his arms the way he used to hold Marguerita in that last exhausted moment of waking.

Bella shifted closer, herself breathing so slowly that Tomas thought she must be already asleep. He remembered, with relief, that his alarm was set for six o'clock; at least they would wake before the children. Then he felt his own hand, as if it had a life of its own, slide in a slow caress from Bella's shoulder to her elbow, touching, in an accidental way, her sleeping breast.

Sleep fled at once, and Tomas felt the sweat spring to his skin. Yet Bella only snuggled closer, breasts and hips flooding through the blanket like warm oceans. Tomas imagined reaching for and lighting a cigarette, the darkness parting once more. A short while ago he had been mourning his youth and now, he reflected, he was feeling as stupid as he ever had. Even with the widow there had been no hesitation. Mostly on his visits they sat in her living room and drank tea; sometimes, by a mutual consent that was arrived at without discussion, they went to her bedroom and performed sex like a warm and comfortable bath. A bath, he thought to himself, that was how he and Bella should become; chaste, warm, comforts to each other in the absence of Abraham. It wasn't right, he now decided, to have frozen his heart to this woman—his daughter-in-law, after all; surely she had a right to love, to the warmth and affection due to a member of the family. *Bella,* he was ready to proclaim, *you are the mother of my grandchildren, the chosen wife of my son. And if you couldn't help shouting, at least you were willing to comfort me.*

Tomas held Bella closer. Her lips, he became aware, were pressed against the hollow of his throat, moving slowly, kissing the skin and now sucking gently at the hairs that curled up from his chest. Tomas let his hand find the back of her neck. There was a delicate valley that led down from her skull past the thick, black hair. He would never have guessed she was built so finely.

Now Bella's weight lifted away for a moment, though her lips stayed glued to his throat, and then suddenly she was underneath the covers, her leg across his groin, her hand sliding up his chest.

Tomas felt something inside of him break. And then, as he raised himself on top of Bella the night, too, broke open; a gigantic black and dreamless mouth, it swallowed them both. He kissed her, tore at her nightgown to suck at her breast, penetrated her so deeply that she gagged; yet though he touched and kissed her every private place; though they writhed on the bed and he felt the cool sweep of her lips as they searched out his every nerve; though he even opened his eyes to see the pleasure on her face, her black hair spread like dead butterflies over Marguerita's linen pillows, her mouth open with repeated climax, the night still swallowed them, obliterated everything as it happened, took them rushing down its hot and endless gorge until Tomas felt like Jonah in the belly of the whale; felt like Jonah trapped in endless flesh and juice. And all he had to escape with was his own sex: like an old sword he brandished it in the blackness, pierced open tunnels, flailed it against the wet walls of his prison.

'Bella, Bella, Bella.' He whispered her name silently. Every time he shaped his lips around her name, he was afraid the darkness of his inner eye would part, and Abraham's face would appear before him. But it didn't happen. Even as he scratched Bella's back, bit her neck, penetrated her from behind, he taunted himself with the idea that somewhere in this giant night Abraham must be waiting. His name was on Tomas' lips: Abraham his son. How many commandments was he breaking? Tomas wondered, pressing Bella's breasts to his parched cheeks.

Tomas felt his body, like a starved man at a banquet, go out of control. Kissing, screwing, holding, stroking: everything he did Bella wanted, did back, invented variations upon. For one brief second he thought that Marguerita had never been like this, then his mind turned on itself and he was convinced that this *was* Marguerita, back from the dead with God's blessing to make up, in a few hours, a quarter century of lost time.

But as he kissed and cried over his lost Marguerita, the night began to lift and the first light drew a grey mask on the window.

By this time he and Bella were lying on their stomachs, side by side, too exhausted to move.

The grey mask began to glow, and as it did Tomas felt the dread rising in him. Surely God Himself would appear to take His revenge, and with that thought Tomas realized he had forgotten his own name. He felt his tongue searching, fluttering between his teeth, tasting again his own sweat and Bella's fragrant juices. He must be, he thought, in Hell. He had died and God, to drive his wicked soul crazy, had given him this dream of his own daughter-in-law, his dead son's wife.

'Thank you, Tomas.'

No parting kiss, just soft steps across the carpet and then one creak as she descended the stairs. Finally, the face of his son appeared. It was an infant's face, staring uncomprehendingly at its father.

Tomas sat up. His back was sore, his kidneys felt trampled, one arm ached, his genitals burned. He stood up to go to the bathroom and was so dizzy that for a few moments he had to cling to the bedpost with his eyes closed. Then, limping and groaning, he crossed the room. When he got back to the bed there was no sign that Bella had been there—but the sheets were soaked as they sometimes were after a restless night.

He collapsed on the covers and slept dreamlessly until the alarm went off. When he opened his eyes his first thought was of Bella, and when he swung out of bed there was a sharp sting in his groin. But as he dressed he was beginning to speculate, even to hope, that the whole episode had been a dream.

A few minutes later, downstairs at breakfast, Tomas found the children sitting alone at the table. Between them was a sealed envelope addressed to 'Dr. Tomas Benares, M.D.'

'Dear Tomas,' the letter read, 'I have decided that it is time for me to seek my own life in another city. Miss Rankin has already agreed to take care of the children for as long as necessary. I hope you will all understand me and remember that I love you. As always, Bella Benares.'

On his birthday, his garden always seemed to reach that explosive point that marked the height of summer. No matter what the weather, it was this garden that made up for all other deprivations, and the fact that his ninety-fourth birthday was gloriously warm and sunny made it doubly perfect for Tomas to spend the day outside.

Despite the perfect blessing of the sky, as Tomas opened his eyes from that long doze that had carried the sun straight into the afternoon, he felt a chill in his blood, the knowledge that Death, that companion he'd grown used to, almost fond of, was starting to play his tricks. Because sitting in front of him, leaning towards him as if the worlds of waking and sleeping had been forced together, was Bella herself.

'Tomas, Tomas, it's good to see you. It's Bella.'

'I know,' Tomas said. His voice sounded weak and grumpy; he coughed to clear his throat.

'Happy birthday, Tomas.'

He pushed his hand across his eyes to rid himself of this illusion.

'Tomas, you're looking so good.'

Bella: her face was fuller now, but the lines were carved deeper, bracketing her full lips and corrugating her forehead. And yet she was still young, amazing: her movements were lithe and supple; her jet-black hair was streaked, but still fell thick and wavy to her shoulders; her eyes still burned, and when she leaned forward to take his hand between her own the smell of her, dreams and remembrances, came flooding back.

'Tomas, are you glad to see me?'

'You look so young, Bella.' This in a weak voice, but Tomas' throat-clearing cough was lost in the rich burst of Bella's laughter. Tomas, seeing her head thrown back and the flash of her strong teeth, could hardly believe that he, a doddering old man, whose knees were covered by a blanket in the middle of summer, had only a few years ago actually made love to this vibrant woman. Now she was like a racehorse in voracious maturity.

'Bella, the children.'

'I know, Tomas. I telephoned Margaret; she's here. And I telephoned Joseph, too. His secretary said he was at a meeting all afternoon, but that he was coming here for dinner.'

'Bella, you're looking wonderful, truly wonderful.' Tomas had his hand hooked into hers and, suddenly aware that he was half-lying in his chair, was using her weight to try to lever himself up.

Instantly Bella was on her feet, her arm solicitously around his back, pulling him into position. She handled his weight, Tomas thought, like the weight of a baby. He felt surrounded by her, overpowered by her smell, her vitality, her cheery goodwill. *Putan*, Tomas whispered to himself. What a revenge. Twenty years ago he had been her equal; and now, suddenly—what had happened? Death was in the garden; Tomas could feel his presence, the familiar visitor turned trickster. And then Tomas felt some of his strength returning, strength in the form of contempt for Bella, who had waited twenty years to come back to this house; contempt for Death, who waited until a man was an ancient, drooling husk to test his will.

'You're the marvel, Tomas. Elizabeth says you work every day in the garden. How do you do it?'

'I spit in Death's face,' Tomas rasped. Now he was beginning to feel more himself again, and he saw that Bella was offering him a cup of coffee. All night he had slept, and then again in the daytime. What a way to spend a birthday! But coffee would heat the blood, make it run faster. He realized that he was famished.

Bella had taken out a package of cigarettes now, and offered one to Tomas. He shook his head, thinking again how he had declined in these last years. Now Joseph wouldn't let him smoke in bed, even when he couldn't sleep. He was only allowed to smoke when there was someone else in the room, or when he was outside in the garden.

'Tomas. I hope you don't mind I came back. I wanted to see you again while—while we could still talk.'

Tomas nodded. So the ant had escaped the honey pot after all, and ventured into the wide world. Now it was back, wanting to tell its adventures to the ant who had stayed home. Perhaps they hadn't spent that strange night making love after all; perhaps in his bed they had been struggling on the edge of the pot, fighting to see who would fall back and who would be set free.

'So,' Bella said. 'It's been so long.'

Tomas, watching her, refusing to speak, felt control slowly moving towards him again. He sat up straighter, brushed the blanket off his legs.

'Or maybe we should talk tomorrow,' Bella said, 'when you're feeling stronger.'

'I feel strong.' His voice surprised even himself—not the weak squawk it sometimes was now, a chicken's squeak hardly audible over the telephone, but firm and definite, booming out of his chest the way it used to. Bella: she had woken him up once, perhaps she would once more.

He could see her moving back, hurt; but then she laughed again, her rich throaty laugh that Tomas used to hear echoing through the house when his son was still alive. He looked at her left hand; Abraham's modest engagement ring was still in place, but beside it was a larger ring, a glowing bloodstone set in a fat gold band. 'Tomas,' Bella was saying, 'you really are a marvel, I swear you're going to live to see a hundred.'

'One hundred and twenty-three,' Tomas said. 'Almost all of the Benares men live to be one hundred and twenty-three.'

For a moment, the lines deepened again in Bella's face, and Tomas wished he could someday learn to hold his tongue. A bad habit that should have long ago been entered in his diary.

'You will,' Bella finally said. Her voice had the old edge. '*Two* hundred and twenty-three, you'll dance on all our graves.'

'Bella.'

'I shouldn't have come.'

'The children—'

'They'll be glad to see me, Tomas, they always are.'

'Always?'

'Of course. Did you think I'd desert my own children?'

Tomas shook his head.

'Oh, I left, Tomas, I left. But I kept in touch. I sent them letters and they wrote me back. That woman helped me.'

'Elizabeth?'

'I should never have called her a murderer, Tomas. It was an accident.'

'They wrote you letters without telling me?'

Bella stood up. She was a powerful woman now, fullfleshed and in her prime; even Death had slunk away in the force of her presence. 'I married again, Tomas. My husband and I lived in Seattle. When Joseph went to university there, he lived in my home.'

'Joseph lived with you?'

'My husband's dead now, Tomas, but I didn't come for your pity. Or your money. I just wanted you to know that I would be in Toronto again, seeing my own children, having a regular life.'

'A regular life,' Tomas repeated. He felt dazed, dangerously weakened. Death was in the garden again, he was standing behind Bella, peeking out from behind her shoulders and making faces. He struggled to his feet. Only Bella could save him now, and yet he could see the fear on her face as he reached for her.

'Tomas, I—'

'You couldn't kill me!' Tomas roared. His lungs filled his chest like an eagle in flight. His flowering hedges, his roses, his carefully groomed patio snapped into focus. He stepped towards Bella, his balance perfect, his arm rising. He saw her mouth open, her lips begin to flutter. Beautiful but stupid, Tomas thought; some things never change. At his full height he was still tall enough to put his arm around her and lead her to the house.

'It's my birthday.' His voice boomed with the joke. 'Let me offer you a drink to celebrate your happy return.'

His hand slid from her shoulder to her arm; the skin was smooth as warm silk. Her face turned towards his: puzzled, almost happy, and he could feel the heat of her breath as she prepared to speak.

'Of course I forgive you,' Tomas said.

Gabriella Goliger

Gabriella Goliger was born in Merano, Italy, in 1949. She has twice been nominated for the Journey Prize and in 1997 was a cowinner. In 1993 she won the Prism International Short Fiction Award. Her first book, *Song of Ascent* (2000), is a collection of linked short stories exploring the lives of a family of Montreal Jews who lives in the shadow of the Holocaust. The book has won the Upper Canada Brewing Company Writers' Craft Award (2001). Goliger's work has also been published in *Coming Attractions* (1998), *Best New American Voices* (2000), *Quintet*, *Parchment: Contemporary Canadian Jewish Writing*, and *Canadian Forum*. She has lived in Montreal, Israel, and Canada's Arctic and now lives in Ottawa. 'Maladies of the Inner Ear' first appeared in *Parchment* in 1997; it combines flashbacks from life in Germany with contemporary life in Toronto.

Gabriella Goliger

Maladies of the Inner Ear

In the Hauptmarktplatz outside Gerda's window all is confusion—the whine of engines, slam of metal doors, footsteps, shouts, murmurs, entreaties, cries. She presses her face into the pillow, but the din continues. Now the noises order themselves into a steady rhythm, a thick *tramp, tramp, tramp* of a thousand boots on flagstones; they approach, recede, approach, recede. Sickening as this is, what follows is worse. For now all is still except for the splash of water from the fountain in the middle of the square. It is a tall, spire-shaped masterpiece of intricate stonework, this fountain—the town's showpiece with its tier upon tier of stone figures from the 12th century. Cascades of water run down the faces and robes of saints, prophets, popes and noblemen, bathe their stone eyes. Inches from her ear, it seems, water pummels the ground with merciless *smacks*. She tosses her head sideways. No escape.

In the bedroom of her luxury apartment in Toronto's Forest Hill, Dr. Gerda Levittson is finally fully awake and staring at a familiar trapezoid of reflected light on the ceiling. The cacophony of the Hauptmarktplatz is over, replaced by a shapeless, nameless roaring. Something like a sea is in her head. It thrashes against the walls of her skull with dizzying, deafening force. It is what Gerda calls her demon and she senses its laughter as she drowns and drowns in noise, is sucked under by foul despair.

With effort, she pushes herself into sitting position. She fumbles in the drawer for her hearing aid and pushes the cool moulded plastic into her ear. As she raps with her knuckles, testing, on the bedside table, this blessed sound from the outer world penetrates. *Tap, tap*. A message of hope, calm and real. She switches on the radio. Late-night jazz. Muffled trumpet notes above the waves.

Outside, the night is black beyond the glow of the streetlamp. It is 2:16 A.M. The sleeping pills that were supposed to deliver her into morning haven't worked. Time, perhaps, to administer a higher dosage. Insomnia is the worst part of the affliction that has tormented her for the past two months. Same for everyone. This fact is confirmed not only by the medical journals and textbooks, but by the sighs and moans of fellow group members. Those like herself, who are new to the misery, have the pale, strained faces and nervous tics of insomniacs.

Each one hears something different. Mr. Somerville, self-appointed chairperson of the group, hears the distant but persistent drone of an airplane. Lucy hears crickets and sometimes, on a very bad day, the sound of smashing china. Bob hears the crackle of radio static, as if his head were caught between channels. 'I keep wanting to adjust the dial,' he says with a wry grin, while his fingers twitch.

Gerda switches on the bedside table lamp and attempts to read more of her novel, but the words swim on the page and the clamour worsens. Learn to live with it, they say in her group. Learn to relax and accept the rushing, roaring wind in the cave as if it were as normal and natural as the ticking of a clock. So it abates, becomes background noise and you can hear yourself think. Interesting phrase. Never, until now, has she realized what it meant, or what its opposite might mean. The steady inner voice that has kept her company for 75 years is now gone, roughly expelled. She won't find it again until the dawn spreads its calm, grey light through her apartment and solid edges reappear—top of the dresser, silver frame around the family portrait circa 1932—father, mother, Ludwig and herself, a plump, bespectacled adolescent.

Friday nights back in Germany. The dinner table laden with gilt-edged serving dishes that offered up smells of roast chicken, dumplings, challah and wine. The family kept the commandments, but in moderation, according to their liberal faith, and in the time-honoured, decorum-loving way of the German Jewish bourgeoisie. On Saturday, although Gerda's father closed the store, he went in to do accounts in the shuttered gloom or to sort through order forms and samples of material—tweeds from England, silks from

Japan. On Friday evening, they all gathered around the dining room table, lit candles, murmured blessings in Hebrew and German and tucked into the courses that the maid put before them. Her father with his stern bulldog face sat distracted, stealing glances at the neatly folded newspaper at his elbow. Her mother, thin and wan in the light of the Sabbath candles, was already showing the signs of illness. The family was able to see her safely to her grave shortly after the first volley of boycotts and decrees and before the Law for the Protection of German Blood and German Honour.

Her brother, Ludwig, was 26, a teacher at the leading progressive, secular school. He was remote and handsome with a neat moustache and wavy hair trained back to show off his high, noble forehead. With his confident laugh, he teased her about her lessons, what she didn't remember or hadn't yet learned. He recited Heine: ' "Oh Germany, distant love of mine . . ." Well, what comes next?' Her cheeks flushed with indignation. She could have told him about the stages of photosynthesis, but he asked the wrong questions.

Her father mumbled his abbreviated version of *Birkat Hamazon*, 'Grace after Meals.' 'Lord our God . . . sustains the whole world . . . food to all creatures . . . may the Merciful One reign. . . .'

Before the amen, and despite entreaties from their mother, Ludwig was up from his chair and dashing toward the hall.

'What a way to behave. You'll spoil your digestion.'

He sat his fedora on his head, blew a kiss and was gone. They knew he was off to the Hauptmarktplatz where young people gathered on Friday and Saturday nights to exchange news and argue politics. But mostly they went to flirt and to court or be courted. Arm in arm, newly matched couples paraded around the perimeter of the square, while those still single clustered in small groups by the fountain. Ludwig was in great demand.

It is dark. It is the middle of the night. Outside, beyond Forest Hill's stately homes, the woods of the ravine lie still in the heavy air. The sweet, rotting smell of late August wafts through the window. She would like to walk outside right now, in her nightgown, into the embrace of the bathwater-warm air but . . . muggers and maniacs. This too is new, this timidity. A few months ago, Dr. Gerda Levittson, despite her age, her deafness, her cane, walked the most secluded paths of the park whenever she pleased. Former patients, whose faces she always remembered although she forgot their names, greeted her with delight. 'It's just not the same since you retired,' an old-timer would say. 'The young ones these days don't know how to listen.'

She went once a month to Rinaldo's Hair Design to have her favourite colour, Sunset Glow, reapplied by Rinaldo's deft hands. Afterward, as she stumped along through the crowds in Yorkville, she chuckled to herself at a passerby's occasional startled glance or indulgent smile. This wonderful parade of fashionable young people in their leathers and silks and studied indifference.

But her heart is no longer in Rinaldo's and Yorkville. The hairdryer bothers her, the smells and most of all being confined in the chair with the hot, sticky plastic apron tied tight around her neck. She wonders whether, beneath the cooing encouragement, Rinaldo has been laughing at her all these years. Her real colour, yellowish grey, has grown back in, pushing the band of orange-red away from her head and looking, for the first few weeks, like a gaudy, badly arranged bandanna.

She reaches under the bed for her notepad and pen to work on the little talk on medications she is preparing for her group.

'*Tinnitus*,' she has written. 'From the Latin, meaning to toll or ring like a bell. It can be almost any kind of noise—a hissing, whistling, crackling, grinding, roaring, thrumming, clicking, chirping, pulsing, rattling, booming (or any combination of these) or even a tune, endlessly, distractingly repeated. It is a symptom, not a disease. Some possible causes: an increase of fluid in the inner ear, pressure on nerve fibres due to infections, tumours, multiple sclerosis, muscular spasms, circulation problems, reactions to drugs, caffeine, alcohol, loud noises, hormonal changes, anxiety, depression, shock.'

Two-thirty A.M. The endless night creeps on its belly.

She reaches for the telephone, longs to hear her name spoken by a friend, words to anchor her, but who at this hour . . . ? Although Hannah Birnbaum in Montreal might be willing to talk, it would be Ernst who would answer the phone, dazed, worried, then somewhat annoyed by her assurances that everything was all right, that she just wanted to chat. And Hannah would be distressed beyond all proportion because her Gerda had always been the strong one. Months ago, Hannah had phoned, depressed and lonely. Gerda, setting out for her afternoon ramble, had suggested joining a group, though she knew full well Hannah was incapable of reaching out to strangers. Later she called back and apologized for her curtness and they reminisced about old times, the youth group in Germany—the outings, flirtations, misadventures.

'Remember,' Hannah said, 'the day I knocked over the bench during the talk on kibbutz life? I almost howled with laughter!'

Hannah had been lovely then, innocent and bumbling as a calf, driven by a restless yearning for nature. On outings in the country she trembled with rapture at the sight of a tumbled-down wall overgrown with wildflowers, while Gerda collected botanical specimens.

Before Hitler, and for many months afterward, the youth group had been about camaraderie, purpose and fun, an escape from cold shoulders and outbreaks of violence on the streets. Serious business, yes, but only to a point. Anyway, who took the Zionist rhetoric literally? Not even the leaders who wrote the manifestos. Ludwig, of course, had always scoffed at the 'little ghetto in Palestine' and at propaganda that stressed divisions between Germans and Jews. One learned to shut out ugliness, to make much of small triumphs, to bear insults—a complaint about the garlicky smell of Jews in the tram—with head held high.

As the noose tightened, friends, one by one, departed for Palestine and America, but Gerda resisted the temptation to join them. Despite the strict quotas, she still hoped for a place at the university and, besides, she was needed at home to help care for her mother, suffering through the last stages of tuberculosis. When everyone, not just the young folks, began talking of emigration, havens had become harder to find.

At what point did she forget to think about Ludwig? Was it when she and her father walked in a daze down the platform at Union Station? It had been sheer luck that they got out when they did. They had been like all the other lost souls without papers, scurrying along the streets, ducking their heads when a Brownshirt appeared. Then, a miracle: a visitor's permit to England and, later, boat tickets to Canada from a cousin, Sheldon, in Toronto.

The last time they saw Ludwig, he was in his cellar flat in Berlin, chain-smoking at the kitchen table, his blue eyes confused and sad. A brief, proud light flared in him when her father tried to persuade him to leave. He could not face more grovelling in the anterooms of consulates. He was determined to wait the Nazis out.

Somehow Ludwig slipped from her mind and, at that moment, it would seem, a cattle car slammed shut. Insane thought, outrageous and utterly symptomatic, according to the psychologists. She cannot bring herself to think beyond the slamming of the door. It shuts and her mind retreats and she is relieved by her lack of morbidity and she is aghast at her cowardice and it goes around and around. A textbook case. Still, she searches for the exact moment she forgot him. She recalls the old apartment on Bathurst Street, her father's bedroom and her own next door, where the radiators in winter gave off too much heat and she sat near an open window letting gusts of wind keep her awake.

She loved the lonely night hours. In those days Gerda Levittson, the medical student living in her father's house, itched for eleven o'clock, for the dreary Friday-evening Sabbath ritual to be over and for her father to plod down the corridor to his bed. Then, laying a towel along the bottom of the door to prevent light from spilling into the hall and arousing her father's peevish anger, she switched on the desk lamp. That fine, intense glare on the printed page. She tunnelled into the text, noted, memorized, added knowledge, brick by brick, to her solid foundations. The late-night stillness, immense and calm, buoyed her. She lifted her head from her books and felt it press against her. Solitude was a muscular embrace.

Friday nights in the Bathurst Street apartment. She and her father sat crowded amid the serving dishes in the dining room, which was cluttered with unnecessary sideboards and chairs. When did her father go back to the strict orthodoxy of his childhood? After the Red Cross telegram, or before? One day, when she had come back from a lab, a gleaming set of crockery, uncontaminated and ready for the new kosher regime, stood on the kitchen counter. A long list of injunctions went with it. On the Sabbath she was not to turn on a light, not to tear a page, not to put pen to paper, not to ride, not to carry any object—not even a book—outside the house. A prayer for rising and for lying down to sleep. A benediction for hearing good tidings and for hearing bad. A chain-link fence of rituals and commandments that invested the minutiae of daily life with enormous significance and kept everything outside at bay. The quaver in her father's voice as he laid down the law made her go along with it, while she planned her respites and escapes. How Ludwig might have teased and waggled a forefinger. She could hear his voice: 'Have you said the benediction for slicing into a cadaver?'

Her father cooked and cleaned while Gerda went to her classes at the university. On Fridays she had to be home in time for the lighting of the candles. When she arrived he was wearing a velvet skullcap—special for *Shabbas*—on his bald, liver-spotted head and it made his jowly face look more withered and pathetic than ever.

He fussed, he shuffled between dining room and kitchen preparing the table—the two challah loaves and their cloth covers, the saltcellar, prayer book, dishes and cutlery. His aged hand held the *kiddush* cup in the air, the dark wine trembling at the brim as he recited the blessing in a gravelly voice. He did the *motzi*, blessing over bread. Slowly his stiff fingers tore off a piece of challah for her, sprinkled salt and placed it by her plate.

When she opened her mouth to say something, his hand flew to his face in an alarmed gesture. No talking between *kiddush* and *motzi*, she remembered. As she ate her salted bread, he hurried to the kitchen to bring out the meal. A pale chicken broth with bits of parsley and droplets of fat, just as his own mother used to make. Roast chicken, potato dumplings, peas and beets. The same dinner repeated itself every Friday, down to the canned dessert peaches and vanilla wafers, imported from Israel. He munched in silence, methodically, without a sign of pleasure or appetite. After sopping the last bit of gravy from his plate with his bread, he launched into a rambling monologue about arcane family customs.

'In your aunt's house they took their salt from a little crystal dish. Do you remember? No, you were too young. A silver-and-crystal dish, part of a set she had. They took a pinch between forefinger and thumb and sprinkled it on the challah. Like this, see? My mother thought it uncivilized, everyone dipping their fingers in the same dish. The thing is, now I don't know what is right. . . .' His voice trailed off, thin and plaintive.

'Ask a rabbi,' Gerda said, her eye on the clock.

'*Ach*, the rabbis here. Pollacks and Russians. They know things, of course. But it's not the same as a rabbi from home.'

Finally, 'Grace after Meals': '. . . for your covenant, which you sealed in our flesh; for your Torah . . . for your laws . . . for life, grace and kindness . . .' His voice was a flat monotone. He couldn't carry the tune at the singing parts, but did not seem to expect her to join in. At the last words he rapped on the table. '*Pflicht getan*.' Duty done.

'Insomnia,' she writes in her notebook, 'is the most troublesome side effect. Medications: anti-spasmodic clonazepan (brand name Rivotril) . . . the tricyclic amitriptyline . . . a specialist from New Zealand prescribes an anti-convulsive . . .'

The group members are proud to have her in their midst. They look to her for answers. 'I know nothing more than you do. There is little substantial research. . . .' No matter. They describe symptoms and wait for her answers. Often she walks out of the meeting more dazed and battered than when she entered. Still she regards the meetings every second Thursday as a necessity. They are fellow shipwrecked travellers. They know, they hear. In their strained smiles and anxious eyes she sees the reflection of her own pain. It is as necessary to be in contact with them as to locate familiar objects in her room after troubled sleep. She envies them their simple-minded faith. They are eager to try herbal remedies, sound-masking devices, reflexology, colour therapy, acupuncture, although, from what Gerda can tell, the results of these treatments are highly inconclusive.

'Chronic *tinnitus* is chronic pain. Our nervous systems are not adapted to absorb the impact of a constant stimulus. Internally generated sound, from which there is no escape, creates an abnormal situation that can call forth the production of noradrenaline, a neuro-chemical that primes our responses. . . .'

The nerve endings in the inner ear quiver. They cannot stop. The liquid around them is in perpetual motion.

One of the more bizarre theories to float out of the pages of the *Völkischer Beobachter* maintained that you could distinguish Jew from

Aryan by the shape of the left ear. Ludwig snorted with delight when he read this. He had his photo taken in left profile and sent it, under the pseudonym Reiner Deutschmann, to the editor. An example of an impeccable Aryan ear. They printed it, with thanks. Ludwig was on top of the world.

The telegram from the British Red Cross was as brief and final as words on a tombstone. 'Ludwig Levittson: last seen Berlin February 1943 boarding transport. Destination eastern territories. Regret no further information at this time.' A scrap of newsprint paper with three badly typed lines, large 'X's over the mistakes and the date on top—September 5, 1946. The end of almost eight years of anxious inquiries, nightmarish rumours, a clutching at hopeful signs and growing certainty of doom. She put it in the file folder marked 'Red Cross,' which she slipped to the back of the drawer.

Her father had sat hunched at the end of his bed, his hands limp in his lap, tears dripping from his nose and chin. First he'd waved the brutal truth away. The telegram was vague, so sparse in detail. What kind of transport and which part of the East, could the Red Cross not find out, could it not have been possible . . . ? Gerda shook her head, grim, determined to end this futile hanging on, this water torture of letters to officials and their carefully worded replies. Finally, he crumpled up and wept, resigned, helpless, exhausted, unrestrained. While horrified at their abundance, Gerda envied him his simple flood of tears. It seemed he would cry the life out of himself. She stroked his shoulders and head, rocked him in her arms, averting her face from his wet, loose cheeks, his odour of age and despair.

As he wept, she planned the days ahead. Her first term of medical school was about to begin. She could not afford to miss a lecture, but could put off long study sessions for a couple of weeks while she kept him company until the worst was over. Then she must drive on with her own life's course.

During the months that followed, she prepared for mid-term exams. She ignored the silence that fell and the burst of chatter that rose up again like a wall when she walked into the med school cafeteria. All those male voices linked in camaraderie and common disdain. She bent her head, cheeks burning, toward her books.

At night, when her overcharged brain would not shut down, she would pick up the anatomy text at her bedside table. She'd trace the course of blood through the body, recite the soothing names of the heart's chambers: superior vena cava, inferior vena cava, atrium, atrio-ventricular valve. Aorta to arteries to minute capillaries where the blood cells push through, one by one by one, transform themselves through intricate chemical reactions, then carry on their timeless, perfect journey back to the heart.

Words roll and buckle on the page. Metal gates *crash*, *smash* against tender membranes already whipped raw. Noise is pain is noise and she is buried in it, six feet under, mouth, nose, ears stuffed with *smash*, *crash* and the *yowl* of the dead. This is not madness, it's a condition, it's all the same.

'Enough now. Stop.' Her frail, cracked voice takes aim at the bedlam. 'Enough of this nonsense.'

She reads aloud. She recites: '*Yitgadal v'yitkadash sh'mei raba . . . Im eshkachekh Yerushalayim* . . . If I forget you, o Jerusalem . . .' Whatever words come to hand until she stands solid again above the waves. '*Tinnitus*, from the Latin, meaning to ring or toll like a bell . . .'

The young ones these days don't know how to listen. Was she a good listener? Was she, really? She certainly knew how to translate the anguished, but vague, complaints into precise symptoms. The files on Mr. X grew fat. Symptoms noted, tests ordered, results collected, medications prescribed, side effects noted, medications changed.

Another scorcher, the radio announcer promises. The sky, glimpsed through the curtains of the kitchen window, has gone from black to milky grey. Streetlights wink, bring the daytime world into faint but unmistakable relief. Later on, the street will lie in dusty, yellow heat, but for now a pleasant breeze parts the kitchen curtains and caresses her face. The ocean roar is beginning to subside. Gerda sips scalding hot chamomile tea to soothe her stomach, which threatens to heave bile. Every bodily function now—a stubborn bowel movement, a fit of tears—can start up the tidal wave in her head. She takes small, wary sips. The stomach above all is a capricious beast that must be treated with respect.

Across the hall, she hears the soft click of a neighbour's door.

Gerda opens her own door to greet Mrs. Paulsen, a pink-cheeked woman about Gerda's age, but younger looking, who is on her way to the garbage chute. Mrs. Paulsen's eyes, limpid and innocent, show that she takes the calm around her for granted. Her movements cause no reverberations. She could not imagine the shroud of echoes Gerda is buried beneath, although she has clicked her tongue and shaken her head over Gerda's ailments.

Back in the apartment, Gerda listens to the radio announcers, a man and a woman, who chatter about tie-ups on the 401 and a stalled truck that's spilled its load of hamburger buns onto the Don Valley Parkway. Morning sounds. A miracle of solid ground through the waves.

Who is she to deserve miracles?

She closes her eyes for just one instant, her attention wanders and look what happens. A row of naked, emaciated men totter above a ditch, topple down into the cold ooze, their mouths open but soundless, their eyes crying out in unspeakable horror. If she had kept that fine-tooled mind more alert, if she had listened for the clanging of the gate . . .

She continues writing: 'Some people find relief through various treatments . . . masking devices that generate white noise . . . cassette tapes with the sounds of nature, ocean waves breaking on a shore.'

There is no cure. Slowly, the mind flattens itself, adjusts, yields to the pounding wash. Slowly, sound and silence are one. A firmament appears in the midst of the waters.

Aryeh Lev Stollman

Born in Detroit in 1954, Aryeh Lev Stollman and his family soon moved across the border to Windsor, Ontario, where he grew up. He attended medical school at McGill University and is currently a neuroradiologist at Mount Sinai Medical Center in New York City. His first novel, *The Far Euphrates* (1997), has been translated into German, Dutch, Italian, and Portuguese and was an American Library Association Notable Book of 1997, a Los Angeles Times Book Review Recommended Book of the Year, and winner of the Wilbur Award and Lambda Literary Award. His second novel is *The Illuminated Soul* (2002). Stollman's short fiction and essays have appeared in the *Fiddlehead*, *Story*, *American Short Fiction*, *Southwest Review*, *Forward*, and *Yale Review* (1996), from which the following story is taken. It demonstrates how the Holocaust intrudes in the lives of a Canadian family a generation later, as a Canadian son looks for answers to mysteries in postwar Germany.

Aryeh Lev Stollman

Die Grosse Liebe

'*The Great Love* was her best movie. I felt so wonderful listening to her and watching her, no matter how many times I saw it.'

As always in our house, the night my mother described the movie in which her favorite actress starred, she spoke the language of her Berlin youth. Not the jumbled clacking of the crowded Scheunenviertel, noisy with the unsteady tongues of immigrants, but the soft, cultivated tones of the beautiful Grunewald, its grand villas overflowing with art and books and music, its gardens, its lawns sweeping down to quiet lakes.

When she pronounced the film's title—*Die grosse Liebe*—it sounded to me, a boy born and growing up in the vast present tense of Ontario, so unlike the marvelous emotion it was meant to convey. Despite the gentle refinement of my mother's voice, that sublime sentiment seemed almost grating and unpleasant. The dense language of my home, the elaborate syntax of my parents' distant, and to me, unknown lives, had suddenly become vaguely unsettling.

The revelation that my mother even had a *Lieblingsschauspielerin*—a favorite actress—was a complete surprise and came on the evening after my father's funeral. My mother had never spoken of actors or movies before. As far as I had known, neither of my parents ever went to the movies, although I was allowed to do so. And, except for one other occasion, the days leading up to my father's funeral were the only times I could remember my mother leaving the vicinity of our house. I never thought to question this behavior. I had simply accepted it as an aspect of her personality. It was never discussed or explained, and I was rather comforted by her generally quiet and steady presence in my childhood world.

I was only twelve at the time of my father's unexpected death and bewildered by my mother's strange disclosure. She had never been talkative. But she had, on that exceptional night in my life, suddenly opened a hidden door and—I could not know it then—would permanently and just as abruptly close it again.

'I saw *The Great Love* maybe fifty times the year it premiered. That was the year I stayed with the Retters. Herr Retter took me to his theater, the Gloria Palace, whenever I was sad and needed to get away. I learned every song by heart.' My mother smiled and caressed one slender hand with the other. 'Sometimes I helped with the projector. I was very mechanical.' Here my mother paused and frowned. 'The Retters had a daughter my age. Ingrid had dark brown eyes and long black hair. She was a big chatterbox and caused a lot of trouble. I was the one with blue eyes and blond hair.' My mother gently smoothed a lock of this same hair from her forehead, shook her head, and smiled again. 'Of course, like most girls we dreamed of becoming actresses.'

When my mother described the movie in which her favorite actress starred, and whose songs she had memorized, we were sitting together on the living room sofa. The last visitor, an old woman neighbor, had just left. My parents had kept mainly to themselves, and there had been few guests at the house after the funeral. Those who did make the visit included several neighbors, the old woman among them, and some business acquaintances who knew my father from his jewelry store. The old woman had silently helped my mother put away the food that had been set up on the dining room sideboard and then clean up the kitchen. Before she left she took my mother's hand: 'I'm very sorry, dear. It's a terrible tragedy. But God is the true judge and we must learn to accept His will.' My mother looked at her blankly and said, 'Thank you.'

Years later, when my mother herself was gravely ill, I took a leave from college to take care of her. She would not allow herself to be admitted to a hospital or permit strangers into the house. I asked her about the old woman. I wondered whatever became of her. My mother lifted her head off her pillow and gave me a surprised look. 'Oh, no. There was never such a person that day.'

'But there was, Mother. She was our neighbor. I even remember what she said—'

'No, you must be mistaken. And now, Joseph, I'm quite tired.'

But I knew I was not mistaken and the old woman really did exist, because I remembered her from that day she helped my mother after my father's funeral. Recently, however, now that I am well into my forties, approaching the ages when my parents died, and I think back to this late exchange with my mother, I find myself increasingly alarmed. I can no longer conjure up a single one of the old woman's features. Did she have a long or a short nose? What color were her eyes? How did she wear her hair? I recall only a sense of her frail, ghostly movements, the vague disruption of the still atmosphere of our house, and her parting words. The details of our house on that day I remember vividly—the carved oak sideboard in the dining room where the food had been set out on silver platters, the speckled green tiles on the kitchen floor over which the old woman passed, and the claret moiré fabric with which the living room sofa was upholstered.

'In *The Great Love* she played a beautiful singer named Hanna. Oma—whom you never met—was named Hanna, too.' My mother had rarely referred to my grandparents except to say proudly that they had been *angesehene Leute*—highly educated and cultured. Her father, she once told me, had composed art songs in the style of Hugo Wolf and no doubt would have been famous had he not died, as she put it, *so vorzeitig*—so prematurely. 'If you had been a girl, I would certainly have named you Hanna.'

The night she told me about her favorite actress in her favorite movie, my mother never looked directly at me. Her eyes skimmed the top of my head and watched the pale blue walls of our living room as if she might be seeing the very same movie, projected there by memory's light. My initial unease at her elaborate reminiscence gave way to an odd comfort and excitement in hearing her talk to me at length as she might have with my father, even if she was in her own world. I had never before considered the mystery of my mother's youth and was now fascinated. I listened carefully and quietly.

While I was growing up, my parents' extreme personal reserve never seemed odd; rather, their conversations seemed dignified and appropriate. In their leisure they read books or listened to records, mostly lieder and opera. We never went away on vacations. Often they spoke about my father's jewelry store. In the background I would hear references to 'a wedding ring with six quadrillions' or 'the young woman who bought the emerald pheasant brooch.' Several nights a week my mother would go over the store receipts. She sat quietly at a small mahogany secretary in the den. A stack of papers would be piled neatly in front of her while she tapped her forehead with the eraser end of a pencil.

Somehow I grew up understanding that one did not ask questions of a personal nature, even to one's parents. I knew that surrounding every human being was a sacred wall of dignity and privacy. My parents never asked such questions as 'What are you thinking, Joseph?' or 'What did you do today?' They never entered my room without knocking. 'Joseph, darf ich eintreten?' my mother would say if she needed to do any cleaning. As far as I could tell she never entered my room when I was out of the house. And I am still taken aback, unsettled, observing people who talk too much, chatter, ask question after question.

My mother told the story of *The Great Love* in extensive detail. After her death, I would increasingly find myself reviewing in my mind's eye the scene of my mother's greatest confidence. When I tried to replay this night in my mind, I would realize to my great dismay that I had forgotten some small detail, some tangential plot line my mother described, and with it, I felt, some irretrievable clue to her life. Sometimes I would experience physical symptoms when my memory failed me. I would break out in a sweat, breathe rapidly, or feel dizzy. And now, years later, the memory of my mother's description is further clouded by my persistent and pathetic attempts to patch those gaps, to move through the doorway she had so briefly opened that evening.

The plot of *The Great Love* was, with its predictable twists and turns, period clichés, and movie-land formulas, fairly simple. And it was of little interest to me at the time.

Paul, a handsome air force pilot on twenty-four hours' leave, attends one of Hanna's sold-out concerts in Berlin. That night, after the concert, during an air raid, fate brings them together in an underground shelter. They fall in love. But love is not easy in wartime. The next day, Paul must go on a dangerous mission. Three weeks later, when he safely returns on furlough, they plan to marry right away, but an unexpected order comes in from the High Command. Once again Paul must leave abruptly. Meanwhile Hanna, disappointed but still hopeful and understanding, goes on with her life and travels to Paris for her next concert.

'In Paris, Hanna stood on the stage in the ballroom of a splendid palace, in front of hundreds of soldiers, many of whom were wounded.' My mother sighed. I kept thinking to myself, Did such places like that ballroom still exist in this crazy world? Yes. Yes. Of course they did! They must. It was an absolutely enchanting scene.

'Hanna wore a black velvet gown with a silver leaf embroidered near the top. Like so.' My mother traced an arc across her bust with her hand. 'Hanna was so elegant, so charming, so warm. She stood onstage before a small orchestra. Her accompanist, a sweet older man, played the piano. She sang a wonderful song about how life had its ups and downs but in the end everything would turn out wonderful. And how she knew that one day her beloved, her soul mate, would return.'

There were tears in my mother's eyes. I had never before seen my mother cry. She had not cried earlier that day at my father's small funeral, nor had she cried when she came into my room the week before, her face pale and drawn. 'I have very bad news, Joseph. Papi was found dead in his store. We now must survive together.'

I asked her only one question that night we sat together on the living room sofa.

'Did Father see it?'

My mother seemed startled by my interruption. 'Oh, no. Papi was in a different hiding place. We weren't married yet.' My mother dabbed her wet eyes with a handkerchief. The tears had stopped. 'Papi was afraid to go outdoors to come to the theater. Someone might see him and catch him. But once when I was able to go to him, I told him about it. At first he was annoyed. He thought it all foolish, vulgar. Not something I should have been interested in. "They are wicked people!" he said. "It's only a love story," I said. Then Papi said he was sorry and listened, just to amuse me.'

After my mother's death, on my first visit to Berlin, I watched *The Great Love* over and over, perhaps five times, all afternoon and evening, at a revival theater on the Kurfürstendamm. Finally the manager came over to me and asked if something was the matter. I said I had come all the way from Canada to see this movie. He shook his head and walked away muttering, 'Noch ein verrückter Fan—Another crazy fan!'

After that a new memory emerged of my mother and her favorite actress in *The Great Love*. It was, I knew from the start, a false memory, but one so insistent in nature that even now hardly a week goes by without it coming to mind as if it had actually happened.

In this false memory that has occurred to me ever since I first came to Berlin and saw *The Great Love* myself, my mother gets up from the sofa where she sat with me that night after my father's funeral. She stands up and begins to sing in a voice that is exactly the voice of her favorite actress. It is a woman's voice, but dark and deep, a voice that hovers between the earth and the heavenly firmament, singing of miracles to be:

Ich weiss es wird einmal ein Wunder geschehen
und ich weiss, dass wir uns wiedersehen!

But in reality, my mother had been sitting the whole time. She never sang any lyrics. And I had never in my life heard my mother sing.

Our house stood on a quiet street at the outskirts of town and, though modest in size, was densely furnished with sofas and chairs, various mahogany and oak side tables, étagères and lamps. Except for the kitchen, heavy draperies hung on the windows of every room, including the bedrooms. My mother kept the house meticulously clean. Though she never left the vicinity of the house and had very little interaction with other people, my mother always dressed very elegantly, even lavishly. She subscribed to several fashion magazines to keep up with the latest styles. She ordered expensive fabrics from a store in Toronto and made her clothes herself. Often when she was working in her sewing room she would call me over. 'See, Joseph, this is a very fine silk, touch it. Feel its weight. Chinese silk is better than Indian. Please hold it out for me so I can see it better,' or 'This cotton comes from Egypt, the land of Nefertiti, the best cotton in the world.'

My mother was also particular about her thick blond hair, which she brushed back from her high forehead and kept gently waved at the temples so it framed her oval face.

My father was always appreciative of my mother's efforts. 'Ute, you are very beautiful tonight,' or 'How elegant you are, Ute,' he would say when he came home from work.

'Danke, Albert.'

My father did the household shopping on his way home from work. From time to time he brought my mother cosmetics, stockings, and even shoes.

Only once, before my father died, can I remember my mother leaving our house. One holiday, I believe it was Yom Kippur or Rosh Hashanah, when I was eight or nine, my father insisted we all go to the synagogue in town. I did not understand why because we had never attended synagogue before and no one ever expressed an interest in doing so. I can still see my mother adjusting a small feathered hat atop her blond hair. The hat had a delicate transparent veil that hung in front of her eyes. Before we left the house she glanced in the hallway mirror. She seemed pleased with her appearance. We drove into town for services. As we walked up the synagogue steps, my mother moved with an uncharacteristic awkwardness, constantly looking down at her shoes. I thought she was afraid of stumbling. At home my mother walked very erect, her tall, slender figure moving gracefully.

In the synagogue I stood between my parents, listening to the unfamiliar melancholy singing. I felt sad and bored. My mother leaned sideways and tugged discreetly on my father's sleeve. We moved out in single file from the crowded pew while the singing continued. Later, when we returned home, she looked at my father. She was pale and trembling.

'Bitte, Albert, nie mehr.'

'Ja, Ute, nie mehr. Nie.'

And we never did attend synagogue again.

When I asked her about that episode before she died, she said, 'No. I never went into a synagogue, even as a child. We were never observant. Maybe you went with your father. Perhaps your father took you once. He was very nostalgic.'

In my boyhood I began a beautiful and, I did not fully realize then, an extremely valuable gemstone collection. I stored my treasures in a velvet-lined leather case that I hid under my bed. This collection was gently but persistently encouraged by my father. Over time he presented me with many precious and semiprecious stones: an oval-cut ruby, a sapphire cabochon, a violet garnet. 'For your birthday,' he would say, or 'For your report card.' My mother would nod and add, 'You must always keep the pretty things Papi gives you. You can take them wherever you go.'

'They are like having *Lösegeld*,' my father once said.

'What?' I had never heard that word.

My mother looked sternly at my father.

'Oh, nothing,' he said. Later I looked the word up. It meant ransom.

Often I would study my collection under the jeweler's loupe he had given me and which I kept on the desk in my bedroom. He had shown me how to scan a stone's surface and, in the case of a transparent stone, its depths. 'A small flaw is a big tragedy if you're a jewel,' he was fond of saying.

Once in elementary school I came home and told my parents that my French teacher, Madame Dejarlais, thought I had an extraordinary gift for languages that might be useful in choosing a career. She was right, because after college I began working in Toronto as a translator for a Canadian corporation that was expanding its business in Europe. My mother smiled pleasantly. She was sewing a hem on a dress.

My father said, 'That is very good news, Joseph. We are happy to hear it.'

My mother looked up from her work. 'Yes, of course. We are very happy to hear it.'

The next day my father gave me a two-carat marquise-cut emerald, the last gift I received from him. My mother said, 'You must always keep the things Papi gives you.'

After Paul safely fulfilled his mission, the one he was called to by the High Command and which postponed his marriage, he was given three weeks' leave. He traveled to Rome to surprise Hanna, who was rehearsing for her latest engagement. They were joyously reunited and decided to marry that very night. Suddenly, as they were making their plans, the phone rang. An officer friend asked him to help and join a new dangerous mission. This time it was not an order but a request. Paul instantly agreed to volunteer.

My mother's voice rose angrily as she described Hanna's reaction. ' "Must you go *volunteer* and leave me just like that when we are about to marry! Without so much as an order! What about us? What about our marriage? Is that so unimportant? I cannot, I will not endure this any longer!"

Then my mother's voice softened. She understood Paul's side as well. 'Paul tried to reason with her. It was wartime and he had his responsibilities. "And what is it you cannot endure," he asked her, "when so many awful things are happening in the world?" '

'But Hanna remained stubborn and so they broke up. Paul, dutifully, left on his mission. After he was gone, Hanna sat down and cried.'

The morning after my father's funeral my mother knocked early on my bedroom door. 'Joseph, darf ich eintreten?'

My mother was wearing a sky-blue satin dress with long sleeves. There were white cuffs at her wrists and white buttons up the front of the dress. I remembered seeing the shimmering fabric when she was working on it in her sewing room, but I had never imagined the finished product. She appeared especially glamorous to me that day, like one of the models in the glossy magazines to which she subscribed.

'I will be back in the evening.' She looked at me to see if I understood, and then added, 'I cannot sell Papi's store. He loved it too much.'

I was puzzled, not because of the sudden and astonishing discarding of what clearly was some form of phobia. I never thought in such psychological terms when I was a child. I was puzzled mainly because it was three miles downtown to my father's store and my mother did not drive. I could not picture her, dressed in white-trimmed, sky-blue satin, walking that distance or, for that matter, traveling on a bus, though it would have been simple to do so.

'I must go now, Joseph. The taxi is waiting.'

For the next two years she went back and forth by taxi from our house to the store. She did not, as far as I know, go anywhere else. I believe the store must have been for her an extension of our home.

I took over from my father and did all the food shopping. My mother would give me a list with the brand names she preferred. Sometimes she asked me to buy certain cosmetics or stockings as my father had done for her before. In her spare time she continued to order material from Toronto and make her own clothes.

My mother turned out to be a skilled businesswoman and was good with customers. She still sold jewelry as my father had but expanded her merchandise to include fine gifts, such as crystal and silver. Though at home she continued speaking to me in German, her English was much better than I had realized, and her accent diminished over the time she worked in the store. Occasionally I would catch her at home with her sewing, repeating some English word out loud until she was satisfied with her pronunciation. Once she caught me watching her. She smiled. 'A good actress must adjust her accent for a new role.'

My mother continued my father's custom of building up my gemstone collection. On the first anniversary of his death, she gave me a one-and-three-quarter-carat round-cut diamond. I examined it that night under my loupe. I scrutinized its brilliant surface table, the glittering facets of its crown and pavilion. Its depths were flawless and fine white. My mother asked if she could enter my room. She took the loupe and examined the diamond herself.

'Yes, it is really an excellent stone. You must keep it with all the things Papi gave you.'

Sometimes after school or on Saturdays I helped my mother at the store. One day, near the second anniversary of my father's death, a short, dark-haired woman came into the store. No other customers were present. The woman wore expensive clothing, large sunglasses, and many rings on her fingers. She walked around the store, browsing. She looked at me, then at my mother. My mother smiled. 'May I help you, please?'

The woman answered in German. 'Yes. Would you show me those bracelets?'

'Natürlich.' My mother leaned over to open the display counter.

The woman took off her sunglasses and glared at the blond hair on my mother's bentover head. 'Feuchtman,' she whispered. 'Feuchtman.' It took me a moment to realize the woman was saying my mother's maiden name. My mother had rarely mentioned it. My mother looked up. She smiled. 'Wie, bitte?' To this day I don't think my mother actually heard or understood that the woman had just called her name. Suddenly the woman whirled around, her scrawny arm outstretched, her fist slamming into my mother's jaw with surprising force. One of my mother's teeth flew out, clattered across the glass top of the display cabinet before falling to the floor.

My mother stood up. Blood gleamed at the corner of her mouth. She was so startled that she did not even bring up a hand to feel the damage on her face.

'Petzmaul! Verräterin!' The woman spat at my mother. 'Bitch! Traitor! You are worse than they were! The evil informer-girl is finally caught!'

The woman ran out of the store and disappeared. I heard a car speeding off, but I was too shocked to run out and look for the license plate. I did not even move from where I was standing.

Finally my mother spoke. Her voice was altered because her lower jaw was now swollen. I could barely make out what she said. When she spoke she did not look directly at me. Her eyes skimmed the top of my head like they did the evening after my father's funeral, when she watched the pale blue walls of our living room and told me about her favorite actress in her favorite movie. She whispered.

'Oh, no. No, no. She is completely mistaken. I would never have worked for them even if they tortured me. I would never turn anyone in. How could I? . . . I had to do something to save your father. . . . No. No. I myself was hiding the whole time, first with the Retters . . .' She became silent. She wiped her mouth and felt her jaw, opening and closing it slowly. She smoothed her blond hair back with both hands. She took in a deep breath and looked directly at me. 'Well, no bones are broken. There is no need to see a doctor. You know I do not go to doctors. Why are you shaking?'

A week later she put the store up for sale.

According to city records, the Grunewald house where my mother grew up was destroyed during the war. Now, in its place, are pretty garden apartments with cobblestone trails meandering down to a small lake. The house of my mother's favorite movie actress in nearby Dahlem, across the street from a forest park, is now a retirement home.

A few years after my first visit, my company established a permanent office in Berlin. I requested a transfer. I thought of renting one of the garden apartments where my mother's house once stood, but none was available. Instead I found an apartment south of the Tiergarten and have lived here almost as long as my parents lived in Canada. At night, from my small balcony, I can see far across the lights of the Kurfüstendamm into the vast city. In *The Great Love*, Hanna had a balcony, too. In one scene she stood there with Paul looking out at the sparkling night sea of Berlin. 'It is like a fairy tale,' she sighed.

'No,' Paul said. 'It is lovelier than a fairy tale.'

I don't think it would be an exaggeration to say I have seen *The Great Love* more than fifty times. First I would go see it any time it was playing at the revival houses, which was surprisingly often. Later, when it became available on video, I began watching it at home. I have also seen my mother's favorite actress in her other movies: *To New Shores*, *In the Open Air*, *Homeland*. But I have found each of these other movies boring and never went to see any of them a second time.

My wife never asks me questions about this peculiar obsession of mine. She thinks only that I am a crazy fan. There are so many other people here who are fascinated with my mother's favorite actress. She is a great cult figure. If you go to the clubs you are bound to find someone dressed up like her, singing her songs, 'Could Love Be a Sin?' or 'My Life for Love.' My wife is glad I have not come to that. 'Ich bin sehr dankbar dafür!' she says. I am thankful for other things. Though we have now lived together for many years, she does not ask me about my family, nor do I ask about hers. I like to think of our life together as in the present, so long as the present maintains its own sense of privacy. Even in *The Great Love*, Paul and Hanna do not ask each other questions of a personal nature.

Lately, now that I am approaching the ages of my parents' premature deaths, when I recall my mother on the night of my father's funeral, I see us sitting on the claret moiré sofa as *The Great Love* is projected on the pale blue walls of our living room. We are watching it together. My mother takes my hand and smiles. She is enjoying herself so much and she hopes I am, too.

After Hanna and Paul break up, Paul leaves on his new mission, the dangerous mission for which he has nobly volunteered. Hanna remains in Rome rehearsing for her big concert.

Her concert is, of course, an amazing success. As she walks triumphantly offstage she is handed a telegram. 'Captain Paul Wendland has been wounded but only slightly. He is in an infirmary in the mountains.' As Hanna returns to the stage and takes her bow, she whispers to her accompanist that she must leave that very night.

'Hanna, when will you return?' he asks sadly, for he is obviously in love with her, too.

'Nie.'

My mother recited this 'Never' with the same restrained tone of conviction, the precise note of love and hope that I later witnessed each time I watched her favorite actress in her favorite movie.

Finally Hanna arrives at an infirmary somewhere in the Alps. Snow-covered mountain peaks are all around. She rushes over to Paul, who is sitting on the terrace, one arm in a sling. 'Perhaps, Hanna, we can try again to get married.' He laughingly points to his bandaged arm. 'This time I really have three weeks' sick leave!'

Hanna smiles. She takes his hand. 'And after the three weeks are over?'

Paul looks up and she looks up, too. Overhead, the sky is so wide and breathtaking. Here and there, glorious shafts of sunlight break through the billowing clouds. And suddenly, in the distance, a squadron of planes appears. And there, of course, to those wondrous heavens, Paul must return. That is where his duty lies.

'Paul turned and looked into Hanna's eyes,' my mother told me. 'Their faces were so beautiful, so full of happiness, it gave me goose-bumps. And then Hanna nodded. Yes. Yes. She would marry him.'

And then my mother turned and looked directly at me for the first time on that extraordinary night in my life. I trembled ever so slightly at the unbearable tenderness of her look. 'If I had been them,' my mother said, rising from the sofa, 'I would gladly have sacrificed all of heaven for love.'

Anne Michaels

Anne Michaels, the daughter of a Russian immigrant, was born in Toronto in 1958. She received her B.A. from the University of Toronto in 1980 and has taught courses in creative writing there. Her first collection of poetry, *The Weight of Oranges*, was published in 1985, and her second collection, *Miner's Pond* (1991), was shortlisted for the Governor General's Award. Music and metaphor, hallmarks of her poetry, find their way into her novel *Fugitive Pieces* (1996), which has been translated into all major European languages and in 1997 won the Chapters/Books in Canada First Novel Award and the British Orange Prize for fiction. The excerpt from her novel focuses on the child Jakob Beer, who has been rescued from his Polish city by the Greek scientist Athos and taken to the island of Zakynthos, where he escapes detection by the Nazis during World War II. After the war Jakob and Athos come to Canada. Michaels's 'poetry after Auschwitz' is evident throughout the narrative.

Anne Michaels

EXCERPT FROM *Fugitive Pieces*

Athos would no longer let me go out on the roof at night.

He had been so careful to maintain order. Regular meals, daily lessons. But now our days were without shape. He still told stories, to try and cheer us, but now they were aimless. How he and Nikos learned about Chinese kites and flew a handmade dragon above Cape Spinari while the children from the village perched on the coast, waiting their turn to feel the tug of the string. How they lost the kite in the waves . . . All his stories went wrong halfway through, and reminded us of the sea.

The only thing that calmed Athos was to draw. The greater his despair, the more obsessively he drew. He took down a battered copy of Blossfeldt's *Elementary Forms* and, in pen and ink, copied the photographs of magnified plants that transformed stems into burnished pewter, blossoms into fleshy fish mouths, pods into hairy accordion pleats. Athos collected poppies, lavatera, basil, broom and spread them on his desk. Then, in watercolours, he made precise renderings. He quoted Wilson: 'Nature's harmonies cannot be guessed at.' He explained as he painted: 'Broom grows in the Bible. Hagar left Ishmael in a clump of broom, Elijah lay in broom when he asked to die. Perhaps it was the burning bush; even when the fire goes out, its inner branches continue to burn.' When he was finished, he gathered what was edible and we used it for supper. Important lessons: look carefully; record what you see. Find a way to make beauty necessary; find a way to make necessity beautiful.

By the end of summer Athos rallied enough to insist that our lessons resume. But the dead surrounded us, an aurora over the blue water.

At night I choked against Bella's round face, a doll's face, immobile, inanimate, her hair floating behind her. These nightmares, in which my parents and my sister drowned with the Jews of Crete, continued for years, continued long after we'd moved to Toronto.

Often on Zakynthos and later in Canada, for moments I was lost. Standing next to the fridge in our Toronto kitchen, afternoon light falling in a diagonal across the floor. About something I can't remember Athos answered me. Perhaps even then the answer had nothing to do with the question. 'If you hurt yourself, Jakob, I will have to hurt myself. You will have proven to me my love for you is useless.'

Athos said: 'I can't save a boy from a burning building. Instead he must save me from the attempt; he must jump to earth.'

⋆

While I hid in the radiant light of Athos's island, thousands suffocated in darkness. While I hid in the luxury of a room, thousands were stuffed into baking stoves, sewers, garbage bins. In the crawl-spaces of double ceilings, in stables, pigsties, chicken coops. A boy my age hid in a crate; after ten months he was blind and mute, his limbs atrophied. A woman stood in a closet for a year and a half, never sitting down, blood bursting her veins. While I was living with Athos on Zakynthos, learning Greek and English, learning geology, geography, and poetry, Jews were filling the corners and cracks of Europe, every available space. They buried themselves in strange graves, any space that would fit their bodies, absorbing more room than was allotted them in the world. I didn't know that while I was on Zakynthos, a Jew could be purchased for a quart of brandy, perhaps four pounds of sugar, cigarettes. I didn't know that in Athens, they were being rounded up in 'Freedom Square.' That the sisters of the Vilna convent were dressing men as nuns in order to provide ammunition to the underground. In Warsaw, a nurse hid children under her skirt, passing through the ghetto gates, until one evening—a gentle twilight descending on those typhus-infected, lice-infested streets—the nurse was caught, the child thrown into the air and shot like a tin can, the nurse given the 'Nazi pill': one bullet in the throat. While Athos taught me about anabatic and katabatic winds, Arctic smoke, and the Spectre of the Brocken, I didn't know that Jews were being hanged from their thumbs in public squares. I didn't know that when there were too many for the ovens, corpses were burned in open pits, flames ladled with human fat. I didn't know that while I listened to the stories of explorers in the clean places of the world (snow-covered, salt-stung) and slept in a clean place, men were untangling limbs, the flesh of friends and neighbours, wives and daughters, coming off in their hands.

★

In September 1944, the Germans left Zakynthos. Across the hills, music from town spun through the air frail as a distant radio. A man rode across the island, his high-pitched yelps and the Greek flag snapping above his head. I didn't go outside that day, though I went downstairs and looked into the garden. The next morning Athos asked me to sit with him by the front door. He carried two chairs outside. Sunlight blared from every direction. My eyeballs jangled in my skull. I sat with my back against the house and looked down at myself. My legs did not belong to me; thin as lengths of rope knotted at the knees, skin dripping where muscle used to be, tender in the strong light. The heat pressed down. After a while Athos led me, dazed, inside.

I grew stronger, each day climbing further down and up the hill. Finally I walked with Athos to Zakynthos town, which gleamed as if an egg had been cracked on the sharp Venetian details and dripped shiny over the pale yellow and white plaster. Athos had described it so often: the hedges of quince and pomegranate, the path of cypresses. The narrow streets with laundry drying from the grillwork balconies, the view of Mount Skopos, with the convent Panayia Skopotissa. The statue of Solomos in the square, Nikos's fountain.

Athos presented me to Old Martin. There was now so little to sell that his tiny shop was mostly empty. I remember standing next to a shelf where a few cherries were scattered like rubies on ivory paper. During the occupations, Old Martin tried to satisfy the cravings of his patrons. This was his private resistance. He bartered secretly with ship captains for a delicacy he knew a customer pined for. Thus, cunningly, he bolstered spirits. He kept track of the larders of the community, efficient as a caterer at a fine hotel. Martin knew who was buying food for Jews in hiding after the ghetto was abandoned, and he tried to save extra fruit and oil for families with young children. The Patron Saint of Groceries. Old Martin's short hair stood up in several directions. If Athos's hair was silver ore, Martin's was jagged and white as quartz. His knobbly arthritic hands trembled as he reached deliberately for a fig or a lemon, holding one at a time. In those days of scarcity his shaking care seemed appropriate, an acknowledgement of the value of a single plum.

Athos and I walked through the town. We rested in the platia where the last Jews of the zudeccha had waited to die. A woman was washing the steps of the Zakynthos Hotel. In the harbour, ropes tapped against the masts.

For four years I'd imagined Athos and I sharing secret languages. Now I heard Greek everywhere. In the street, reading signs for the farmakio or the kafenio, I felt profanely exposed. I ached to return to our little house.

In India there are butterflies whose folded wings look just like dry leaves. In South Africa there is a plant that's indistinguishable from the stones among which it grows: the stone-copying plant. There are caterpillars that look like branches, moths that look like bark. To remain invisible, the plaice changes colour as it moves through sunlit water. What is the colour of a ghost?

To survive was to escape fate. But if you escape your fate, whose life do you then step into?

⋆

The Zohar says: 'All visible things will be born again invisible.'

The present, like a landscape, is only a small part of a mysterious narrative. A narrative of catastrophe and slow accumulation. Each life saved: genetic features to rise again in another generation. 'Remote causes.'

Athos confirmed that there was an invisible world, just as real as what's evident. Full-grown forests still and silent, whole cities, under a sky of mud. The realm of the peat men, preserved as statuary. The place where all those who have uttered the bony password and entered the earth wait to emerge. From underground and underwater, from iron boxes and behind brick walls, from trunks and packing crates . . .

When Athos sat at his desk, soaking wood samples in polyethylene glycol, replacing missing fibres with a waxy filler, I could see—watching his face while he worked—that he was actually traipsing through vanished, impossibly tall Carboniferous forests, with tree bark like intricate brocades: designs more beautiful than any fabric. The forest swayed one hundred feet above his head in a prehistoric autumn.

Athos was an expert in buried and abandoned places. His cosmology became mine. I grew into it naturally. In this way, our tasks became the same.

Athos and I would come to share our secrets of the earth. He described the bog bodies. They had steeped for centuries, their skin tanning to dark leather, umber juices deep in the lines of palms and soles. In autumn, with the smell of snow in the dark clouds, men had been led out into the moor as sacrificial offerings. There, they were anchored with birch and stones to drown in the acidic ground. Time stopped. And that is why, Athos explained, the bog men are so serene. Asleep for centuries, they are uncovered perfectly intact; thus they outlast their killers—whose bodies have long dissolved to dust.

In turn I told him of the Polish synagogues whose sanctuaries were below ground, like caves. The state prohibited synagogues to be built as high as churches, but the Jews refused to have their reverence diminished by building codes. The vaulted ceilings were still built; the congregation simply prayed deeper underground.

I told him of the great wooden horses that once decorated a synagogue near my parents' house and were now desecrated and buried. Someday perhaps they would rise in a herd, as if nothing had occurred, to graze in a Polish field.

I fantasized the power of reversal. Later, in Canada, looking at photographs of the mountains of personal possessions stored at Kanada in the camps, I imagined that if each owner of each pair of shoes could be named, then they would be brought back to life. A cloning from intimate belongings, a mystical pangram.

Athos told me about Biskupin and its discovery by a local teacher out for an evening stroll. The Gasawka River was low and the huge wooden pylons perforated the surface of the lake like massive rushes. More than two thousand years before, Biskupin had been a rich community, supremely organized. They harvested grain and bred livestock. Wealth was shared. Their comfortable houses were arranged in neat rows; the island fortification resembling a modern subdivision. Each gabled home had ample light as well as privacy; a porch, a hearth, a bedroom loft. Biskupin craftsmen traded with Egypt and the Black Sea coast. But then there was a change in climate. Farmland turned to heath, then to bog.

The water table rose inexorably until it was obvious that Biskupin would have to be abandoned. The city remained underwater until 1933, when the level of the Gasawka River dropped. Athos joined the excavation in 1937. His job was to solve the preservation problems of the waterlogged structures. Soon after Athos made the decision to take me home with him, Biskupin was overrun by soldiers. We learned this after the war. They burned records and relics. They demolished the ancient fortifications and houses that had withstood millennia. Then they shot five of Athos's colleagues in the surrounding forest. The others were sent to Dachau.

And that is one of the reasons Athos believed we saved each other.

*

The invisible paths in Athos's stories: rivers following the inconsistencies of land like tears following the imperfections on skin. Wind and currents that stir up underwater creatures, bioluminescent gardens that guide birds to shore. The Arctic tern, riding Westerlies and Trades each year from Arctic to Antarctica and back again. On their brains, the rotating constellations, the imprint of longing and distance. The fixed route of bison over prairie, so worn that the railway laid its tracks along it.

Geography cut by rail. The black seam of that wailing migration from life to death, the lines of steel drawn across the ground, penetrating straight through cities and towns now famous for murder: from Berlin through Breslau; from Rome through Florence, Padua, and Vienna; from Vilna through Grodno and Lodz; from Athens through Salonika and Zagreb. Though they were taken blind, though their senses were confused by stench and prayer and screams, by terror and memories, these passengers found their way home. Through the rivers, through the air.

When the prisoners were forced to dig up the mass graves, the dead entered them through their pores and were carried through their bloodstreams to their brains and hearts. And through their blood into another generation. Their arms were into death up to the elbows, but not only into death—into music, into a memory of the way a husband or son leaned over his dinner, a wife's expression as she watched her child in the bath; into beliefs, mathematical formulas, dreams. As they felt another man's and another's blood-soaked hair through their fingers, the diggers begged forgiveness. And those lost lives made molecular passage into their hands.

How can one man take on the memories of even one other man, let alone five or ten or a thousand or ten thousand; how can they be sanctified each? He stops thinking. He concentrates on the whip, he feels a face in his hand, he grasps hair as if in a passion grasp, its matted thickness between his fingers, pulling, his hands full of names. His holy hands move, autonomous.

In the Golleschau quarry, stone-carriers were forced to haul huge blocks of limestone endlessly, from one mound to another and back again. During the torture, they carried their lives in their hands. The insane task was not futile only in the sense that faith is not futile.

A camp inmate looked up at the stars and suddenly remembered that they'd once seemed beautiful to him. This memory of beauty was accompanied by a bizarre stab of gratitude. When I first read this I couldn't imagine it. But later I felt I understood. Sometimes the body experiences a revelation because it has abandoned every other possibility.

⋆

It's no metaphor to feel the influence of the dead in the world, just as it's no metaphor to hear the radiocarbon chronometer, the Geiger counter amplifying the faint breathing of rock, fifty thousand years old. (Like the faint thump from behind the womb wall.) It is no metaphor to witness the astonishing fidelity of minerals magnetized, even after hundreds of millions of years, pointing to the magnetic pole, minerals that have never forgotten magma whose cooling off has left them forever desirous. We long for place; but place itself longs. Human memory is encoded in air currents and river sediment. Eskers of ash wait to be scooped up, lives reconstituted.

How many centuries before the spirit forgets the body? How long will we feel our phantom skin buckling over rockface, our pulse in magnetic lines of force? How many years pass before the difference between murder and death erodes?

Grief requires time. If a chip of stone radiates its self, its breath, so long, how stubborn might be the soul. If sound waves carry on to infinity, where are their screams now? I imagine them somewhere in the galaxy, moving forever towards the psalms.

⋆

Alone on the roof those nights, it's not surprising that, of all the characters in Athos's tales of geologists and explorers, cartographers and navigators, I felt compassion for the stars themselves. Aching towards us for millennia though we are blind to their signals until it's too late, starlight only the white breath of an old cry. Sending their white messages millions of years, only to be crumpled up by the waves.

Michael Redhill

Born in Baltimore, Maryland, in 1966, Michael Redhill has lived in Toronto most of his life. Educated in the United States and Canada, he spent seven years completing a three-year B.A. degree in acting, film, and, finally, English. Since 1988 he has published five collections of poetry, had eight plays of varying lengths performed, and worked as a cultural critic and essayist. He has been an editor, a ghostwriter, an anthologist, a scriptwriter for film and television, and, in leaner times, a waiter, a house painter, and a bookseller. Currently he is the managing editor of *Brick*, the literary journal founded by Michael Ondaatje. His most recent books are *Martin Sloane*, a novel nominated for the Giller Prize, *Light-crossing*, a collection of poetry, and *Building Jerusalem*, a play, all published in 2001. He lives with his partner and two sons in Toronto. The eponymous protagonist of *Martin Sloane* divides his time between Canada, the United States, and Ireland, just as part of his dual identity is split between the American artist Joseph Cornell and his Jewish roots on his mother's side of the family. 'Crossing' is one of the major themes in *Martin Sloane*.

Michael Redhill

EXCERPT FROM *Martin Sloane*

Martin's father wanted to make a detour into St. Joseph's Church, to thank the Virgin.

Colin, their mother said, You're not taking any child of mine into a church. Even to thank the Virgin.

He's half a child of Christ, love. We shouldn't push our luck now.

What if it's the Christ half got sick?

All the more reason to thank the Virgin for prayers answered.

They argued like this for a few moments; Martin and Theresa had been through these attempted detours many times. Their father still clung to his stray hope that he'd get the four of them into a church one day. As usual, they saw his shoulders slump a little and their parents walked back toward them.

Why don't you make one of us Catholic and one of us Jewish? Theresa asked. Then there won't be any more of this half and half business.

And which would you be, Theresa? asked her father.

I'd be Catholic and Martin would be Jewish. Then there'd be one of each, a Jewish boy, a Catholic girl, a Jewish mum, a Catholic dad.

I think not, said Adele. We don't need to be divided against each other. Lord knows there's enough trouble already. You can still thank God, Theresa, without praying to the Virgin.

But I like the Virgin. She has a pretty face.

There would be no more discussing it. They turned up the street and walked straight home, but Martin's father said in his mind, Hail Mary full of grace, the Lord is with thee. Blessed art thou amongst women and blessed is the fruit of thy womb, Jesus. Pray for us sinners now, and at the hour of our death. Amen, and they all knew he was doing it because his lips were moving. Adele nudged him with her elbow and shook her head at him, but she was also smiling. That was the way of their family. [. . .]

Cramped, salt-reeking Galway was more unpleasant than Martin had feared, and later it got worse. It was a fake city, like the painted booths of a county fair, the shop windows displaying dusty magazines ajumble with creaky toys and faded corsets, the druggist's shelves thinly stocked, although bile beans and bullet-shaped suppositories were available everywhere, as if the main activity in Galway were egestion. That seemed right: this was life in the form of an aftermath, and all the colourless days and nights to come seemed very much the product of a nourishment now mulched to fetidness.

At the beginning, they'd lived with the Hannahs, old friends of their mother's who lived in an apartment above Donnellan's, a furnishing shop where the sounds of dowels being whacked into holes could be heard at all hours. The four of them slept like stowaways in a room separated by a curtain from the rest of the Hannahs (there were the parents, the eldest boy, Malcolm, the girl, Sheila, and Gabriel, the youngest at eight). Never in his life had Martin felt such remorse; so much that despite his fear of darkness and eternity, he wanted to die and set his parents and even his sister free. If his continuing life had pulled them clear across the country, then only his death would release them back to where they belonged. But he believed he was too much a coward ever to set them free that way. The only saving graces were the gas lamps that cast an orange light in brilliant cones up to the night sky, and the horses beneath them, those noble animals, running their carriage errands.

Don't stare at them too hard, Theresa said, or they'll blow up.

This reproach stung him as she knew it would. It had been a terrible thing to dynamite King George on the very day of the London coronation. Their mother had been very upset about it, but their father muttered bitterly as they passed through Maynooth: Art criticism. He should have been sitting on an ass. There'd been a period of silence, after that.

Standing at his new, but temporary, window, Martin tried to consolidate old visions with new ones. But he couldn't see a church spire here without pressing his cheek to the glass and looking aslant down the street. And here they seemed to be in the thick of the city, but there was no centre to look toward: it was all sprawl. Across the way, a tailor's dummy stared out blankly over the cobble.

The radio played a commercial.

Oh, is that an electric toaster, Mary? Goodness, it must be expensive to use!

Mary chided that electricity was cheap. I must show you my electric cooker and iron, she said. And I have the neatest little electric fire in my bedroom.

There were nine of them in a five-room apartment. The Sloanes had come from their red-bricked, iron-gated house on Iona to the life of indigents. In the mornings, their father would set out to find them a house, while their mother and Mrs. Hannah busied themselves with shopping and cooking. Out on the streets, going quietly in and out of the shops, it all felt so ephemeral—like an ill-chosen vacation spot rather than real life. Martin was on one side of his mother, safely separated from Theresa on the other. Mrs. Hannah showed their mother the best place to buy apples, the best covered buttons, the best cheese shop. Over the bridges spanning the branches of the Corrib, down the cramped medieval streets with their smells of damp and crumbling brick. They crossed the Dominick Street Bridge and went up by Nun's Island and the old jail, but then somehow the river was to their right again (as it had been before they crossed the bridge), and still flowing down into the bay, although they had not turned around or crossed the street.

Martin, stop pulling on me, said his mother.

He turned back around. Mrs. Hannah? How many rivers are here?

Just the one, she said. All the way to Galway Bay, that's a song. And she sang it, dispelling none of his confusion. How could a river change direction? Mrs. Hannah had a sharp little voice, not like his mother's, but his mother had not sung anything for a long time.

The Hannahs' children were in a private school up past Newcastle Road where the university was. Their father proudly walked them every morning, his pockets full of unhulled hazelnuts, and he sounded like a game of dice walking out the door with the three of them. How shameful, Martin thought, that his own mother would be seen in public with two children out of school in May. Although she seemed to be enjoying the change of habit, and smiled down at him and Theresa often.

Feeling okay, honeylamb? she'd say, stroking his cheek with her fingers.

This is the temple, Mrs. Hannah said one afternoon. Everyone calls it the St. Augustine Synagogue—can you imagine? It was like all the other shops on St. Augustine Street, only it featured a placard with Hebrew writing in the window. The curtains were drawn behind it. Seeing a synagogue brought Martin fresh feelings of guilt.

New members welcome all the time, said Mrs. Hannah.

I'll keep my word, said their mother, shaking her head. But maybe I'll come with you and Michael one evening.

I want to come, said Theresa. I feel more and more Jewish every day.

You'll honour your father's wishes as you do mine.

They walked on, but Martin's spirit felt bruised by his own sins.

That afternoon, Mrs. Hannah boiled the cod for the evening meal and put all of the oatmeal in a pot of water to soak until morning. It was to become a pot of flummery. The best kind of invalid cookery, she told Martin.

I'm not an invalid, though, he replied.

Soon you'll be right as rain. She held his head in her hands and squeezed. She smelled like butter going bad and he noticed his own mother looking unhappily at her friend. He knew then that they were only at the Hannahs because they had no other option, and Mrs. Hannah's friendship was not one his mother wanted particularly. He understood that there was something about these people that his mother had walked away from; only duty (on the part of the Hannahs) and great need (that was their portion) had drawn the two families together.

He looks like your da, Adele. Martin squirmed between Mrs. Hannah's hot hands. She turned his head down and laughed. A little spray of red straight from Poland.

His mother came over from the table where she'd been sitting and smoothed down his hair. Both women gripped his skull in their hands, like they were testing a melon. It's more likely straight out of Antrim, I'd think. From those Antrim Sloanes.

Mrs. Hannah released him. I love his colour. We've all black hair to our flanges, look at us, like dark purebreds! She clapped her hands, her eyes shining. She nodded at Malcolm, who was sitting with a book on the couch. That one, he looks like we brought him straight from Palestine.

I was born in England, the boy protested.

You were right, said Mrs. Hannah. The future is in people of all different types coming together. No stopping it, anyway. You were right to ignore the prating of your friends. People can be backwards, as we know.

I'm sure you remember when I came back with Colin to Hammersmith. It must have been hard to hear all the things people were saying. Wasn't it?

Oh it was, it was, said Mrs. Hannah, pushing her fish back down into the frothing water. But you know how hard it is to talk sense to some people.

Yes, said his mother, staring at the back of Mrs. Hannah's head. I do know.

That night, at dinner, they tried their best to eat Mrs. Hannah's meal. It was called kedgeree, and it smelled exactly like the streets: of mildew and salt.

Malcolm, Sheila, and Gabriel cleaned their plates, and Gabriel, sitting beside Martin, rescued him by quietly offering to finish his supper. When dinner was over, Martin's father spoke.

Well, I'm glad to be able to share happy news. Our little streak of bad luck is at an end. He raised a glass of water to the rest of the table. I've found us a house.

Their mother was beaming. You didn't tell me!

It was a surprise.

Where is it, then?

It's a beautiful house in St. Mary's Terrace, down on Taylor's Hill. A beautiful little house behind a gate. We'll have you over when we're settled, he said to their hosts, and drink to your graciousness and hospitality.[. . .]

They lasted two more years. Their hearts softened a little toward the place, but it never yielded to them. Colin Sloane hired a felt cutter in the fall of 1938, just as the hints of war were building over Europe. Business was good; enough to keep them all going.

In the spring of 1939, the Spanish Civil War ended and Hitler annexed Slovakia. The Cadburys moved from number four St. Mary's Terrace to a nicer address in Salthill, and Hannah Mosher took ill in Montreal. Martin had never seen a telegram before—a man came to the door with a yellow sheet of paper on which were glued strips of words. It said, MOTHER ILL STOP WIRING MONEY FOR PASSAGE STOP FATHER. He watched his mother read the message and her face lifted and she was staring, her eyes white like the boy's in the story William had once told him.

That night she explained to him and Theresa that she had to go overseas. She didn't know how long she would be gone, but she would write to them all, and before long they would all be together again. Their father sat half in the dark, folding the telegram into smaller and smaller squares.

He's finally got his revenge, he said. Your father. Duped, he was, now he's getting you to take the rest of the trip.

Don't be morbid, Colin. Are you saying he's lying about my mother?

Not lying, but it's convenient, isn't it. See now, his daughter's an Irishwoman married to a Mick, he'll do anything to turn back the clock. She went to the stairs and motioned for him to come, but he stayed rooted to his chair, disconsolate, and it frightened them to see him that way. No need to have this talk in private, Addie. The kids should know how ashamed your father is.

My father loves me, and he loves his grandchildren as well as their father. So don't be twisting this into something you can't twist back. Honestly, Colin, and with my mother sick enough that my father would spend the money on a telegram! You should know to think of something more than yourself!

For the love of God! he said. If she died without warning, you'd have no choice.

That would suit you well, wouldn't it? Well, I have a choice, and I'm going. And if you're finished talking your nonsense, I'll be upstairs to pack.

She turned her back to him and proceeded up the stairs, and he rose and bellowed behind her: Just when we're getting settled, aye! This! A curse on us all! They'd never heard him raise his voice before, and Martin saw his face was red, and his cheeks were shaking. This is all my fault, he said miserably.

Theresa edged her way around her father's paralyzed form and went up the stairs behind her mother. When his father sat, Martin followed her up, giving a wide berth to the throbbing, mussed head of his father. Upstairs, the two of them watched their mother pack, their sullen faces hovering behind the open lid of the case. She folded her silk bed-gown into a gleaming square that smelled of spice and lavender, and she tucked it into the corner. Martin put his hand on it; its formlessness was disheartening, knowing it would cover the miles of darkened sea with his mother's body in it, but him back on another coast.

Are you worried about the boat? she asked him.

No, he said. You'll be fine, I know. You almost went the first time. When you met Dad. Good things happen on boats.

Will you have enough to eat? asked Theresa.

They have food for the whole journey. She closed the lid and sat beside Martin and touched his hair. It was unbearable, as their father had said, that just as their lives were settling that such an upset would occur.

I want you to be patient and treat your father well. He'll recover from his bad mood. No matter what happens for good or bad, family is all we have. Do you understand? She turned to each of them to receive their acknowledgements.

Martin knew that he would do anything for her then, to save her, to take away the pain that she was surely feeling for her own mother. When he'd imagined how his death would have saved the family, it was the image of his mother's grief as he was buried that ultimately made him want to live, even if it destroyed all their other dreams. Right then he knew that everything that was chosen in life created a single path and destroyed all the alternatives, and that meant, probably, that you could not choose how to live and also be happy. It was true here: his mother could not choose to remain in Galway and so not be with her mother. Nor could she go to her and also be spared the anguish of watching her die and upsetting her family. There was no choice that did not amplify pain elsewhere; it was a cruel balance. It could only and ever be so, or it would not be at all.

She leaned down and kissed him on the downy hair at his crown, and pulled Theresa in toward her as well. His sister was crying, silently tears went down her face, even though her expression was still. Then she placed Theresa's hand over his, and without words they both knew any feud between them was to end here. As they left her, they passed their father in the hall, his face ashen and knowing.

The next day, their mother climbed the gangplank and disappeared into the giant ship. It turned around in the bay and pointed out toward the sun, then put on steam and began to get smaller. The ocean was huge, and dark, and cold. Martin tried not to think about it.

Afterwards, they did their best to return to normal life, but normal life had been suspended. The house was eerily silent without her, and they all went about their various tasks in the sun-starved house quietly, as if they were in mourning and risked offending the gravity of their circumstance. They saw that their father had begun talking to himself—at least it seemed that way with his lips moving—and when he sometimes gave breath to the shapes of words, they heard bits of their mother's instructions to him: *the lever*, or *Wednesdays*. It was comforting to hear her channeled through him, and even more so when he attributed an action to her, such as when he added an egg to chopped steak, or squeezed a lemon over half a cantaloupe to help it keep its colour in the icebox.

In the mornings, they saw that he sometimes pulled down both sides of the bed and then made both sides, even though her side was untouched.

The first week passed. Theresa did the laundry as best she could, and Martin swept up the halls and the kitchen. But their father began to fade. He said to Martin, See what God will take away? and his eyes were a little unfamiliar, as if they were vigilant for something Martin could not see coming.

As the days went by, it became clearer that their father was not going to be able to keep up. The meals, which had at first been hearty, if flavourless, grew smaller, and then became alarming. One night, he put plates of raw rice in front of them, with lashings of hot tomato sauce across it. Let it sit a moment to soften, he told them. Theresa sneaked out next door after supper and wept in Mrs. Raleigh's arms. The next day, large tubs of stew and hot breads and jars of pickles began appearing, and the Raleigh girls secretly told their friends that the Sloanes had become family members because they could not feed themselves and were being nourished on their mother's cooking.

The nights were difficult. Martin woke up feeling a cold pall had enveloped the house, and for the first time since before he became ill, Theresa pulled back her covers for him and let him nestle against her. At night, alone in the house without their mother, sharing a bed was the only way of dealing with the anxiety of distances. Their grandmother (whom they had never met, in fact) was surely dying, but in a part of the world so far away that neither of them could conceive of the kind of love that would drive a person to go that far.

By August, their mother's letters began arriving, and she described the city of Montreal as if it were more like Dublin than Dublin had been: the smell of fresh bread everywhere, the river full of ships, and horses in the streets. Of course, many of the people spoke French, but it was charming. It had been hot, in fact the summer there had been unbearable. She wrote to their father that he would love the city: it was surmounted by a hill with an iron cross atop it, and at night it was lit up like a beacon to the faithful. It was taller than Nelson's pillar, she wrote.

Their father read and reread her letters, as if the sound of her voice could actually rise off the page, material. Each letter (and now they arrived with regular frequency, each about a month and a half old), told more of a life in a place it was becoming clear to him she would never return from. The letters became imploring in tone, saying that she missed them all dearly, and she signed some of them *je vous adore*. Finally, in September, she sent a telegram, as her own father had, and begged them to sell everything and come to Canada. Her mother had stabilized, but she could not leave. No, she did not want to leave. There was no argument from Martin or Theresa—they missed her too much to consider such a thing as a country or a home of any importance, but their father was grief-struck anew. Galway was the edge of the very known world to him, and although he had no relations but a brother in Belfast, his country was all of who he was. But he had foreseen having to leave, as he had said to Martin. God will find you and drive you out.

They began to divest themselves of unnecessary possessions, and before long, all possessions seemed unnecessary. The grandfather clock, which had paced Martin's entire life with a stately tick and gong, went. Then the sofas and the beds. Their father sold his business to his felt cutter, who changed the shop's name to Caprani. He'd come from Naples.

Passenger travel had been restricted out of Galway since the sinking of the *Athena* off the Hebrides earlier in the month. (Gabriel had told Martin that the cries of the dying were heard in Sligo.) They waited until late October for the shipping lanes to reopen, and the sea was buff and cold, the waves even near the shore tipped white. A hansom cab took them down to the docks to wait with the hundreds of others for whom this ship was their first chance to leave Ireland since the end of the summer. The massive form of the M.S. *St. Louis* stood against the black sky, taking on passengers who moved slowly up a gangway and through a dimly lit door to the insides.

Martin stood with his father, the smell of the damp thatch behind them in the Claddagh, the pong of salt all around. Theresa had pushed forward already into the throng of waiting passengers, and he could see her by the new hat their father had made for her. A lady's hat, he'd said, for a young lady. Above them, the passengers taken on in Dover, in Dublin, in Cork waved from the foredecks, the plumes of steam and grit chuffing out of the funnels, the horses quietly moored to their posts as the porters unloaded the carriages. This was the great ship's last stop before it would sail over the Atlantic to Halifax and then Montreal.

Source Acknowledgments

Excerpt from Leonard Cohen, *The Favourite Game* (Toronto: McClelland and Stewart, 1963), 11, 15–16, 66–68, 102–3, 117–20. © Leonard Cohen 1963. Used by permission, McClelland and Stewart, Ltd. *The Canadian Publishers.*

Excerpt from Mordecai Richler, *Barney's Version* (Toronto: Knopf, 1997), 187–201. Copyright © 1997 Mordecai Richler. Reprinted by permission of Knopf Canada, a division of Random House of Canada, Ltd.

Excerpt from David Solway, *Random Walks* (Montreal: McGill-Queen's University Press, 1997), 86–93. © David Solway 1997. Used by permission of the author.

Miriam Waddington, 'Mrs Maza's Salon,' in *Apartment Seven* (Toronto: Oxford University Press, 1989), 1–8. Copyright © 1989 by Miriam Waddington. Reprinted by permission of Oxford University Press Canada.

Chava Rosenfarb, 'A Friday in the Life of Sarah Zonabend.' Translated by permission of the author. Translated by Goldie Morgentaler.

Naïm Kattan, 'The Dancer' is a translation of 'La danseuse,' in *La distraction* (Montreal: Hurtubise HMH, 1994), 49–59. © Éditions Hurtubise HMH, coll. 'L'Arbre,' 1994. Translated by permission of the author. Translated by Phyllis Aronoff.

Excerpt from Monique Bosco, *Sara Sage*, translated from *Sara Sage* (Montreal: Hurtubise HMH, 1986), 12–21. © Éditions Hurtubise HMH, coll. 'L'Arbre,' 1986. Translated by permission of the author. Translated by Phyllis Aronoff.

Excerpt from Régine Robin, *The Wanderer*, trans. Phyllis Aronoff (Montreal: Alter Ego Editions, 1997), 5–17, 132–33. Reprinted by permission of the author and translator. Translation copyright © 1997 Phyllis Aronoff. Originally published as *La Québécoite* (Montreal: XYZ éditeur, 1993), 232 pp., ISBN 2-89261-080-X.

Excerpt from Robert Majzels, *Hellman's Scrapbook* (Dunvegan ON: Cormorant Books, 1992), 7–19. Reprinted by permission of Cormorant Books and the author.

Excerpt from Robert Majzels, *Apikoros Sleuth* (Toronto: Mercury Press, forthcoming), printed from the manuscript version by permission of the author.

Robyn Sarah, 'Looking for My Keys,' in *Promise of Shelter* (Erin ON: The Porcupine's Quill, 1997), 115–27. Reprinted by permission of the author.

Judith Kalman, 'Personal Effects,' in *The County of Birches* (Vancouver: Douglas and McIntyre, 1998), 61–68. Copyright © 1998 by Judith Kalman. Published in Canada by Douglas and McIntyre, Ltd. Reprinted by permission of the publisher.

Norman Levine, 'By a Frozen River,' in *Champagne Barn* (New York: Penguin, 1984), 153–64. Reprinted with permission of Key Porter Books from *By a Frozen River: The Short Stories of Norman Levine*. © Norman Levine, 2000.

Matt Cohen, 'The Sins of Tomas Benares,' in *Café Le Dog* (New York: Penguin, 1985), 75–101. Courtesy of Stickland. Copyright © 1983 by Matt Cohen.

Gabriella Goliger, 'Maladies of the Inner Ear,' in *Song of Ascent* (Vancouver: Raincoast, 2000), 111–25. Copyright © 2000 by Gabriella Goliger.

Aryeh Lev Stollman, 'Die Grosse Liebe,' in *The Dialogues of Time and Entropy* (New York: Riverhead Books, 2003). Copyright © 1996 by Aryeh Lev Stollman. Used by permission of Riverhead Books, an imprint of Penguin Putnam, Inc. Originally published in *Yale Review* 84, no. 3 (1996): 75–87.

Excerpt from Ann Michaels, *Fugitive Pieces* (Toronto: McClelland and Stewart, 1996), 43—54. Copyright © 1996 by Anne Michaels. Used by permission, McClelland and Stewart, Ltd. *The Canadian Publishers*.

Excerpt from Michael Redhill, *Martin Sloane* (Toronto: Doubleday Canada, 2001), 142, 221–25, 265–70. Copyright © 2001 by Michael Redhill. Published by William Heinemann. Reprinted by permission of The Random House Group, Ltd., and by permission of Doubleday Canada, a division of Random House of Canada, Ltd.

In the *Jewish Writing in the Contemporary World* series

Contemporary Jewish Writing in Austria
An Anthology
Edited by Dagmar C. G. Lorenz

Contemporary Jewish Writing in Britain and Ireland
An Anthology
Edited by Bryan Cheyette

Contemporary Jewish Writing in Canada
An Anthology
Edited by Michael Greenstein

Contemporary Jewish Writing in Germany
An Anthology
Edited by Leslie Morris and Karen Remmler

Contemporary Jewish Writing in Hungary
An Anthology
Edited by Susan Rubin Suleiman and Éva Forgács

Contemporary Jewish Writing in Poland
An Anthology
Edited by Antony Polonsky and Monika Adamczyk-Garbowska

Contemporary Jewish Writing in South Africa
An Anthology
Edited by Claudia Bathsheba Braude

Contemporary Jewish Writing in Switzerland
An Anthology
Edited by Rafaël Newman